Strategic Planning for Correctional Emergencies

Robert M. Freeman, Ph.D.

Cover art by Mactronics, Washington, D.C.
Editorial Services by Gravel Hill Communications, Beltsville, Md.
Composition by Design Consultants, Gainesville, Va.
Printed in the U.S.A. by Graphic Communications Inc., Upper Marlboro Md.

Cover Photos: *Top*, courtesy Federal Correctional Institution, Talladega, Ala.; *middle*, courtesy Mark S. Schreibner, Missouri Dept. of Corrections; *bottom*, courtesy Maryland Division of Correction.

Library of Congress Cataloging-in-Publication Data
Freeman, Robert M. 1947-
      Strategic planning for correctional emergencies/Robert M. Freeman.
      p.   cm.
      Includes bibliographical references.
      ISBN 1-56991-052-9 (pbk.)
      1. Prison administration. 2. Prison administration—United States. 3. Emergency
management. 4. Emergency management—United States. I. Title.
HV8759.F74 1996
365'.068'4—dc20   96-24867
                                                      CIP

This publication may be ordered from:
      American Correctional Association
      4380 Forbes Boulevard
      Lanham, MD 20706-4322
      1-800-ACA-JOIN

Table of Contents

Preface by Reginald A. Wilkinson... *v*

Introduction: It Won't Happen Here 1

1   Golden Rules of Strategic Planning... 7

2   Establishing Facility Vulnerability 15

3   Lining Up the Ducks.. 23

4   Specialized Teams and the Life Cycle of Emergencies............................... 29

5   Emergency Plan Activation: Setting the Stage 41

6   Inmate-precipitated Emergencies: General Principles of Mitigation................... 49

7   The Rumblings of Inmate Discontent: Early Warning Signs........................... 59

8   Work Stoppages, Hunger Strikes, Escapes, and Walkaways 65

9   Violence in Inmate-precipitated Emergencies: General Principles of Mitigation....... 71

10   Sexual Assaults and Suicide 77

11   Nongang-Related Minor Disturbances and Gang-related Minor Disturbances........ 83

12   Riots and Hostages... 89

13   The Rumblings of Staff Discontent: Early Warning Signs 101

14   Facility Fires and Technological Emergencies....................................... 107

15   Floods, Hurricanes, and Tornadoes 115

16   Earthquakes, Severe Winter Storms, and Forest Fires................................ 127

17 Urban Unrest, Terrorist Activity, Hazardous Material Accidents, and
    Nuclear Incidents 133

18 Evacuation 143

19 Emergency Medical Management 151

20 Emergency Management of Public Information 161

21 Testing the Emergency Plan 169

22 Communication Failures: The Ultimate Threat to Strategic Planning 175

23 Raising the Phoenix from the Ashes: Meeting the Physical and Psychological
    Challenges of Recovery 183

24 Managing the Tidal Wave of Post-Emergency Inmate Litigation 193

25 Healing the Silent Wounds 205

References 211

Appendix: Samples of Emergency Procedures Checklists from Maryland Department
          of Corrections 217

Preface

This book addresses the extensive spectrum of topics and issues correctional managers must consider as part of the overall management of a correctional facility. As you read this book you will find yourself face-to-face with emergencies that have occurred in correctional environments. This book puts forth the lessons learned from these emergencies and, more important, how you can be more prepared if you and your facility are faced with an emergency situation.

As chief executive of a large correctional agency, I was required to provide leadership during one of the worst prison riots in the history of this country. The Easter 1993 riot at the Southern Ohio Correctional Facility in Lucasville, Ohio, is the type of event every correctional administrator dreads. That eleven-day siege was extremely costly. Correctional Officer Bobby Vallandingham was murdered. Nine inmates were executed by fellow inmates. An entire cellblock was ripped apart from floor to ceiling. Over 2,000 individuals worked twenty-four hours a day to resolve the crisis and free the hostages. The Ohio National Guard, Ohio State Highway Patrol, local law enforcement and emergency personnel, and the facility's own special teams accrued thousands of hours of overtime. Three years later,

the State of Ohio is still dealing with the aftermath of that tragedy.

The challenge of that massive effort required that I apply not only my own years of experience and training, but those of hundreds of department staff and local and state responding agencies. It is incumbent on us, as leaders, to be prepared to confront, respond to, and recover from such incidents.

The ultimate goal of all correctional administrators is to manage a facility or agency in such a way that emergencies are prevented. However, despite our best efforts, there are times when we cannot control the actions of others or, for that matter, of mother nature. As a result, strategic planning must become an integral part of our day-to-day operation. *Strategic Planning for Correctional Emergencies* walks you through the various steps that encompass emergency planning.

Preparing for the worst case scenario may seem overly cautious and unnecessary in light of the fact that, in general, correctional facilities are operated in a safe, secure, and humane manner on a daily basis. Yet, each year there are several correctional emergencies that require an organized and planned response. A knowledgeable correctional leader will eschew reactive incident management in favor of preventive and preparatory management that addresses the immediate situation, develops a response plan, resolves the incident, and recovers—returns the prison or agency to normal operations.

This book addresses a number of valuable preventive measures that can be used to reduce the risk of many types of incidents. Beyond prevention, correctional facilities must be prepared for any emergency by developing a system capable of identifying, containing, responding to, managing, and recovering from any type of incident from minor to catastrophic. This book identifies a multitude of incident types and presents information critical to planning and preparing for them, should they occur. Helpful information on incident management is included for inmate-precipitated events, such as sexual assaults, suicides, work stoppages, hunger strikes, escapes, gang unrest, and minor and major disturbances. The book also includes advice on working with staff problems as well as natural emergencies, such as fires, floods, and tornadoes. External hazards, such as technological emergencies, urban unrest, terrorism, hazardous waste, evacuation, and even nuclear incidents, also are covered.

The chapters dealing with crucial tangential issues, such as dealing with the media, emergency medical management, and communications, demonstrate that we cannot resolve crises in a vacuum. We must work together with other agencies, the media, legislators and other public officials, family members, and others. The era of circling the wagons and keeping a closed shop during correctional emergencies is long gone.

The staff of the Ohio Department of Rehabilitation and Correction, a proud and resilient group of professionals, will attest to the importance of the three final chapters: Raising the Phoenix from the Ashes—Meeting the Physical and Psychological Challenges of Recovery, Managing the Tidal Wave of Post-Emergency Inmate Litigation, and Healing the Silent Wounds. Each of us, in our own way, is still dealing with the events that began on April 11, 1993. Adrenaline, courage, and hope kept us strong throughout the riot. Resilience, patience, adaptability, and teamwork are the qualities necessary to deal with the personal, professional, and political aftermath.

Ohio was not unprepared for a riot in 1993. We had in place Disturbance Control Teams, Hostage Negotiation Teams, Sniper Teams, Public Information Teams, and the like. However, our state of readiness perhaps was dwarfed by the unprecedented growth in our inmate population, staff, and number of facilities. Our readiness had been untested for many years at a time.

As a corrections manager you should ask yourself, "Am I doing the best I can do to prepare my agency before an emergency occurs? When an emergency happens, are we in a position to respond quickly and appropriately? Will our response be implemented in the most professional, cost-effective, and incident specific manner possible?" *Strategic Planning for Correctional Emergencies* helps you answer these crucial questions confidently and completely. I commend the author and encourage every reader to move past the conceptual phase and into the implementation phase until readiness is part of your agency's culture.

Reginald A. Wilkinson
Director, Ohio Department of Rehabilitation
 and Correction
President, American Correctional Association,
 1996-1999

Introduction

It Won't Happen Here

Are You Prepared for a Correctional Emergency?

October 25, 1989—Camp Hill, Pennsylvania

Routine afternoon activities of the 2,600-bed State Correctional Institution at Camp Hill in Camp Hill, Pennsylvania, were being carried out in uneventful fashion. Staff meetings were coming to a close. Line movements from the education building to the cellblocks in Groups II and III were orderly. Recreational activities were proceeding smoothly on both the main stockade field and the Group I field. Kitchens I and II were preparing for the evening meal. At 3 P.M., I had finished the last meeting of the day and was sitting down to open the afternoon mail when my institutional line rang. Picking up the phone, I heard my deputy superintendent for operations say: "Superintendent, an inmate coming in from main stockade just assaulted an officer at E-Gate. We have an officer down, and inmates are refusing to lock up in Groups II and III."

Two minutes later, I was in the deputy's office, located inside the fifty-two-acre institution in a cellblock/office/infirmary complex designated as Group I. I had entered the institution to get a face-to-face briefing on the assault, anticipating no personal danger to myself, because in my mind, it was still a routine day at Camp Hill. Standing at the windows in the deputy's office a few minutes later, looking in the direction of E-Gate, I watched Group II and III correctional officers running for their lives towards us, pursued by hundreds of screaming inmates. As the officers reached Group I, we opened the security doors. When all the officers were safe, we armed as many as we could with batons from the Restricted Housing Unit. My entire chain of command was trapped inside the institution, less than one hundred yards from the main gate and safety, with no hope of escape. There was nothing to do except activate the institution emergency plan, wait for the anticipated inmate assault on our location, and hope the state police would arrive in time.

The hand-held radios in the Group I command post suddenly came alive with the screams of block officers. Unable to flee their posts, some Group I and II block officers had locked themselves in the switchboxes controlling the door-locking mechanisms. As we listened, officers yelled that inmates were trying to break down the block walls to get to them. As the afternoon dragged on, the radios, one by one, went silent. By 5 P.M. we knew the last officer had been taken hostage. Then inmates began using captured radios to tell us what they were going to do to the hostages if their demands were not met.

April 29, 30, and May 1, 1992—Los Angeles, California

The California Department of Corrections had to evacuate 438 reentry and restitution inmates from eight regional community correctional centers in Los Angeles and return them to their parent institutions because of urban riots triggered by the not-guilty verdict in the Rodney King police brutality trial. The evacuations were necessary for two reasons: to protect the safety of staff and inmates put under threat by the proximity of the centers to the rioting and to prevent inmates from joining the rioters (DiMaggio 1992:3-4).

August 23, 1992—Miami, Florida

The Federal Prison Camp on Homestead Air Force Base had to be evacuated because of Hurricane Andrew. Sixty-three staff and 146 inmates were evacuated to the Metropolitan Correctional Center (MCC). Homestead Air Force Base was destroyed and MCC-Miami sustained significant damage during the hurricane. No lives were lost (Samples 1992:108-10).

April 11, 1993—Lucasville, Ohio

The tragedy at the maximum security Southern Ohio Correctional Facility in Lucasville began at 2:50 P.M. on Easter Sunday when one group of inmates attacked a correctional officer processing inmates into L-Block and another group attacked a corridor officer, taking his keys and baton. Officers responding to a silent alarm rushed to help as inmates raced to overpower other officers and release inmates confined to their cells:

> By 3:10 p.m., L-Block was lost to the inmates, and the longest prison siege in U.S. history where lives were lost had begun. Correctional Officer Robert Vallandingham and nine inmates were murdered during the disturbance. Thirteen correctional officers were held hostage—five throughout the entire 11-day ordeal. More than 2,000 people from corrections special teams, the Ohio State Highway Patrol, the Ohio National Guard, FBI and local law enforcement agencies assembled with one goal—to end the siege and bring the remaining hostages out alive (Wilkinson 1994:64).

July 1993—Missouri, Illinois, Iowa, Minnesota, and Wisconsin

Correctional facilities were damaged or destroyed by a period of unprecedented flooding that occurred in the Midwest (Spertzel 1993:159).

August 21, 1994—Detroit, Michigan

The normal routine was in place at the Ryan Correctional Facility in Detroit, Michigan, until early Sunday morning when:

> . . . [S]omeone outside the fence tossed the inmates a bolt-cutter and a shotgun with shells. The men traversed two fences and around large spools of razor

ribbon. It is believed to be the largest escape in Michigan in 70 years (Detroit Free Press 1994:1).

Ten inmates escaped and were picked up by a getaway car. By Monday, August 22, 1995, four inmates had been arrested, and a fifth inmate was found dead of unknown causes, although a drug overdose was suspected. The escape happened ten weeks before Governor John Engler faced reelection. Accusations flew, four correctional officers were suspended, and union-management conflict flared. The finger-pointing had begun, and a major controversy was under way.

August 14, 1995—Shamokin, Pennsylvania

Officer Joseph Gricoski attempted to quiet inmate Leon Robinson in the dining hall at the State Correctional Institution at Coal Township near Shamokin, Pennsylvania. Officer Gricoski was punched in the face, and other inmates jumped into the assault on Gricoski and two officers, Arnold Hayle and Samuel Stewart, who had come to his aid. Gricoski was knocked unconscious and received severe facial injuries, Hayle suffered facial injuries and bruises on his upper back, and Stewart received a broken jaw and fractures to a cheek bone and the area around one eye. The investigation of the disturbance focused on four related activities: the assaults in the dining hall, assaults in the yard outside the dining hall, disturbances in E–Block, and inmates assaulting other inmates in the chapel (The Evening News 1995).

Corrections Officer Aldo Mirarchi also was involved in the disturbance:

Mirarchi had been trained for the moment with tactics on hostage

negotiation. He walked out of the prison that same day uninjured—and was hailed yesterday as one of several heroes who used new and improved state training to avert tragedy (Russell 1995:B1).

August 28, 1995—Copenhagen, Denmark

Twelve Danish convicts, walking in the exercise yard of the Vridsloeselille state jail took advantage of a bulldozer crashing through the perimeter wall by escaping through an opening wide enough to run through. Two of the inmates were arrested within hours. Police were at a premier soccer league game during the escape. The bulldozer reportedly was operated by the outside accomplice of one of the inmates walking in the exercise yard (*USA Today* 1995).

September 5, 1995—Puerto Rico

Sixty-four inmates in three Puerto Rican jails took advantage of power outages caused by hurricane Luis to escape confinement. As of September 7, 1995, thirty-two of the inmates remained on escape status (*Patriot News* 1995e:2).

October, 1995—Allenwood, Pennsylvania; Talladega, Alabama; Memphis, Tennessee; El Reno, Oklahoma; and Greenville, Illinois

In less than one week, the Federal Bureau of Prisons experienced a series of inmate disturbances at five federal prisons. Property damage was estimated to be in the millions of dollars and twenty-six people were injured. As a result, the entire Federal Bureau of Prisons went into lockdown status. There was speculation that the uprisings were the result of the failure of the U.S. Congress to change the penalties for possession of crack cocaine, which are more severe than the penalties for possession of powder cocaine (*Patriot News* 1995d:B9).

November 8, 1995—Blair County, Pennsylvania

Three inmates escaped from the Blair County Prison by breaking into a crawl space housing the prison laundry's water heater, wiggling through a small space, and knocking out a three-foot-by-three-foot heater panel. This allowed access into the county garage, where the inmates stole a 1986 Ford Bronco. They drove into Altoona, where they stole an Oldsmobile Cutlass (*Patriot News* 1995c:B3).

December 29, 1995—Honduras

Twenty-seven inmates in the Tela jail located in the Caribbean coast injured two correctional officers during an escape timed to take advantage of the end of the visiting period. The inmates were armed with machetes, clubs, and knives (Clayton 1996:24).

January 11, 1996—Mississippi

Two burglars escaped from a county jail because a contractor installed a new door upside down, and it didn't work. Two inmates used a light fixture to open the latch. Staff had not realized the door was upside down because the lock had a metal block around it to prevent people from jimmying it (Associated Press 1996).

October 26, 1989—Camp Hill, Pennsylvania

Activation of the emergency plan had been successful, and the State Correctional Institution at Camp Hill had officially been declared secure at approximately 10 P.M. on

October 25. The next day, institutional staff were beginning the process of returning the facility to a state of normal operations, confident that the emergency was over. At 6 P.M. I received a phone call from the main gate officer informing me that inmates were loose and attacking the Group I complex. Minutes later, I witnessed from the main gate, the stunning sight of hundreds of screaming inmates sweeping across the institution grounds in two well-defined waves of attack. Many inmates were yelling, "Last night we gave you a riot! Tonight we're giving you a war!" Their target was the offices where some of my staff and I had been trapped the day before. Within minutes, firebombs were thrown through the windows. The deputy superintendent for operations and fifty staff (many of them commissioned officers) were trapped in a building that was soon ablaze. Camp Hill was lost to the inmates in less than five minutes.

By 7 A.M. the next morning it was all over. Sixty-nine staff, many of whom had been taken hostage or trapped in burning buildings, and forty-one inmates had been injured. Eighty percent of the buildings on the fifty-two-acre reservation were vandalized, burned to the ground, or suffered extensive smoke damage. Six of ten cellblocks were gutted so severely that it was a year before the last block was restored for occupation. The interior fence of a two-fence perimeter security system had been breached. Camp Hill was no longer a functional institution.

Preparing for Correctional Emergencies—Strategic Planning

Involvement in an emergency is unlike any other correctional experience. I have a colleague who says about deer hunting: "You don't know what it's all about until you've dragged a body out of the woods." Correctional emergencies are like that. You have to experience an emergency to truly understand the complexity of the long-term responsibilities and issues it can create. In *Strategic Planning for Correctional Emergencies,* I present a conceptual framework that will help prepare readers for the day when they have to drag their "body out of the woods."

Strategic planning is a proactive strategy that begins during the site location phase of new facility construction and continues for the rest of the facility's existence. Chapters 1 through 5 present a general foundation for strategic planning by examining basic principles and requirements for an effective emergency plan. Chapters 6 through 17 examine twenty-five specific correctional emergencies in terms of their life cycle. Chapters 18 through 20 discuss the specialized activities of evacuation, emergency medical management, and emergency management of public information. Chapter 21 suggests a comprehensive approach to testing the emergency plan. Chapter 22 examines the role of a variety of types of communication failures in causing inmate-precipitated emergencies. Chapters 23 through 25 examine general issues that should be addressed when an emergency, especially a major inmate-precipitated emergency, is over.

This book is written for two audiences. The first audience consists of those dedicated professionals in the field of corrections who need a ready reference book when they are working on their emergency plan. The second audience consists of college students who are preparing for a career in corrections. The extensive index will help you find specific information quickly.

Chapter 1

Golden Rules of Strategic Planning

*T*he main problem seems to be that individual criminal justice agencies tend to be reactive rather than future-oriented in their decision-making operations . . . there can be no meaningful regional or systemwide planning without individual agencies first being able to establish their own orderly, systematic, and continuous processes of setting objectives, anticipating the future, and bringing these anticipations to bear on critical present decisions (Nanus 1974:345).

A correctional emergency is any event that can (1) disrupt the orderly operation of a facility; (2) cause deaths, injuries, and property damage within the facility; and (3) jeopardize the safety of the community. Correctional administrators are responsible for developing emergency plans for correctional emergencies. Strategic planning is most effective if it is done in accordance with six basic rules:

1. Do not assume "good" inmates will remain "good" inmates in an emergency.

2. Planning is organized around the emergency life cycle: mitigation, preparedness, response, and recovery.

3. Every facility is unique and requires an individualized emergency plan based on information and analysis provided by the best and brightest on your team.

4. Assign specific tasks to specific individuals and hold those individuals responsible for their assignments.

5. Ensure the format of every emergency plan within the system is standardized in terms of format, emergency definition, and the emergency response structure.

6. Details count.

Rule One

Do not assume that "good" inmates will remain "good" inmates in the event of an emergency. Erving Goffman (1961), in his classic study of the total institution, notes that inmates have two types of adjustment to confinement: primary and secondary. Primary adjustment involves going by the rules, attending programs, and not presenting problems for staff. Staff see inmates displaying primary adjustment as being with the program—"good" inmates. Secondary adjustment involves a rejection of both the program and staff through rebellion—rule violations, attempted escapes, and other behavioral problems. The inmate displaying secondary adjustment is the "bad" inmate.

When an emergency occurs, "good" inmates, even though they are not responsible for the emergency, quickly may see the personal benefit of taking advantage of the situation. Strategic planning should assume that every inmate under the jurisdiction of the plan has the potential to become a serious problem and should be managed accordingly. This would appear to be an obvious rule, as it is in escapes or riots, but it is a rule that may be overlooked in the event of natural emergencies or noninmate-precipitated emergencies (such as urban riots) where staff may be inclined to assume that because they and the inmates share a common goal (survival), this mutual goal will inhibit inmate acting-out. Maximum inmate control is an essential consideration in correctional strategic planning.

Rule Two

Planning is organized around the emergency life cycle: mitigation, preparedness, response, and recovery (Federal Emergency Management Agency 1990:2).

Mitigation

Mitigation activities are those that either prevent the occurrence of an emergency or reduce the community's vulnerability in ways that minimize the adverse impact of a disaster or other emergency (Federal Emergency Management Agency 1990:2).

There is some debate about the validity of using the word "prevention" in strategic plan-

ning. In the early 1970s the term "disaster prevention" was widely used. However, in recent years the less optimistic term "mitigation" has come into fashion:

> *. . . the reason for the evermore widespread use of the term mitigation seems to be in its inherent sense of realism. Prevention has sometimes been found misleading, inasmuch as many disasters cannot be prevented from taking place. Mitigating, that is to say damping, the worst effects of violent and sudden natural hazards, is well within the realm of reality . . . .* (United Nations Disaster Relief Organization 1989:2).

"Mitigation," a term commonly used in community disaster management, has been defined as "actions taken to prevent or reduce the risks from natural hazards" (National Research Council 1991:3). However, mitigation as a process is most valuable if it is applied within the context of "reducing vulnerability in all its forms" (Blaikie *et al.* 1994:222). Correctional mitigation is a proactive approach that focuses on maintaining the integrity of life; the physical plant; security (internal and perimeter); and lifeline services, such as water, food, sanitation, medical, fire protection, and communications systems. Correctional mitigation is an ongoing, sequential process that operates at three levels:

Level 1—Prevention of a specific emergency

Level 2—Reduction of the probability of occurrence of a specific emergency

Level 3—Reduction of the negative consequences of a specific emergency

Level 1—Site-Location Mitigation. Level 1 is the most desirable level. Prevention represents a zero probability of occurrence for a specific emergency, a situation that saves staff a multitude of headaches. Level 1 mitigation is possible in some natural emergencies (floods, hurricanes, and forest fires) and human emergencies (urban unrest or nuclear power plant accidents). Through site-location mitigation, the emergency is prevented because the facility has been constructed in an area where that specific emergency does not occur. For example, administrators concerned about hurricanes understand that the hurricane itself cannot be prevented. Yet, strategic planning that concentrates on constructing facilities in a region where hurricanes do not occur will prevent the facility from being vulnerable to hurricanes. If prevention is achieved through site-location mitigation, no further mitigation activities are necessary.

No matter how effective the strategic planning process, a zero probability of occurrence for inmate-precipitated emergencies, facility fires and technological emergencies, and some types of natural and human emergencies cannot be guaranteed. If level 1 cannot be achieved, staff should direct their activities towards level 2 mitigation.

Level 2—Reducing the Probability of Occurrence. If there is any chance a specific emergency will occur, strategic planning should direct staff activities towards creating a set of conditions that will make it more difficult for the emergency to occur. Administrators concerned about the possibility of a riot may attempt level 2 mitigation by providing staff activities, such as adequate counseling, educational, training, and

recreational programs; having an inmate grievance system; and the monitoring of inmate groups and leaders by the Intelligence Unit, to reduce their opportunity for planning a riot.

Despite the effort put into level 2 activities, the fact that there always will remain some chance, no matter how small, of the emergency occurring, mandates that staff activities also must be directed towards achieving Level 3 mitigation.

Level 3—Reducing the Consequences. For facilities located in a hurricane-risk area, the reduction of consequences will require using appropriate hurricane-resistant construction methods. For riots, reduction of consequences will require using specialized assault teams operating in a physical environment designed to limit inmate mobility and contain disturbances to a limited area.

Mitigation is not static. Mitigation is a process that should become part of the daily routine for every staff member. It is an ongoing process by which staff are alert to changes in the internal environment of the facility as well as changes in the external environment that might affect the facility negatively. Effective mitigation requires two commitments:

- Mitigation activities should be incorporated into the budgetary process. Planning is useless without funding.

- All physical plant projects, proposed policy changes, and proposed modification of procedures/programming should be reviewed in terms of three questions:

  1. Does this project/proposal/modification increase facility vulnerability to an emergency?

2. If so, what type of emergency?

3. Once the specific emergency has been identified, what mitigation activities will be most effective in reducing facility vulnerability?

Preparedness

> *Preparedness activities, programs, and systems are those that exist prior to an emergency and are used to support and enhance response to an emergency or disaster. Planning, training, and exercising are among the activities conducted under this phase* (Federal Emergency Management Agency 1990:2).

Preparedness complements mitigation by providing staff with the guidelines and training they need to reduce the consequences of a specific emergency. Preparedness plays a role in both response and recovery and has four primary goals: (1) to anticipate as many emergency situations as possible; (2) to develop an adequate resource base; (3) to prepare all staff to function in a safe, efficient manner designed to maintain security while minimizing injury, loss of life, and property damage; and (4) to effectively test staff capabilities.

Response

> *Response involves activities and programs designed to address the immediate and short-term effects of the onset of an emergency or disaster. It helps to reduce casualties and damage and to speed recovery. Response activities include direction and control,*

warning, evacuation, and other similar operations (Federal Emergency Management Agency 1990:2).

Response involves those activities designed to protect life and property through the coordinated use of all available internal and external resources during the emergency. Response has three primary goals: (1) to carry out the emergency plan in a professional manner, (2) to minimize the damage and casualties that would delay a speedy and efficient recovery, and (3) to provide information that will improve the effectiveness of future strategic planning. It is during response that defects in strategic planning will become obvious.

Recovery

> *Recovery is the phase that involves restoring systems to normal. Short-term recovery actions are taken to assess damage and return vital life-support systems to minimum operating standards; long-term recovery actions may continue for many years* (Federal Emergency Management Agency 1990:2).

Recovery involves developing a blueprint for returning the facility to a state of normal operation as quickly and as safely as possible once response has been completed. Recovery has four primary goals: (1) to meet all the immediate basic life, safety, and security needs of inmates and staff; (2) to return the facility to a state of normal operations as quickly as possible; (3) to incorporate lessons learned from the emergency into the future operation of the facility; and (4) to meet the long-term needs of inmates and staff.

Each phase of the emergency cycle involves specific conditions that should be anticipated. Strategic planning is incomplete if all four phases of the emergency life cycle are not thoroughly evaluated during development of the emergency plan. For purposes of illustration, the four phases of the emergency life cycle have been discussed as though they exist independently of each other; in reality, there is an overlap between mitigation and the other phases. Preparedness, response, and response activities, in a very real sense, may be considered mitigation activities occurring at different points in time.

Rule Three

As with every aspect of correctional management, there is a right way and a wrong way to plan for correctional emergencies. The wrong way to plan for correctional emergencies is to borrow another facility's emergency plan and play fill-in-the-blanks with your staff. The right way to plan is to understand that every facility is unique and requires an individualized emergency plan based on the information and analysis provided by the best and brightest on your team.

Rule Four

Assign specific tasks to specific individuals and hold those individuals responsible for their assignment. Emergency response should not be a seat-of-the-pants activity. As many activities as possible should be preplanned and assigned to specific individuals who are trained to perform specific activities during any given emergency. The language of the emergency plan should be clear and precise, with a chain

---

Strategic planning should be based on the following assumptions:

- The purpose of an emergency plan is to maximize the ability to protect lives, the community, and property during an emergency.

- An emergency can occur without warning, at any time of the day or night.

- When an emergency occurs, minutes count. Rarely is there time to stop and develop an on-the-spot response to an unexpected event.

- The initial reaction of staff to an emergency, no matter how well anticipated, may be shock and disbelief—an emotional reaction that can make a bad situation worse if staff have not been properly trained.

- The unexpected may occur in an emergency plan—develop as many back-up procedures as possible.

- The initial emergency, even if response is successful, may generate secondary emergencies. A failed escape attempt may create a hostage situation. A hostage situation may trigger a riot. Evacuation of inmates may provide the opportunity for escapes or assaults.

- An emergency at another facility may affect your facility negatively. The ripple effect of riots, for example, should not be ignored in strategic planning.

- Strategic planning is an important administrative responsibility.

- All emergencies, no matter how destructive, provide the opportunity to learn and increase the capability to be better prepared for the next emergency.

- Simple plans are the most effective.

of command clearly established by name or position. An effective emergency plan provides very specific information: who does what, how they do it, where they do it, and when they do it.

Rule Five

Ensure the format of every emergency plan within the system is standardized in terms of format, emergency definition, and the emergency response structure.

Format

The emergency plan may be in the format of an operational manual, with text explaining specific assignments and providing comprehensive descriptions of emergencies and assignments. Or, emergency plans may consist of brief explanations of the behavior expected by staff in specific emergencies and provide a checklist of actions designed to implement situation-specific strategies. The Maryland Division of Corrections, for example, uses the checklist system to standardize responses at its twenty-seven state correctional facilities. (See examples in the Appendix.) Regardless of the system used, adjustments should be made for the unique features of each facility, but a standardized format will reduce confusion.

Definition

An essential element of standardization is a uniform definition of the various types of emergencies that can confront correctional administrators. The Maryland Division of Corrections, for example, has a master plan, "Directive 110–24," that establishes a system of six emergency categories.

Category 1 includes relatively minor emergencies, such as a brief hunger strike, that may result in a partial or complete lockdown but can be managed by facility staff. Category 2 includes incidents, such as a major disturbance, that, in addition to resulting in a partial or complete lockdown, require the assistance of community law enforcement and support services. Category 3 involves an emergency so severe that staff have lost control of all or part of the institution. The response phase includes retaking control from inmates. Category 4 involves emergencies in two or more facilities within a geographic region. Category 5 includes incidents occurring simultaneously in more than one region. Category 6 involves an emergency, such as a natural disaster, a hazardous waste spill, or an urban riot, that may spread into the area of the facility.

Staff anywhere in the Maryland Division of Corrections know what it means when they hear that a Category 3 emergency has just occurred at a Maryland facility. Standard categorization of emergencies eliminates confusion and misdirected responses that can occur when each facility develops its own system for defining emergencies.

Response Structure

Correctional systems historically have used a traditional command-and-control structure for responding to emergencies: response is directed through the established chain of command. Thus, the facility administrator, once alerted that there is an emergency, is responsible for activating the emergency plan and directing staff activities in accordance with that plan.

At least one correctional system, the Arizona Department of Corrections, has gone a different route in strategic planning. It uses an incident management system that differs from the traditional command-and-control structure. This system will be discussed in Chapter 5.

Rule Six

Details count. Major elements of a plan may be impressive on paper, but if critical details have been overlooked, staff may find themselves unable to respond to an emergency as effectively as expected. For example, early in his career as a superintendent, this author and his staff spent a lot of time developing what we considered to be a flawless emergency plan. We were proud of our efforts and were confident that all the bases had been covered. The test of the plan involved response to a fire in a housing unit located in the center of the facility. Fifteen minutes into the test, we were embarrassed to find that although the plan called for local fire trucks to enter the facility through the rear sallyport, no one had ever measured the rear sallyport to determine if those fire trucks would have enough clearance to enter. The fire trucks could not fit through the rear sallyport. One fire truck narrowly avoided being hung up in the gate. The trip back to the front of the facility, where the sallyport fortunately had sufficient clearance, could have been very costly if the fire had been real.

Correctional administrators should plan in detail for the worst possible emergencies while hoping those emergencies will never happen. Strategic planning brings together three critical elements: an awareness of vulnerability, readily available resources, and specific life cycle staff activities. Individuals who buy insurance do so with the hope that they never will have to use it. Strategic planning operates on the same principle.

Chapter 2

Establishing Facility Vulnerability

O ne day in late 1991, a shift commander at a Maryland prison called the
Maryland Emergency Management
Agency (MEMA) to ask if MEMA staff could
review an emergency plan he was preparing for
his facility. It was a simple phone call, but ultimately it led the state to restructure its prison
emergency plans and training and to consolidate
the facility plans into a uniform statewide policy
(Mascari 1993:148).

Strategic planning should produce two sets
of emergency plans: (1) a master emergency
plan outlining the specific responsibilities and
functions of central office staff in the event of
an emergency at any facility in the system;
and (2) a separate local plan for each facility,
including boot camps and community-based
residential facilities. The heart of effective
strategic planning is the Emergency Planning
Committee.

Establishing the Emergency Planning Committee

There should be a central office emergency
planning committee and a facility emergency
planning committee. Staff selected for the
Emergency Planning Committee should be

senior-level individuals who possess the
personal skills, experience, and institutional
memory necessary for engaging in thoughtful
analysis, planning, and evaluating. They also
must have the administrative authority to
ensure strategic planning is comprehensive
and successful.

The Central Office Emergency Planning Committee

The central office Emergency Planning
Committee, chaired by the agency administrator, has five specific functions:

1. **Taking General Oversight Responsibility.** Oversight responsibility begins with
developing an official mission statement that
establishes the need for developing,
disseminating, implementing, testing, and
reviewing/modifying an appropriate emergency plan at each facility within the system.
After the mission statement is developed, the
central office Emergency Planning Committee
should address the issue of providing support
to facilities experiencing an emergency. This
support may be in the form of sending staff to
the facility to provide on-site assistance, coordinating a systemwide correctional response,

and intervening in disputes between correctional staff and representatives of the state emergency management and law enforcement agencies expected to assist in facility response. Central office resources should be documented in a central office master plan.

Oversight also includes reviewing all facility emergency plans annually; participating in the emergency postmortem, at both the facility and central office level; and appropriately monitoring to ensure every test of a facility emergency plan is a genuine test of readiness that holds staff accountable.

For the central office Emergency Planning Committee to effectively carry out these oversight responsibilities, a formal, written schedule of activities should be developed and enforced. This schedule should include (1) setting dates for review of facility emergency plans, evaluating test results, and reviewing modifications suggested by actual use of the plan; and (2) establishing a schedule of dates on which specific central office staff are expected to present their critiques of assigned sections of the facility and central office plan. The Emergency Planning Committee will standardize the amount of time that may elapse between review and modification of any emergency plan and the number and type of emergency plan tests per calendar year.

2. Securing Financial Resources. The agency administrator should include in the annual budget request to the legislature a specific request for funds necessary for mitigation, preparedness, and response, with a contingency fund for estimated recovery costs. A specific emergency plan funding request forces legislators to think about strategic planning by reminding them of their obligation to provide appropriate funding levels.

3. Mandating Inclusion of Contract Vendors in Strategic Planning. An increasing number of correctional facilities are contracting basic inmate services to private, for-profit vendors. All contracts should contain an accountability clause that requires vendors to participate in strategic planning and to ensure the availability of specific personnel, supplies, and materials in the event of specific emergencies.

4. Ensuring Legal Review of Emergency Plan Policy. The agency position on sensitive subjects, such as suspending routine administrative policies during an emergency and using lethal force, should be reviewed by legal counsel.

5. Coordinating Interagency Cooperation Beyond the Local Level. Interagency cooperation is essential to successfully develop and implement emergency plans on a systemwide basis. Representatives of all agencies expected to respond to a facility emergency should be involved in all phases of strategic planning. Representatives may be from the state or federal level, as well as those from the local level.

The Facility Emergency Planning Committee

The facility Emergency Planning Committee, chaired by the facility administrator, should endorse the agency mission statement, develop a written time frame for facility Emergency Planning Committee activities in line with the central office Emergency Planning Committee time frame, and engage in six specific functions:

1. Coordinating the Facility Emergency Vulnerability Analysis. The foundation for any emergency plan is the facility preemergency vulnerability analysis and a post-emergency vulnerability analysis. All vulnerabilities, once identified, should be prioritized in terms of degree of disruption to the operation and the likelihood of death or serious injury.

Photo courtesy Capitol Communications

Analysis of a facility's vulnerability is an essential function of the Facility Planning Committee.

2. Determining Resource Availability. Different types of emergencies require different types of resources. Once the facility vulnerability to emergency has been established, the facility Emergency Planning Committee should identify all necessary internal and external resources, establish their on-hand availability, and secure external sources for each category of resource needed. Private vendors who provide direct services to inmates should be considered an external resource and be required to participate in strategic planning.

3. Securing Funding. The facility administrator should include in the annual budget request to the agency administrator a specific budget amount for developing, testing, and modifying emergency plans. Funding for specific mitigation activities should be emphasized in the budget request.

4. Coordinating Interagency Cooperation at the Local Level. The Emergency Planning Committee should ensure coordination of planning activities with representatives of all external local resources during all phases of strategic planning.

5. Archiving. The ready availability of a wide range of reference documents plays a critical role in planning for all phases of the emergency life cycle. To ensure these documents are protected, each facility should create an archive in a location no inmate can access, even in an emergency. Blueprints, aerial photographs of the facility and surrounding area, diagrams of utilities, and any other documents providing information about the physical plant and the community in which it exists should be stored in this archive.

6. Ensuring the Quality of Preparedness. An emergency plan is worthless if staff are not trained and the plan is not realistically tested. Facility Emergency Planning Committee members should have a personal and professional commitment to ensure appropriate levels of staff training, participate in emergency plan exercises, thoroughly review the critiques of emergency plan testing, implement as quickly as possible any recommended modifications, and ensure staff are held accountable for their performance in all phases of strategic planning.

The ability of a facility Emergency Planning Committee to effectively perform depends on the analysis of two situations: facility preemergency vulnerability and post-emergency vulnerability.

The Preemergency Vulnerability Analysis

This analysis identifies emergencies that may threaten the facility. Four basic emergency categories are as follows:

- Inmate-precipitated emergencies, such as riots, hostage situations, escapes, walkaways, gang fights, work stoppages, hunger strikes, sexual assaults, and suicides

- Facility fires and technological failures

- Natural emergencies, such as hurricanes, floods, tornadoes, earthquakes, forest fires, major plague-like epidemics, and life-threatening winter storms

- Human emergencies, such as nuclear accidents, hazardous waste spills, bomb threats, urban riots, and terrorist activities, such as bomb threats or acts of biological, chemical, or nuclear terror in the community around the facility

The Federal Emergency Management Agency (1993:14-15) identifies emergencies in terms of five elements: historical, geographic, technological, human error, and physical. These elements can serve as a foundation for the facility Emergency Planning Committee preemergency vulnerability analysis.

Historical

The Emergency Planning Committee should evaluate the history of the facility. Have specific emergencies occurred at that site in the past that may occur again? Are there patterns of emergencies that history suggests have a high probability of repeating? Patterns at the institutional level would include the following:

- Frequent escapes because of defects in the physical perimeter of the facility, or outdated supervisory policy and procedures, or a faulty classification system

- A high incidence of gang-related activity within the facility because of proximity to an urban area with a high concentration of warring gangs

- Frequent walkaways from outside work details because of proximity to a major interstate highway

- Periodic inmate work stoppages

- Cellblock fires every New Year's Eve because this is the way inmates historically have celebrated the arrival of the new year

Patterns at the community-based level may include the following:

- Frequent failures to return to the facility because of inmate proximity to the old neighborhood

- Urban unrest that threatens the facility

- Proximity to transportation routes with a history of hazardous material accidents

The Emergency Planning Committee should not be concerned with just the physical plant of the facility. It also should be sensitive to any issues of personnel, policy, procedure, and classification that make the facility vulnerable to emergencies.

Geographic

The issue here is: What can happen because of the physical location of the facility? The Emergency Planning Committee should focus concerns on proximity to (1) flood plains, seismic faults, dams, and bodies of water; (2) companies that produce, store, use, or transport hazardous materials or products; (3) major transportation routes or airports; and (4) nuclear power plants. What is the geographic history of the area? Is it prone to earthquakes, flooding, hurricanes, tornadoes, forest fires, or life-threatening snow/ice storms? If geographic history suggests a high degree of vulnerability to a specific emergency, how often does the emergency occur and how accurate is the weather forecasting?

Technological

Technological emergencies include any interruption or loss of a utility service, power source, life support system, information system, or equipment needed to maintain the integrity of the physical plant. Staff should know the location of electric and water cutoffs for each building. What are the possible negative consequences of a failure in the perimeter electronic security system, electronic locking mechanisms, heating/cooling system, electrical system, communications system, plumbing/sewage system, and visual surveillance systems?

Human Error

The Emergency Planning Committee should be particularly interested in accidents, such as fires or hazardous waste spills. In addition, although technically not an issue of human error, the possibility of terrorism can

no longer be ignored. It is not as unthinkable as it once was that a terrorist group (domestic or international) might someday target a correctional facility for some act of terrorism designed to effect mass inmate escape or drive home an ideological point.

Physical

Every physical plant has design flaws that somehow evade detection until it's too late to correct them without incurring extraordinary expense. The goal of the Emergency Planning Committee should be to identify these flaws, determine their impact on any given emergency situation, and plan accordingly. For example, if electronic locking mechanisms in a facility tend to short out during electrical storms, giving inmates the opportunity to exit their cells on their own, then the Emergency Planning Committee should ensure this eventuality is covered in the emergency plan. Analysis of the physical plant should include any structural features of the facility that may create problems, hinder emergency response, or assist response and evacuation/escape routes and exits from buildings within the facility and from the facility itself.

Prioritization of Emergencies

The preemergency vulnerability analysis should establish a list of potential emergencies. The next step is to develop a probability-ranking that establishes which emergencies have the highest probability of occurrence. Emergencies may be ranked on a scale of one to five, with five representing the highest probability of occurrence and one representing the lowest probability.

Emergencies most likely to occur should be allocated the most planning time, and resource allocation should be distributed accordingly. Generally, inmate-precipitated emergencies have the highest probability of occurrence; however, other categories of emergencies should not be ignored. Administrators of facilities located in areas with a history of urban unrest, on flood plains, on the coast, near geological fault lines, or within ten miles of nuclear power plants should consider the possibility of urban riots, floods, hurricanes, earthquakes, or nuclear power plant melt-downs. Administrators of facilities whose walls or fences border busy streets should plan for civilians attempting to assist an escape.

At the conclusion of the preemergency vul-nerability analysis, emergencies with the high-est probability of occurrence will have been identified. Two examples are given as illustra-tions. In the first example, the facility is a max-imum security facility in the desert Southwest located a hundred miles from any major met-ropolitan area, with no major highway system within ten miles. The Emergency Planning Committee at this facility might develop the following probability of emergencies:

Emergency Probability Ranking

• Riots	5
• Hostage situations	5
• Inmate work stoppages	5
• Escapes/walkaways	3
• Gang fights	2
• Utility failures	2
• Winter storms	1
• Epidemics	1
• Terrorist activities	1
• Hurricanes	1
• Floods	1
• Forest fires	1
• Earthquakes	1
• Dam collapse	1

• Nuclear accidents	1
• Urban riots	1
• Hazardous waste spills	1

The second example is a community cor-rections center located in a metropolitan area on the coast of Florida. This facility lies on a flood plain, is surrounded by major highways, one of which is less than a hundred yards from the facility, and the area has a history of both hurricane activity and urban riots. The Emergency Planning Committee for this facility might establish the following probabil-ity of emergencies:

Emergency Probability Ranking

• Escapes/walkaways	5
• Hurricanes	5
• Floods	5
• Urban riots	4
• Hazardous waste spills	4
• Hostage situations	2
• Utility failures	2
• Terrorist activities	2
• Riots	1
• Inmate work stoppages	1
• Gang fights	1
• Winter storms	1
• Epidemics	1
• Forest fires	1
• Earthquakes	1
• Dam collapse	1
• Nuclear accidents	1

In addition to being aware of facility and community conditions, correctional adminis-trators should be sensitive to the effect of high-profile national situations. Correctional staff throughout the nation were concerned that a guilty verdict in the O. J. Simpson trial would lead to negative inmate reaction, espe-cially if there were reaction-riots in Los Angeles or other cities. In October 1995, the entire federal prison system went into lock-down because of riots reportedly triggered by the U.S. Congress' refusal to change the penalties for possession of crack cocaine (*Patriot News* 1995d:B9). During any high-profile legal or political situation, with elements of perceived racial injustice, the mood of the inmate population should be monitored carefully.

The Post-emergency Vulnerability Analysis

Problems aren't over once the emergency has been managed. In fact, some very serious problems may be ready to appear just when staff believe they are home free. If staff are not prepared, post-emergency problems may present as great a threat as the emergency itself. The Emergency Planning Committee should assess post-emergency vulnerability during recovery. This analysis should keep in mind the first rule of planning: "good" inmates don't necessarily stay good in an emergency

situation. Post-emergency issues of concern fall into two primary areas: physical plant and inmate management.

Physical Plant

The Emergency Planning Committee should anticipate, and plan for, the probable consequences of the following:

- disrupted staff access to the facility
- breaches in the perimeter security system
- disabled electronic monitoring equipment
- loss of electric power
- disruption of communication lines
- ruptured gas mains
- water and smoke damage
- structural damage to the cellblocks and other high-use areas
- air, water, or food contamination
- explosions
- building collapse
- fires
- trapped staff and inmates
- chemical release
- disruption of sewage lines
- loss of heating and cooling capability
- loss of housing capability

The specific questions to be asked are as follows:

- What advantage do any of the above provide to inmates interested in creating additional problems for the correctional staff?

- What actions can staff take to minimize the advantage these situations create?

- What threats do these events present to life and safety?

Photo courtesy Capitol Communications

After an emergency has been managed, the Emergency Planning Committee should assess post-emergency vulnerability.

Inmate Management

The Emergency Planning Committee should determine in advance how best to manage inmates during recovery and establish procedures to meet the following needs:

- health and safety
- food, water, clothing, and shelter
- medical attention
- communication with family
- personal property storage

Chapter 3

Lining Up the Ducks

*I*n a correctional institution there must be a
division of work if inmates are to be
guarded and fed, problems and paperwork
attended to, and payroll maintained. However,
because security and watchfulness are everyone's
responsibilities, everyone should be familiar, at
least to a certain extent, with several other tasks
to be able to fill in during emergencies. In some
systems, for example, riot plans call for secretaries
to take positions in certain gun towers to free correctional officers for more specialized and
dangerous duties (Houston 1995:210).

An emergency plan developed without a
thorough knowledge of available resources is a
flawed plan that, when implemented, will
result in a mad scramble to try to locate
important resources at a time when minutes
and hours are critical. Effective strategic planning includes predetermining the type and
source of resources necessary for any given
emergency. Resources are inventoried on the
basis of the type of resource (human, materials,
and physical plant) and the source of the
resource (internal or external).

Internal Resource Inventory

The internal resource inventory consists of
all human and material resources available

within the facility before response. The physical plant is counted as an internal resource.

The Internal Human Resource

The primary human resource within the
facility is the staff whose activities are directed
through the formal chain of command. If the
emergency is not inmate precipitated, selected
inmates also may be a resource.

Staff. Most correctional staff can be relied
on to respond to an emergency, but willingness to respond is not enough. The old days of
everyone chaotically rushing to the scene of an
emergency to lend a helping hand, even
though he or she didn't have any information
about the situation, are long gone. The complexity of modern corrections requires a formal
division of labor to meet the challenge of the
emergency life cycle. This division of labor will
be discussed in chapters 4 and 5.

Inmates. Unless the emergency is inmate
precipitated, it may be possible to use carefully
selected inmates as a source of labor. Many
inmates have specialized construction skills
that can be of value during the life cycle of
emergencies such as hurricanes or floods.
Inmates with no skills still can help by

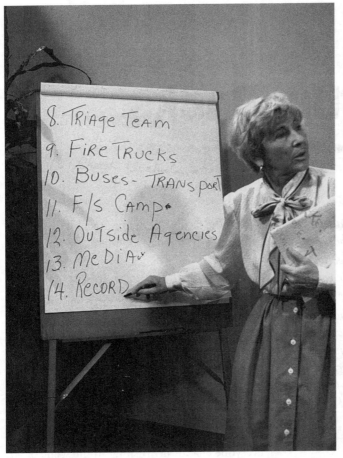

8. Triage Team
9. Fire Trucks
10. Buses - Transport
11. F/S Camp•
12. Outside Agencies
13. Media•
14. Record

Photo courtesy Capitol Communications

Both internal and external resources should be considered when planning for correctional emergencies.

that has been damaged. A supervisor should be designated for each detail of inmates classified as suitable for emergency services. Using inmates as workers in emergency situations is most feasible if work supervisors already have established a supervisory relationship with the inmates assigned to the work group.

If an emergency has been precipitated by inmates, it still may be possible to use the services of carefully selected inmates during recovery. Because this option may invite retaliation from other inmates, it should be considered carefully before it is taken. If inmates are used during recovery, they should be short-timers, eligible for transfer to community-based corrections or early parole.

The Internal Materials Resource

A preemergency security response inventory and materials and supplies inventory should provide the number and location of specific items that may be reasonably anticipated to be necessary during response and provide a baseline for calculating any additional resources necessary during recovery. A security response inventory may account for the following:

boarding up windows, shoveling snow drifts, or sandbagging a dike or riverbank.

Strategic planning includes developing and maintaining a periodically updated list of inmates who have specialized skills and a list of unskilled inmates who have been classified as suitable for manual labor during an emergency. The classification process should determine which of these inmates will be permitted to work outside the facility or under minimal, or intermittent, supervision within a facility

• Inmate control devices, such as metal handcuffs, leg irons, plastic cuffs, waist belts, and padlocks and chains for securing cell doors whose locking mechanisms have been sabotaged by inmates during an emergency

- Emergency control equipment, such as handguns, shotguns, rifles, automatic weapons, ammunition, batons, stun guns, canisters of mace, canisters of crowd-control gas, security vests/helmets/gloves/shields, and bullhorns

- Hand-held radios, batteries/charging stations, and flashlights

- Spare parts for all electronic monitoring and security devices, both perimeter and interior

- All tools, knives, cutting torches, barber equipment, and any implement (by type and location) that can be converted into a weapon by an inmate

- Fire fighting equipment, by type and location

- Vehicles, by type and location

The materials and supply inventory provides the quantity of items on hand (and the time before depletion if not replenished on schedule) during normal facility operation. If specific items are destroyed during the emergency, the preemergency inventory provides a ready reference for purchasing as staff work to quickly replenish supplies during recovery. This inventory can save many hours of need estimation, especially if staff who normally possess inventory knowledge are not available during recovery. The inventory should include the on-hand quantity of the following:

- **Food Items**—canned fruit; canned vegetables; sugar; flour; canned/powdered milk; butter; meats, including bacon and sausage; eggs; fresh milk; bread, rolls, biscuits, and/or ingredients for baking; condiments; soft drinks; fresh produce; TV dinners; serving trays; utensils (knife, spoon, fork); glasses; and bottled water and auxiliary sources of water

- **Inmate Clothing**—shirts, pants, underwear, stockings, light jackets, winter jackets, shoes, boots, belts, and suits

- **Cell Furnishings**—bed/mattress, sheets, blankets, towels, pillows, personal hygiene items (toilet paper, soap, combs, toothbrush/paste, and feminine hygiene needs), desks, lightbulbs/light fixtures, toilets, sinks, mirrors, pencil, paper, and envelopes

- **Medical Needs**—Medications, syringes, surgical equipment, wrappings, stretchers, crutches, braces, medical evaluation equipment (stethoscopes, X-ray, EKG), and eyeglasses

The Physical Plant. The physical plant of any given facility will have features that can either help staff or create opportunities for problems. Of specific interest are the following:

- The nature and status of all locking mechanisms (both cell and security doors)

- The location of entrances and exits of every building

- The location of any access to roofs of buildings

- The placement of any interior fences and the location of interior gates

- The status of perimeter security systems and any breaches in perimeter integrity (by means of gates or visual blindspots)

- The existence of any within-perimeter tunnel system that can be accessed from inside the facility

• The location of all tool storage areas within the facility

• The extent and nature of any vehicular traffic within the perimeter

• The location of all entrances and exits to the facility

• The location of all highways and roads within a one-mile radius of the facility, with designation of the intersections most appropriate for establishing roadblocks and crowd-control activities

• The location of all buildings or recreation areas suitable for temporary inmate housing

Ignorance of the specifics of the physical plant can have disastrous consequences if any of these features of the physical plant represent a vulnerability not recognized earlier or if their potential usefulness in response and recovery is overlooked. The time to find out which feature is an asset and which represents a vulnerability is during mitigation, not during response and recovery.

External Resource Inventory

Emergencies limited to only a small section of the facility or emergencies involving a small number of inmates may be managed successfully by facility staff. However, many emergencies are beyond the scope of facility staff. Serious emergencies may require immediate access to external resources. The Camp Hill riots, for example, required the services of 3,000 law enforcement and emergency services personnel during response to the second riot. An astonishing variety of external resources (human and material) were used during recovery. Strategic planning always should assume that any given emergency can exceed the management capacity of facility staff and effective response and recovery will require access to community resources.

External Human Resources

External human resources may be obtained from the following:

• **The Community**—local police, hospital/emergency medical services staff, firefighters, medical evacuation lifeflight units, correctional facility staff, business community, and utility representatives

• **The State**—the state police, National Guard, emergency management agency, state department of transportation, regional hospitals, state and county correctional facilities, and commercial vendors with resources that exceed those of local vendors

• **Surrounding States**—commercial vendors who may be able to supply equipment and essential materials not available in adequate quantities from state vendors and additional rescue work volunteers

• **The Federal Government**—military, specialized medical units, the Federal Emergency Management Agency, the Federal Aviation Agency, and the Federal Bureau of Prisons

The emergency plan should list the names and organization of every individual who may be called on in the event of an emergency by address of the organization and primary and secondary telephone numbers where the individual may be reached. An alternative always should be designated in case the individual originally identified is not available. The specific ability of each individual to provide a particular service, material, supply, or equipment should be recorded in the emergency plan.

External Materials Resources

Regardless of the size of the preemergency inventory, an emergency may leave staff without the equipment and supplies necessary for an efficient recovery. Massive destruction of the physical plant may create a severe threat to the ability of staff to meet even the most basic inmate needs during recovery if inadequate emergency planning has occurred. A list of commercial vendors and agencies that can provide essential recovery equipment and supplies should be included in the emergency plan. Staging areas for the delivery of all equipment and supplies should be included in the emergency plan, with specific directions given to all vendors. The emergency plan should provide at least both a primary and a secondary source for the following items:

- **Food.** The entire range of food items eventually will have to be obtained, although TV dinners, which are handy if the kitchens have been destroyed, may be provided on a temporary basis. The vendors for all food items should be large commercial vendors; the local grocery store is unlikely to have enough goods on hand for recovery.

- **Potable Water.** If the available water is contaminated, or the plumbing has been destroyed, or no is longer accessible to inmates, an immediate priority will be obtaining a reliable source of potable water. The National Guard usually can provide water buffaloes that will address water needs.

- **Temporary Kitchens.** If facility kitchens have been destroyed, or are too badly damaged for immediate use, the National Guard or military bases can provide portable field kitchens.

- **Portable Toilets.** If inmate housing is no longer usable, it will be necessary to provide temporary toilet facilities, which are available from commercial vendors in large quantities.

- **Medical Supplies.** These items can be brought in from commercial vendors with relative ease, although there should be several sources listed in the emergency plan for items such as insulin and heart medication.

- **Portable Emergency Lighting.** Portable lighting may be necessary in buildings, on facility grounds, and outside the perimeter. Portable lighting may be obtained from the local emergency management agency or the National Guard.

- **Clothing, Bedding, and Personal Hygiene Items.** These items may be obtained from other correctional industries if they are part of the product line. If correctional industries cannot be of help, these items may be loaned from other correctional facilities or obtained from commercial vendors whose operation is large enough to provide large quantities of these items on short notice.

- **Inmate Control Equipment.** Handcuffs, leg irons, and waist belts may be difficult to find in sufficient supply if adequate planning has not been accomplished. Inmates maintained outside their normal living quarters, as 1,800 inmates were for three days at Camp Hill, must be secured. To have available thousands of pairs of handcuffs (especially the plastic cuffs that must be replaced often) it may be necessary to establish contacts with local, state, and national vendors. Cell doors sabotaged by inmates may be secured by padlocks and chains, but it can be frustrating to attempt to locate several thousand same-keyed padlocks if a national vendor has not been previously determined.

• **Mass Evacuation Vehicles.** The worst case scenario for any emergency involves evacuating large numbers of inmates. In this situation, the facility should have contact information readily available to arrange for commercial buses to relocate as many inmates as possible at one time. The best source for buses is either a commercial transportation company or the local school district. The inability of commercial vendors to provide buses should be established before contacting local school districts. Their obligation to transport students makes them a last resort.

Coordinating Resources

Strategic planning should provide for a Memorandum of Agreement between the facility and every agency expected to assist in an emergency. This Memorandum of

Agreement should provide for (1) a mutual command post, (2) a joint chain of command to direct staff, (3) mutual agreement on decisions, and (4) criteria for determining when law enforcement staff may leave the facility.

The importance of this last item should be stressed. Without specific criteria for releasing law enforcement personnel, there may be a premature release that plays into the hands of inmates planning to take advantage of the situation created by the initial emergency. Inmates may plan riots or escapes during response and activate those plans while staff are focused on recovery, as happened at Camp Hill in 1989.

Chapter Four

Specialized Teams and the Life Cycle of Emergencies

When a group of people coalesce to pursue some commonly agreed upon objective, an important transformation takes place within an organization. One often observes this occurrence during times of crisis . . . . People give selflessly of themselves, work long hours in adverse conditions, and sometimes even risk their own lives to save others. In these situations, people show how deeply they care for one another (Wright 1994:55).

Before the 1971 Attica riot, correctional facilities often responded to emergencies with a seat-of-the-pants approach that involved grabbing the nearest available staff, issuing hastily prepared orders, and then sending terrified officers into life-threatening situations they were not trained to handle. This approach significantly increased the potential for unnecessary death, injury, and property loss. There are at least fifteen types of specialized teams to be considered as a resource in strategic planning. The number of teams any given facility needs depends on the facility's size and resource base. In the following discussion, it is assumed that every team will play a role in preparedness.

The Fire Safety Team

Headed by a fire safety officer, this team consists of staff capable of receiving specialized training in fire prevention, response, and rescue, as well as in the control and management of hazardous substances.

Deployment Phase

Mitigation, response, and recovery

Goals

- To attain the specialized knowledge necessary to manage fires and hazardous substances accidents

- To effectively communicate that knowledge to staff and inmates through appropriate training

- To coordinate all fire/hazardous substances accident activities with community fire departments

- To effectively respond to all fire emergencies and hazardous substances emergencies

Selection Criteria

- A stated interest in the subjects

- Relevant experience

- The ability to analyze problem situations and develop logical responses

- The ability to communicate effectively

- The ability to respond calmly to crisis situations

- The physical ability to meet standardized requirements for victim rescue procedures

The Correctional Emergency Response Team

Correctional Emergency Response Team officers receive special training in the strategies and techniques best suited for controlling the behavior of disruptive inmates. Team activities range from responding to a minor disturbance to advancing a full-scale assault on a facility under the control of rioting inmates.

Deployment Phase

Response and recovery

Goals

- To efficiently and effectively respond to any emergency in which the number of inmates involved is too large for the regular complement of officers to manage effectively and safely: riots, cellblock takeovers, large-scale refusals to lock-up, hostage situations, and escapes and escape attempts that have led to other types of emergencies

- To help law enforcement units in any assault too large for the team to manage

- To locate and render ineffective any booby traps developed by inmates before response or recovery

- To locate and safely extract hostages

- To provide surveillance and security of inmates during recovery

Selection Criteria

Correctional Emergency Response Team membership should be based on past performance that has proven the officer's ability to do the following:

- Maintain calm under conditions of extreme stress.

- Exhibit maturity when confronted by angry, hostile inmates displaying a high level of verbal animosity.

- Resist the temptation to use excessive force.

- Respond immediately to orders, yet be able to show initiative when it is needed.

- Do not personalize the emergency.

- Engage in an assault on a defended position manned by combative inmates where booby traps may be encountered.

- Safely extract hostages.

The Hostage Negotiation Team

The taking of hostages is most likely in the event of an inmate-precipitated emergency, but hostage-taking is a possibility during any type of emergency. If hostages have been taken, their successful release automatically becomes a priority. The first administrative impulse may be to use the Correctional

Photo courtesy Bowden Institution

The expertise of many areas of the institution can be called on for a specialized team. Bowden Institution's Critical Incident Stress Debriefing Team and Organizing Committee.

Emergency Response Team to rescue the hostages, but history has taught the risk inherent in armed solutions to hostage situations. In 1971, the Attica riot was resolved by force and ten staff hostages were killed by "friendly fire." A Rand study found that 75 percent of all hostages who died were killed during an assault intended to rescue them (Jenkins *et al.* 1977). However, at Camp Hill, the release of hostages was negotiated successfully during both riots.

Deployment Phase

Response

Goals

- To establish verbal contact with inmate leaders

- To establish the identity and status of each hostage

- To structure communications to emphasize the value in not allowing the hostages to be harmed

- To negotiate the safe release of all hostages

- To provide explicit surrender instructions to the inmates once hostages have been released

- To obtain information during negotiations that will assist an assault if it becomes necessary

Selection Criteria

The hostage negotiation team may be drawn from both treatment and custody staff and should include both primary and secondary negotiators. Members of the team should be selected on the basis of the following criteria:

- A knowledge of the facility, the inmates, and human behavior

- The intelligence to practice conflict resolution

- A high tolerance for frustration

- The ability to remain calm regardless of provocation

- The ability to handle the stress of a process that, if unsuccessful, can lead to the death of hostages

- Possession of strong verbal skills

- A position in the chain of command that does not have the authority to set policy or make major decisions

- An ability to work with Correctional Emergency Response Team officers

Administrators should not be negotiators. A key element in negotiating is the ability to say that the negotiator doesn't have the power to grant inmate demands and must pass them along through the chain of command. This allows negotiators the advantage of buying time, an option not open if negotiators have the power to grant demands. There is a tendency to put counselors and psychologists on the negotiation team automatically, but the ability to negotiate depends on more than formal education. Other staff may have the personality and verbal skills to be extremely useful in communicating with inmates in volatile situations, even though these staff have never set foot in a college classroom. Lack of a formal education should not automatically preclude membership on this team.

In facilities with Hispanic inmates, at least one negotiator should be bilingual in English and Spanish. If this is not possible, and the hostage takers don't speak English, the only recourse is to have either a bilingual inmate or civilian volunteer translate. Because this situation creates a serious potential for miscommunication that can get hostages killed, every effort should be made to ensure that at least one negotiator is fluent in Spanish if there are non-English-speaking Hispanic inmates in the facility.

The Intelligence Unit

Intelligence gathering is extremely valuable during all phases of the emergency life cycle.

Deployment Phase

All phases

Goals

• To develop inmate sources of information

• To develop staff sources of information

• To identify inmate leaders

• To identify staff who violate the rules

• To function as an early warning system for inmate-precipitated emergencies or staff discontent that can make the facility vulnerable to inmate activity

• To determine any inmate plans to precipitate an emergency during recovery

At Camp Hill, if facility staff knew that inmates were planning to launch a second night of riots, a different set of decisions might have prevented the second riot.

Selection Criteria

This can be a difficult unit to staff because its members must be willing to interrogate staff, as well as inmates, and develop the chain of evidence that can lead to administrative disciplinary action against staff or prosecution of staff. The unit should be composed of correctional officers who are at least at the sergeant level and should not be used for any activity not directly related to the gathering of intelligence. Staff on this team should have the following:

• Strong analytical and communication skills

• Ability to establish the case for disciplinary action against staff

• Ability to interrogate without resorting to physical force

• Organizational ability necessary for chain-of-evidence procedures

• Ability to present themselves well in a courtroom setting

The Medical Response Team

Deployment Phase

Response and recovery

Goals

- To triage injured staff and inmates in accordance with accepted emergency medicine criteria

- To treat injuries on-site

- To coordinate treatment with local hospitals

- To identify dead staff and inmates

Selection Criteria

Because this team engages in tasks that require specialized knowledge, and are subject to government regulations, team members should possess the following:

- A valid state medical license

- Knowledge of emergency medical procedures

- The ability to handle simultaneous medical emergencies while remaining calm

- The ability to work outside an infirmary setting in the midst of chaos and disorganization

- Sound diagnostic judgment

The Special Transportation Unit

Deployment Phase

Response and recovery

Goal

- To safely and efficiently evacuate staff and inmates from a facility

Selection Criteria

In many states, these individuals are required to have a commercial vehicle operator's license. In addition, they should have the following:

- Ability to handle large commercial vehicles under a wide range of negative driving conditions

- Ability to use appropriate initiative under highly stressful conditions

- Ability to enjoy driving and view an evacuation as a test of personal skills

- Sufficient mechanical ability to diagnose vehicle breakdowns and effect simple repairs if a mechanic is not readily available

The Damage Assessment Team

Deployment Phase

Recovery

Goals

This team is responsible for accurately evaluating the status of the following:

- All cell locking mechanisms, cellblock security door locking mechanisms, the security doors on any other type of living unit in which inmates will be confined during recovery, and access doors to tunnels or plumbing chases

- Perimeter security system (fences, walls, monitoring devices, towers, and gates)

- Interior fences designed to limit inmate movement

- Electrical, plumbing (including shower rooms), and heating/cooling systems in the cellblocks and other housing units that must hold inmates immediately

- Electrical, plumbing, and heating/cooling systems in buildings providing support inmate services, beginning with the kitchen(s)

Cell door locking mechanisms should be examined immediately. During any type of emergency there will be inmates willing to use the opportunity to sabotage locking mechanisms. As the Damage Assessment Team conducts its evaluation, reports should be flowing back to the command post. As soon as the first report of significant damage comes in, the Damage Repair Team should be activated.

Selection Criteria

The team should include specialists in plumbing, electricity, locking mechanisms, surveillance and perimeter technology, heating/cooling, and construction who can perform assessments under extremely trying conditions. These individuals must:

- Have an expert knowledge of their specialty

- Know the facility so well they can work under extreme conditions of hardship

- Be able to control their emotions when they see shops or pet projects that have been destroyed by inmates

- Understand the need for special alertness if the emergency has been other than emergency precipitated and they are using inmates to assist in assessment

Photo courtesy Incident Management System at Arizona Dept. of Corrections

During a simulated disturbance, an officer with a video camera arrives to record the incident. Incident Management System, Arizona Department of Corrections.

- Have the physical stamina and health to work twelve-hour shifts that may involve physical exertion

- Be able to prioritize repair needs

The Damage Repair Team
Deployment Phase
Recovery

Goals
- To quickly and efficiently effect facility repairs in accordance with priorities set by the Damage Assessment Team

- To ascertain any damage missed by the Damage Assessment Team and recommend an appropriate adjustment of priorities

Selection Criteria
Maintenance staff selected for this team must:

- Be able to supervise inmate work crews that may be agitated and emotional

- Have the physical stamina to work twelve-hour shifts in conditions requiring extraordinary physical exertion

The temptation to combine the Damage Assessment Team and the Damage Repair Team and begin repairs only when damage assessment has been completed should be avoided. Once damaged security locking mechanisms have been identified, it is imperative they be repaired immediately. At the same time, it is imperative to determine the status of the rest of the physical plant. This can be accomplished efficiently in a large facility only if two teams are operating simultaneously. If

the size of the facility staff does not permit two teams, then locking and other security mechanisms should have priority for both status identification and repair.

The Escapee Recovery Team
This team may be either a separate team or a subset of the Correctional Emergency Response Team.

Deployment Phase
Mitigation and response

Goals
- To determine all possible escape routes from a prison or jail

- To determine all possible routes into the community if the perimeter of a prison or jail is successfully breached

- To develop an understanding of the geographical area surrounding any community-based facility

- To conduct all searches in a manner that does not endanger the public or embarrass the agency

- To effect the safe capture and return of any inmate who has fled a correctional facility

- To avoid the use of excessive force

Selection Criteria
Because this team may have to operate within the community and outside facility routine, team members must:

- Be able to communicate with the public, including inmate family members, as well as with law enforcement personnel

- Have the knowledge necessary to exercise sound judgment in the use of lethal force to effect capture

- Be knowledgeable about first aid in case staff or escapees are injured and medical staff are not readily available

- Be able to "think like an inmate on the run"

- Have a thorough knowledge of all possible escape routes and hiding places along those routes

- Have highly developed observation skills and the ability to notice the smallest detail when tracking an inmate

- Have the emotional control necessary to avoid the use of excessive force against an escapee who has led officers on a long, tiring chase

The Post-traumatic Assessment Team

Deployment Phase

Response and recovery

Goals

- To determine the emotional status of inmates and staff throughout response and recovery

- To provide on-site crisis intervention

- To refer inmates, staff, and families to post-emergency therapy if necessary

- To use a monitoring system that tracks staff and inmates in need of long-term mental health services

- To educate staff and inmates to the signs of post-traumatic stress disorder and a method of referral if those signs appear

- To periodically assess staff and inmates for signs of post-traumatic stress disorder

- To conduct an ongoing psychological assessment of staff and inmates to detect indicators of future participation in violent behavior and provide appropriate intervention to prevent such behavior

Selection Criteria

This team should be composed of psychiatrists, psychologists, counselors, and chaplains. These individuals should be able to do the following:

- Communicate with staff and inmates in varying stages of emotional reaction and discomfort

- Conduct psychological assessments under difficult circumstances

- Engage in long-term monitoring of staff and inmates to determine if the delivery of psychological services has been effective

The Criminal Prosecution Team

This team should include some, or all, members of the Intelligence Unit, but it should be under the command of a high-ranking correctional officer, such as the major.

Deployment Phases

Response and recovery

Goals

- To identify all inmates who have engaged in criminal behavior during an emergency and gather evidence necessary to successfully prosecute them

- To practice proper chain-of-evidence and evidence preservation procedures in all cases

- To coordinate the administrative and criminal prosecution of inmate rule violators

- To assist other staff during the prosecution phase

Selection Criteria

The Criminal Prosecution Team should begin work as soon as the facility has entered a state of emergency. The development of evidence for criminal prosecution can begin as soon as the team arrives on the scene. The members of this team must be able to do the following:

- Understand and effectively use specialized training in interrogation techniques, evidence location and identification, legal documentation, and courtroom behavior and preparation

- Use specialized equipment, such as tape recorders for making a record of all telephone contacts with inmate ringleaders and radio transmissions by inmates in possession of staff walkie-talkies and documenting the statements of injured staff or inmates; cameras and video tape equipment to document emergency events as they occur and provide a follow-up record of damage done to the facility; and highly sensitive directional microphones, infrared sensing devices, and cameras with telephoto lenses that can be set up in towers or other locations that permit safe recording of inmate activity

- Humanely, but effectively, debrief staff and inmates injured, or taken hostage, by inmates

---

Debriefing Staff and Inmate Victims

Any staff, or inmates, who are injured by inmates participating in the emergency should have their injuries photographed and videotaped as soon as they are brought in for treatment. The more graphic the evidence, the more likely the jury is to convict. If possible, the identities of the inmates inflicting the damage should be ascertained and recorded at the time of treatment. The injured person should not be badgered for information, but the most vital information often is secured immediately after injury has been inflicted. Too long an interval between treatment and debriefing may result in the loss of valuable information concerning the events and the inmates involved in them.

Debriefing should establish:

- The chronology of events that led to the victimization of the staff member or inmate

- The identity of inmates involved in the victimization of the staff member or other inmate

- The identity of staff witnesses to the victimization

- The identity of inmate witnesses to the victimization

- The specific behavior of the inmates who are to be prosecuted

- Any statements made by the inmates before, during, or after the victimization

The Litigation Response Team

This team is rarely, if ever, developed until staff belatedly realize, at some point during recovery, that they eventually will have to respond to large numbers of inmate lawsuits.

Deployment Phase

Recovery

Goals

• To anticipate the most likely issues inmates will focus on in post-emergency litigation

• To debrief all decision makers in anticipation of litigation

• To formulate a response to potential major litigation issues before the lawsuit is received

• To prepare staff for testimony in court

• To manage all aspects, including appeals, of the agency response to post-emergency litigation

• To evaluate all actions taken by staff and recommend changes in procedures that will make future actions legally defensible

Selection Criteria

Team members should be attorneys and investigators trained in legal investigation. In the event of a major prison riot, there most likely will be a coordination between in-agency attorneys and attorneys from the Attorney General's Office.

The Information Management Team

This team will be divided into two groups: a command post recording group and a media/community information group.

Command Post Recording Team

Deployment Phase

Response and recovery

Goals

• To accurately record rapidly developing events while maintaining strict confidentiality

• To maintain a written (as well as audio log, if resources permit) of all major decisions, significant incoming information, telephone calls and their content, and discussions that occur in the primary and secondary command posts

• To participate in all debriefing sessions conducted by the Post-Emergency Litigation Response Team

Selection Criteria

Individuals on this team should be able to do the following:

• Rapidly and accurately record information under stressful conditions

• Maintain confidentiality of all records

• Participate in settling disputes of recollection during the post-emergency litigation phase

Media/Community Information Group

Deployment Phase

Response and recovery

Goals

- To provide accurate and timely media information

- To provide accurate and timely information to relatives of staff and inmates

- To coordinate the management of the thousands of phone calls that can pour in during response and recovery

Selection Criteria

Members of this communications team should be able to do the following:

- Manage news conferences

- Brief decision makers on information to be presented at a news conference

- Write news releases

The type of emergency will determine the need for a specific specialized team.

The Inmate-precipitated Emergency

Response Teams

- Correctional Emergency Response Team
- Hostage Negotiation Team
- Medical Management Team
- Information Management Team
- Escapee Recovery Team

Recovery Teams

- Intelligence Unit
- Special Transportation Unit
- Damage Assessment Team
- Damage Repair Team
- Post-traumatic Assessment Team
- Criminal Prosecution Team
- Litigation Response Team
- Information Management Team
- Architectural Assessment Team
- Fire Safety Team
- Stepdown Committee

Fires and Technological Emergencies/the Natural Emergency

Response Teams

- Medical Management Team
- Special Transportation Unit
- Intelligence Unit
- Information Management Team
- Fire Safety Team

Recovery Teams

- Damage Assessment Team
- Damage Repair Team
- Post-traumatic Assessment Team
- Information Management Team
- Litigation Response Team
- Architectural Assessment Team
- Stepdown Committee

The Human Emergency

Response Teams

- Medical Management Team
- Special Transportation Unit
- Intelligence Unit
- Information Management Team
- Damage Assessment Team
- Damage Repair Team
- Fire Safety Team

Recovery Teams

- Post-traumatic Assessment Team
- Information Management Team
- Stepdown Committee

The specific role of each team member during each category of emergency should be clearly established. Training should emphasize developing appropriate responses to a variety of real-life situations and understanding the role each individual and team is to perform when the emergency plan is activated.

- Professionally handle hostile phone calls and questions from the media and the public

- Professionally manage and meet the needs of both print and visual media

The Architectural Assessment Team

This highly specialized team addresses the issue of modifying physical plant design. This team applies lessons of the past to buildings of the future.

Deployment Phase

Recovery and mitigation

Goals

- To comprehensively evaluate every emergency to determine the physical plant's role in the development of the emergency and any hindrance or assistance that plant design contributed to the response and recovery phases

- To recommend specific modifications to the facility's physical plant

- To recommend specific modifications to any facility in the design stage or approval stage of construction

Selection Criteria

The members of this team should be able to do the following:

- Understand the complexity of facility design and construction

- Understand security needs

- Translate blueprints, or at least understand the rudiments of blueprint reading

- Analyze the role of the physical plant during all phases of an emergency and communicate meaningful recommendations in an understandable manner to decision makers

The Stepdown Committee

Deployment Phase

Recovery

Goals

- To return the facility to normal operations as quickly as possible without endangering staff, inmates, or the community

- To determine and direct the daily activities of staff as they attempt to return the facility to normal operation

- To effectively address short-term inmate needs in the immediate aftermath of the emergency

- To recommend long-term changes that will improve overall facility mitigation, response, and recovery

Selection Criteria

This committee should be chaired by the chief administrative officer of the facility and members should include all department heads, commissioned officers, and union representatives.

Chapter 5

Emergency Plan Activation: Setting the Stage

*A*fight breaks out on the recreation yard
*of a Federal Correctional Institution. It
quickly spreads to the gymnasium and
nearby common areas of the institution, then to
several housing units. Inmates begin to break into
offices and storage areas, destroying property and
setting fires. Disturbance Control and Special
Operations Response Teams from this institution
and two nearby federal correctional facilities are
immediately activated. The institution alerts the
local sheriff's office, which provides staff to bolster
perimeter security. The Disturbance Control
Squad and Special Operations Response Team
restore order, containing damage and preventing
serious injuries* (Federal Bureau of Prisons
1994:5).

If resources are to be used effectively during
response, strategic planning should provide
written guidelines for activating the communications tree, establishing a command post for
response/recovery direction and coordination,
remaining on post during response, managing
post evacuation, deploying specialized teams,
evacuating civilian visitors, and using inmate
work cadres. These guidelines make clear to
staff what is expected of them.

The Communications Tree

The communications tree is the official
chain of command for the agency and every
facility contained within that agency. Because
it is already in place and routinely used, the
communications tree provides a standardized,
efficient method of coordinating information
flow during response and recovery. The communications tree is the most effective means of
activating the emergency plan.

During an emergency, the roots of the communications tree are located in the facility control center, or whatever other central location
is best suited for rapid communication of
information. All staff should be subject to a
standing order that as soon as they become
aware of an emergency situation they are to
notify the control center and provide as much
information about the situation as they can.

The type of information needed will
depend on the type of emergency. Once notified, control center staff should call the facility
administrator, advise of the information
received, and request permission to activate the
emergency plan. This request presents the first
critical decision for the facility administrator.

Immediate activation may be premature and may cause unnecessary panic and waste of time and energy. Failure to activate the emergency plan immediately may result in unnecessary loss of life and property. If the plan is activated, the facility administrator should advise executive staff and the agency administrator that an emergency situation exists and the emergency plan has been activated. Executive staff should contact their department heads who, in turn, should advise their respective subordinates.

In a large facility it may be necessary to notify hundreds of staff that an emergency has occurred. On-duty staff may be notified by means of telephone, hand-held radio, a bell or whistle emergency alarm procedure, or all three methods. However, many staff with specific emergency response responsibilities may be off duty. To quickly and efficiently notify off-duty personnel, a periodically updated telephone directory of report-to-work primary and secondary numbers where each member of the work force may be reached day or night should be contained in the emergency plan.

The primary number usually will be the home phone number. The secondary number represents locations where an employee is most likely to be reached if not at home. When staff are reached at home, they should be ordered to report to work. If someone other than the employee answers the phone and asks to take a message, the caller should first confirm that the employee is absent from home, then make certain the message to report to work is given to an adult, not a child. However, if a child is the only person available to take a message, the caller should give the message to report to

work and repeat the call at a later time. If the employee is not at home, then the secondary phone numbers should be used.

Because emergencies, by definition, often are unanticipated, it may be that key individuals in the chain of command are absent when the emergency occurs. In this case, the chain of command fills in any communication gaps. For example, if the major is on vacation, the deputy for operations will be responsible for notifying the shift captains.

There always will be staff who cannot be reached through the communications tree. As a backup, the emergency plan should include the names and call letters of television and radio stations willing to include an "All essential staff report to work" message in their coverage of the emergency. The emergency plan should designate the name of the staff member responsible for making this request to the media.

Staff who hear about the emergency through the media and call in to ask if they may be of any assistance should be directed to stay at home until contacted by their supervisor. The switchboard operator should not put this type of call through to the supervisor. Supervisors will have enough to do and cannot afford to waste time on unnecessary calls. Only staff with a designated emergency response responsibility should be allowed on facility property during response. Staff who do not have a designated role, but who show up with the intention to help out will just get in the way and can make a bad situation worse.

The Command Post

Response to any emergency should be coordinated by staff located in a predetermined command posts. There are two types of command posts: primary and secondary.

The primary command post is outside the facility and provides direction and coordinates response. The secondary post may be located inside the facility for use during recovery as the location from which supervisors coordinate recovery efforts with the primary command post. Because many emergencies are inmate precipitated, it is critical that the primary command post be in a building outside the facility, even if this post is nothing more than a mobile trailer brought in for emergency use. Decision makers must remain in the primary command post until it has been established that the facility is secure beyond any doubt.

Regardless of the type of emergency, a basic rule of thumb is that key decision makers should never be vulnerable to being taken hostage or injured. At Camp Hill, after the first riot, when staff were under the assumption the institution was secure, a second riot broke out and approximately fifty staff (including the entire chain of command, except for the author) were trapped inside a secondary command post firebombed by rioting inmates.

Photo courtesy of Ohio Department of Rehabilitation and Correction

The Ohio Department of Rehabilitation and Correction practice its emergency plan activation.

Staff Who Remain on Post

If staff are expected to remain at their posts during response, and are able to safely do so, the emergency plan must specify their responsibilities. For example, the specification for block officers might be as follows:

1. Order all inmates to their cells.

2. Lockdown the block.

3. Secure all outer block doors.

4. Ensure telephone contact with the primary command post is established.

5. Report in to the primary command post on a regular basis.

6. Reassure inmates and listen to their concerns and fears.

7. Constantly assess the physical security of the block to determine if any inmates are attempting to break out.

8. Observe the surrounding area through any available windows and report any unusual or significant inmate activity to the primary command post.

Staff Unable to Remain on Post

If staff are driven from their posts, the emergency plan should list emergency relocation sites outside the facility to which they can report. The emergency relocation site may be a parking lot, a field, or an outside building, such as a barn. The main criterion for emergency relocation sites is that they are in an area where staff exiting the facility will not interfere with the deployment of response personnel rushing to the facility. If staff are not expected to remain at their posts, and can exit the facility safely, the emergency plan should direct them to the emergency relocation site where they can wait until it has been decided if, and when, their skills will be needed. Staff not immediately needed for response should be sent home so they will not get in the way of those staff with response duties.

Activation of Specialized Teams

If on-duty staff are members of a specialized team, the emergency plan should specify their deployment site, any equipment they need to bring with them, any equipment they will be issued once they report, and a procedure for other staff to "double up" to cover their normal duties. If team members are off duty, the

Photo courtesy Anthony Carnevale, Director of Public Affairs, Mass. Dept. Of Correction

Simulated exercises, Massachusetts Department of Correction.

strategic plan should specify the deployment site to which they should report. The emergency plan should establish a medical triage area inside the facility (usually the infirmary) and outside the facility in case the emergency makes the infirmary site unusable. All off-duty medical staff should be placed on standby or brought in immediately, depending on the type of emergency.

Removing Civilians from Harm's Way

Inmate visitors and any other noncorrectional staff who happen to be in the facility at the time of the emergency should be escorted to their vehicles and ordered to leave the facility immediately. In the case of visitors of inmates, it may be necessary to obtain law enforcement assistance to facilitate their orderly exit.

Activation of Inmate Labor Teams

Unless the emergency is inmate precipitated, supervisors should brief inmate work cadres concerning their jobs during response and recovery and provide them with appropriate equipment and clothing.

As soon as activation has occurred, the facility is in a position to respond. But who is responsible for directing that response? There are currently two direction structures in existence: the traditional command-and-control structure and the Arizona Department of Corrections Incident Management System.

The Traditional Command-and-Control Structure

This structure requires emergency plan activation by the facility administrator or appropriate designee in the event of the administrator's absence:

> *During an emergency situation, the Warden, or highest ranking official on duty, shall have absolute and total authority for decisions made affecting the institution, the emergency and security of the premises* (Avoyelles Correctional Center 1995:9).

All response direction comes from the facility administrator through the regular chain of command. Line staff take their orders through this chain of command just as they would during normal facility operation. The traditional corrections approach to emergency response is to have the most senior staff provide direction.

The Arizona Department of Corrections Incident Management System

The Arizona Department of Corrections Incident Management System was implemented under the guidance of Director Samuel A. Lewis, with the goal of effectively managing resources in such a way that small problems don't have the time to become big problems. The Incident Management System is distinguished from the traditional command-and-control structure in that the first correctional officer, regardless of rank, to identify an emergency in progress becomes the incident commander charged with directing the response:

> It is important to note that active participants in the incident or its resolution cannot assume command, nor should they attempt to set up the command post. The first arriving officer on the scene not directly involved in the incident is to assume command . . . . The Incident Commander establishes command by giving an initial report to applicable staff (Arizona Department of Corrections 1993:2).

The incident commander has the authority to direct the activities of superior officers in accordance with the established emergency plan. Superior officers arriving on the scene do not automatically assume command as would be the case in the traditional command-and-control structure:

> Command is normally transferred **ONLY** to improve the quality of the command organization and the effectiveness of the incident being managed . . . . Transfer of command **may** occur as supervisors senior to the current Incident Commander arrive on the scene and determine the need for a higher level of authority to be the Incident Commander (Arizona Department of Corrections 1993:3).

Thus, the arrival of a ranking officer on the incident scene does not mean command has been transferred to that officer. Command is transferred only when a specific transfer-of-command process has been initiated and completed. Off-site chain-of-command employees, such as the agency administrator or central office directors, who want to provide direction or advice may do so without assuming command. Specialized response teams report to the incident commander, even if senior officers are in the area.

The Incident Management System also provides that radio communication be in the form of plain text, that is, no call signs or confusing code labels. All transmissions use the job title of the individual involved in the communication. If the officer assigned to escort is being radioed, the term of address will be "escort."

Initiating a Twelve-Hour Emergency Staffing Schedule

An effective response and recovery requires more than the usual eight-hour shift. The emergency plan should provide direction for placing all essential staff on a twelve-hour schedule until normal operations have been resumed. Predetermination of this schedule will save countless hours of frustration and confusion. However, note that although correctional administrators readily acknowledge that twelve hours is long enough for any staff to work during an emergency, they generally are reluctant to leave the facility themselves until response is complete and the facility is declared to be secure. The result of too many hours on the job without relief can be extreme fatigue and mistakes in judgment and decision making. The emergency plan should address this critical issue in one of three ways:

1. The facility administrator and deputies rotate command on a twelve-on-twelve-off basis.

2. High-ranking, experienced central office staff relieve the facility administrator on a twelve-on-twelve-off basis.

3. The agency administrator selects a senior facility administrator from another facility to relieve the facility administrator on a twelve-on-twelve-off basis.

In any case, the periodic relief of key decision makers should be addressed by the emergency plan, otherwise, a bad situation may be made worse by fatigue accumulated over several stressful days:

> *On October 26, many of the correctional officers and administrators at Camp Hill were in a state of extreme exhaustion. Considering the events of the previous 24 hours, that is understandable. This exhaustion undoubtedly contributed to the failure to assess, and respond to, the security situation within the institution in an adequate manner. The presence of fresh administrative personnel to provide assistance and a "second opinion" might well have lessened this failure* (Pennsylvania House Judiciary Committee 1990:15-16).

Emergency Keys

Each correctional institution should have several sets of emergency keys that will give access to all areas. These keys should be tested routinely and color coded. In an exercise, make sure staff have access to each area of the institution.

Chapter 6

Inmate-precipitated Emergencies: General Principles of Mitigation

*N*onviolent inmate disturbances include hunger strikes, sit-down strikes, work stoppages, voluntary lockdowns . . . excessive numbers of inmates reporting for sick call, and the filing of grievances by nearly everyone in a cellblock or even in the entire institution. Violent inmate disturbances include . . . assaulting officers; sabotaging the electrical, plumbing, or heating systems; burning or destroying institutional property; and taking control, with or without hostages, of a cellblock, a yard, or an entire prison (Bartollas and Conrad 1992:421).

Strategic planning for inmate-precipitated emergencies tends to be approached solely in terms of preparedness and response. This approach makes the fatalistic assumption that these emergencies are inevitable and all staff can do is be prepared to respond when they occur. Although it is foolish to assume a zero probability for any inmate-precipitated emergency, it is equally foolish to assume that level 1 and 2 mitigation is impossible.

Inmate-precipitated emergencies include escapes, walkaways, work stoppages, hunger strikes, minor disturbances, gang-related disturbances, riots, and hostage situations. These emergencies differ from other types of emergency in three critical aspects:

1. **Source of the Emergency**. The inmates are the source of the emergency. They cannot be used as a resource during preparedness and response. Their ability to contribute to recovery activities may be severely limited.

2. **Staff Emotions.** Staff may experience a sense of betrayal and anger when inmates engage in disruptive behavior that upsets orderly facility operations and harms the public image of the facility. These feelings of betrayal may negatively influence decision making, particularly in the area of the use of force. Staff who are proud of their facility and truly believe they are doing the best they can under difficult circumstances may experience intense anger when inmates engage in disruptive behavior, especially when that behavior is embarrassing, for example, an inmate escaping from a visiting room by mingling with civilians when visiting hours are over, or walking off while on outside work detail, or committing a crime while on furlough. The most

intense anger and feelings of betrayal will occur in a riot.

3. **Staff Under the Physical Control of Inmates.** Staff may be hostages or barricaded in buildings in areas under inmate control. Feelings of fear, anxiety, and anger that staff normally experience during an emergency will be intensified by this frightening confirmation of just how vulnerable all staff are to victimization by the inmates they are expected to control. Hostages, trapped staff, and killed or injured staff represent a troubling complication during response and recovery.

Level 2 Mitigation

Adequate Levels of Inmate Programming

Numerous books have been written on the rehabilitative value of inmate programming, with an emphasis that such programming is a valuable means of correcting inmate behavior and preparing the inmate for reintegration into society (Stojkovic and Lovell 1992, for example). However, maximizing programming availability also serves the goal of level 2 mitigation. Inmates who are occupied with meaningful work, vocational training, and educational programs may have more of a stake in helping maintain order in a facility than inmates who are bored and frustrated by the lack of opportunities to use their time constructively. Programs and job opportunities are critical to the effective management of any facility, but particularly one that is crowded.

Before the Camp Hill riots, one-third of the 2,600 inmates were idle and every program had long waiting lists. This degree of idleness and lack of opportunity creates feelings of

hopelessness, anger, and frustration that easily can turn into violence, particularly when inmates are being denied parole because they have not met the requirements of their treatment plans. Failure to qualify for parole sets up a vicious cycle: crowding increases, the waiting lists grow, and even more inmates are denied parole. The Pennsylvania Senate Judiciary report on the Camp Hill riots noted:

> *Superintendent Freeman stated the programs for inmates were inadequate. In the past, when Camp Hill had 900 inmates . . . . There were 53 full-time educational and vocational instructors. By the time Camp Hill had reached 2,600 inmates, we had 25 full-time and part-time vocational and educational instructors because of cutbacks in the budget* (Pennsylvania Senate Judiciary Committee 1990:17).

Monitoring of Inmate Activity

Not all inmate-precipitated emergencies are spontaneous. Most escapes and hunger strikes are planned in advance, as are most, if not all, instances of gang-related activity. Riots and other major forms of inmate disturbance are not necessarily spontaneous events that correctional staff and administrators are powerless to predict. The potential for inmates to make the conscious decision to engage in a systematic process of riot planning over a period of months is very real. According to the report on the 1989 Camp Hill riots issued by the Pennsylvania Senate Judiciary Committee:

> *There were indications that the activities by disruptive groups*

played a part in the uprising. There was testimony from many witnesses who stated their belief that the riots were fomented by an Islamic splinter group (Fruit of Islam) which, in a well organized manner, took advantage of inmate discord. Some staff said they believed the institutional conditions provided the perfect base for a small organized group of terrorists to create discord . . . . (Pennsylvania Senate Judiciary Committee 1990:13).

Systematic and ongoing use of the Intelligence Unit as an early warning system is essential. Information gathered by the Intelligence Unit should be analyzed immediately and brought to the attention of the facility administrator as quickly as possible. To prevent delays in communication, the chief of the Intelligence Unit should report directly to the facility administrator. Recommendations always should accompany the analysis.

Monitoring is not just a function of the Intelligence Unit:

> *. . . the BOP's correctional worker concept—which stresses that every employee is a correctional worker first and a specialist second— means that every staff member is a potential source of information, analysis, and action. All employees—no matter what their job specialty—are trained in security procedures and trained to be alert to unusual inmate activities and behavior . . . .*

In addition to this philosophy of individual staff as an element of level 2 mitigation, the Federal Bureau of Prisons has created an organizational structure that provides a formal process of level 2 mitigation: the unit management system. Unit management creates a division of labor that requires a multidisciplinary team of correctional officers, case managers, mental health personnel, counselors, and clerical staff to manage inmate housing units. Inmates and staff interact directly on a daily basis and get to know each other on a more personal level than might be possible otherwise: "In the prison setting, communication is a major element in preventing misunderstandings and mistakes that can lead to serious incidents . . . ."

As an added benefit, inmates develop confidence in the credibility of staff, making it more likely that the inmate population will accept management decisions. That, in turn, is a major factor in preventing institutional disturbances (Federal Bureau of Prisons 1994:7-8).

Direct Supervision of Inmates

Not all correctional facilities use the unit management system. A number of facilities in recent years have moved toward indirect supervision of inmates in the housing unit by building enclosed unit control centers that physically prevent staff-inmate contact. This practice physically isolates officers from the daily routine and lives of inmates. Although many officers feel safer working in an enclosed housing unit control center, indirect supervision is a practice that can send two negative messages to inmates: that officers are afraid, and that officers are not concerned about inmate safety. An officer in a unit control center, busy with paperwork, may not see an inmate assaulting a staff member or another inmate until it is too late. This is an especially critical issue in view of the research findings that 48 percent of prison assaults occur in the housing unit, and 20 percent of these assaults were inmate assaults on staff (Zausner 1985).

Closed-circuit television and unit control centers have their value, but they cannot replace the benefit of direct supervision policies that encourage close physical contact between correctional officers and inmates in their housing unit. Direct supervision policies keep officers circulating among the inmates. This allows for constant visual inspection, followed by a search if necessary, of all areas of the unit. Direct supervision also increases the opportunity for conversations that can serve as early warning systems of problems to come. During testimony concerning the Camp Hill riots, a block sergeant testified:

> *People probably think they (inmates) are on one side of the bars and we are on the other. That's not true, they are around us every day and the only way we can survive each day is by earning their respect. You earn their respect by interacting with them* (Pennsylvania Senate Judiciary Committee 1990:16).

Level 2 and Level 3 Mitigation

The control elements to be discussed at this point can be useful for both level 2 and level 3 mitigation. In terms of level 2 mitigation, these control elements can reduce the probability of occurrence of an emergency by restricting inmate opportunity to engage in disruptive behavior. In terms of level 3 mitigation, if disruptive behavior does occur, these same control elements can reduce the negative consequences of that behavior by limiting inmate freedom of movement and access to certain items.

Control of Movement Within the Housing Unit

The ability of inmates to engage in disruptive behavior is limited if they can be securely confined in a housing unit. The probability of escapes, gang fights, and riots can be greatly reduced if inmates are securely confined. If there is a disturbance, the ability to confine inmates can reduce the consequences of that disturbance:

> *Camp Hill management recognized years ago that the cell locking devices were antiquated and that doors and windows were of doubtful integrity. In recognition of this problem, Camp Hill received a cost estimate in July 1988 to upgrade cell block locks, doors and windows. At that time, the estimated cost was $10 million. The proposal was discussed with the Department of Corrections . . . was apparently determined to be a low priority*

item, and . . . was not considered further (Adams, Leader, and Irvis 1989:48).

The requested upgrade of Camp Hill's cell block locking system certainly would have reduced the consequences of the first riot by reducing the probability of a second riot.

Control of Movement Within Nonhousing Buildings

All buildings within the perimeter of the facility should use solid steel exterior doors and solid steel interior grille doors that are locked when not in use and can be quickly locked in response to an emergency. The ability of staff to compartmentalize any building reduces inmate opportunity for disruptive behavior and, during an emergency, can save lives by preventing the taking of hostages. To facilitate level 2 and 3 mitigation, each building servicing inmates should have at least one permanently assigned officer per floor. However, easily locked doors are of no value if the facility has window air conditioners without bars around them. The Pennsylvania House Judiciary Committee review of the 1989 Camp Hill riots noted:

> *Over the course of the years, air conditioners had been installed in openings in the exterior walls of almost all the buildings within the perimeter fence at Camp Hill, other than the cell blocks. The removal of these air conditioner units provided easy access for inmates into these buildings. In particular, the control center for the institution, was vulnerable to*

inmate assault for this reason (Pennsylvania House Judiciary Committee 1990:11).

Inmates also entered a number of other buildings through window air conditioners, most notably the supervisor's office in the main kitchen, in their attempt to take staff hostage and look for weapons and keys. In this case, level 3 mitigation would consist of removing all window air conditioners or installing bars around them in the windows.

Inmate Movement Within the Perimeter

When inmates are not in a building, the next issue of control becomes their ease of movement within the perimeter of the facility. Interior fencing is invaluable for controlling inmates within a facility. It provides a physical barrier to unauthorized inmate movement and has the added benefit of not blocking the vision of officers during line movements or recreational activities. Interior fencing can reduce the probability of escapes during routine operation or emergencies. It also reduces the consequences of a disturbance by reducing the ability of inmates to take down the entire facility. The Governor's Commission on the 1989 Camp Hill riots noted:

> *Minimal interior fencing, single-line chain link of moderate height topped with razor ribbon, separated Groups 2 and 3 from the furniture factory, Groups 2 and 3 from the Group 1 and administrative areas, the power plant, and the Main Stockade Field. The Commission recommends*

that a review of interior security barriers be conducted at Camp Hill and other institutions to ensure that it is adequate to control inmate movement and contain disturbances (Adams, Leader, and Irvis 1989:51).

Facilities should be designed to minimize blind spots (alleys and corners where inmates can easily evade line-of-sight detection) and large multitiered cellblocks with limited direct-observation capability. The ability of officers to see as much inmate activity as possible at any given time reduces the probability of disruptive behavior by facilitating detection and response. Staff are safer during routine facility operation, as well as during response and recovery, if there are few blind spots from which an ambush can be successfully launched.

Tool/Flammable Substance/Keys/ Weapons Control

When inmates engage in a disturbance, or are planning disruptive behavior, one of their first objectives is to secure keys, weapons, walkie-talkies, and tools that can be converted into weapons and/or flammable substances. Therefore, all keys, weapons, and radios should be stored in a building outside the facility. If this is not possible, they should be stored in a vault inside a secure control center designed to withstand heavy assault for at least an hour. Personnel working inside a facility should not be permitted to carry keys that open doors, gates, or tunnels that permit access to the outside. Drugs in the medical area also should be secured in a vault or in a reinforced storage area. All maintenance shops should be located in buildings outside the

perimeter. The final report of the Governor's Commission to investigate disturbances at Camp Hill noted:

The Commission has also received evidence regarding the location of trade shops inside Camp Hill. These trade shops provided inmates on Wednesday and again on Thursday with a variety of tools and equipment, including: a chain saw, an acetylene torch, fuel tanks, screwdrivers, sledgehammers, hedge trimmers, poles, gas cans, and other potentially lethal instruments. Inmates also gained access to utensils and knives from the kitchen and razors from the barber shop (Adams, Leader, and Irvis 1989:50).

It is not just during a riot that tools and keys become security issues. During the routine operation of the facility, inmates may steal tools and knives from their work areas and use these items to later attempt an escape or assault. Level 2 mitigation in this case takes the form of a visual control system: all tools and keys should be kept on a tool/key control board that is checked regularly by a supervisor. The most effective visual control system is a board that has the shape of the specific tools and keys outlined. Regular inventories of keys and tools should be checked against a master inventory list.

Because vehicles represent a potential method of escape, every facility should have a policy regulating the use of vehicles inside the perimeter. New facilities should be designed to preclude the interior use of vehicles. The Governor's Commission noted:

> *The Commission recommends a review of the use of vehicles inside a prison's perimeter. On October 25, 1989, inmates seized control of vehicles and rammed interior fences and gates and the inside perimeter fence. Vehicles inside the perimeter pose a security danger to the facility. One can only speculate as to what might have happened if the vehicle that breached the inside perimeter fence had exploded* (Adams, Leader, and Irvis 1989:50-51).

Access to the Community

The physical control of access to the community can be achieved by a perimeter security system of guard towers, double fences (at least twelve feet apart) with razor ribbon, lighting, electronic movement detection systems, mobile patrols, security cameras, a cleared area of at least 100 feet between the outer fence and the nearest trees or bushes, and appropriate alarm systems. There should be a clear line of sight between perimeter posts and a system of communications between perimeter posts and the control center that includes both phones and walkie-talkies. Post orders for perimeter security personnel should include directions to watch for intruders on the property and instructions for stopping and questioning any unauthorized individuals who have come onto the property, especially if they are in an area that would not normally see civilian traffic. Guard towers should have 360 degrees of vision, and mobile patrol schedules should be random to prevent easy prediction

Funding

There is a need for funding to address issues such as the following:

- Internal fire fighting capability of the facility
- Interior fencing designed to limit inmate mobility
- Vulnerability of wood modular units to fire
- Adequacy of key and tool control systems
- Ability to service vehicles outside the perimeter
- Vulnerability to inmate seizure of maintenance shops inside the perimeter
- Overall status of housing unit security systems
- Presence of blind spots
- Status of all perimeter security systems
- Availability of evacuation vehicles
- Presence of window air conditioners
- Adequacy of security systems in all nonhousing buildings
- Construction deficiencies that may facilitate inmate-precipitated emergencies
- Adequacy of communications systems
- Ready availability of riot-control equipment
- Adequacy of storage facilities for materials and supplies needed during recovery
- Adequacy of staffing levels
- Adequacy of medical facilities
- Availability of external resources
- Availability of communications with the providers of external resources
- Availability of staging areas
- Ability to store inmate personal property

of patrol movements. The distance between any structure and the inner fence always should be greater than an inmate can jump.

Buildings should not be part of a fenced perimeter system, even in a minimum security facility. For example, Pennsylvania's State Regional Correctional Facility at Mercer originally was designed with the administration building and medical complex as part of the single perimeter fence. Inmates wishing to escape could use the door handles of the door leading into the medical complex to boost themselves onto the roof. Half a dozen steps later, they were in position to lower themselves to the ground outside the facility. Level 2 mitigation in the case of the Mercer Facility involved stringing rolls of razor ribbon across the top of perimeter buildings and fences.

Access to all tunnels, gates, and sallyports should be secure at all times. Tunnels should be secured from the inside and gates and sallyports secured from the outside to minimize inmate access through them. During the aftermath of the Camp Hill riots, specially trained state troopers searched the underground steam tunnels for missing inmates. Blueprints stored in an outside building would help staff and troopers involved in this type of search.

Mitigation and the Budget Process

Strategic planning as a source of justification for budget requests often is overlooked by correctional administrators. Once the activities necessary to achieve the three levels of mitigation have been identified through the strategic planning process, funding for these activities should be included in all budget documents. Whether the budget document concerns the operation and/or proposed renovation of

existing facilities, rehabilitation of emergency-stricken facilities, or design and construction of new facilies, mitigation information can provide compelling justification for a variety of physical plant, staff, and programming requests.

Unfortunately, the most compelling justification for mitigation resources comes from an actual emergency. After the emergency, frequently there is an opportunity to correct past errors in design by changing the physical plant during the reconstruction phase of recovery. Although recovery can be a very painful time, the bright side to the situation is that the facility finally may receive the mitigation funding its administrators have been seeking for years. A veteran correctional administrator once stated: "Every time there's a riot, half of us cries and half is happy because we know it means more attention and probably more money for everything—salaries, programs, you name it" (DiIulio 1987:33).

After the 1989 Camp Hill riots, the Governor's Commission recommended:

> *As Camp hill is renovated, consideration should be given to upgrading cell block walls. As is well known, Camp Hill's cell block walls were constructed of hollow block. The corrections officer's switch boxes are likewise vulnerable and need reinforcement. The cell locking mechanisms should be completely replaced* (Adams, Leader, and Irvis 1989:49).

Ultimately, the decision was made to demolish the cell blocks at Camp Hill and replace them with modern housing units designed to handle the type of inmates housed at Camp Hill during the riots. Wooden frame modular housing units that were quick to burn have been replaced by steel and concrete units highly resistant to fire. To date tens of millions of dollars have been spent on projects designed to achieve mitigation.

Chapter 7

The Rumblings of Inmate Discontent: Early Warning Signs

*S*ergeant Baker cited increasingly foreboding, classic signals that portend grave problems. "You hear rumblings, but you hear rumblings all the time . . . things just weren't right at the mainline (when most of the inmate population is at the dining hall for meals). There were less people coming down eating. It was quieter. People that normally come up and talk to you, they walked by and didn't say anything" (Pennsylvania Senate Judiciary Committee 1990:19).

Level 2 mitigation of inmate-precipitated emergencies involves more than physical plant assessment and policy formulation. It involves systematically gathering and interpreting critical information about changes in inmate behavior as part of a proactive approach that is significantly different from the traditional reactive approach of inmate emergency management:

> The increased pressures of prison crowding, the costliness of violent disturbances and the scarcity of resources have forced correctional administrators to consider the value of proactive management.

> One of the easiest ways to adopt this proactive style is to establish an environmental scanning process, which can be accomplished through the development of comprehensive management information systems (Labecki 1994:108).

The primary emphasis in environmental scanning is to systematically acquire and analyze information that will allow level 2 mitigation in the form of the following:

1. Identifying a specific inmate action that is in the process of being planned

2. Determining that conditions are right for a spontaneous eruption of inmate disruptive behavior with an identification of the most likely forms such behavior will take

Sources of Information

An effective environmental scanning system relies on three sources of data: long-term statistical indicators, short-term behavioral-observation indicators, and inmate informants.

Long-term Statistical Indicators

The potential for trouble can be viewed as increasing if there is an annual increase (or sudden month-to-month increase) for general population inmates and disciplinary unit inmates in the number (or percentage) of behaviors listed in the following categories:

• Inmate-on-staff assaults

• Inmate-on-inmate assaults

• Incidents of disruptive behavior

• Inmate-set fires

• Officers reporting minor, moderate, or serious injuries at the hands of inmates

• Reports of urine, feces, or food thrown at staff by inmates

• Inmate use of weapons

• Incidents in which cut or stab weapons were used

• Incidents in which minor, moderate, or major injuries were sustained by staff or inmates

• Incidents that officers resolved with the use of force

• Inmates involved in incidents who have no prior history of involvement in such activity

• Lawsuits filed

• Formal inmate complaints filed. Any increase in the number of complaints should be evaluated in terms of patterns. Are there "hot" issues appearing time and again that need to be addressed immediately?

• Complaints received from family, friends, inmate advocacy groups, or politicians protesting or questioning specific policies or general conditions of confinement

• Staff use of lethal force

• Attempted/successful escapes

• Walkaways from outside work details

• Failure to return from furlough

• Inmate demands to speak to the media

• Inmates found in possession of weapons

• Incidents of verbal defiance of staff

• Letters to the facility administrator and/or agency administrator

Every correctional system should have a routine reporting procedure (weekly or monthly) in place that requires every facility to provide the central office with the data described here. Data analysis staff can provide an early warning system by comparing each report to preceding reports for each facility as well as comparing facilities to each other to determine if there are long-term statistical indicators of impending problems.

Short-term Behavioral Observation Indicators

Inmates who are aware that an inmate-precipitated emergency has been planned may engage in certain tell-tale behaviors that are in themselves significant, or that reinforce the concern generated by the identification of any of the long-term statistical indicators. Such behaviors may include the following:

• Refusal to go to recreation, movies, or meals

• Warnings to family and friends not to visit the facility

• Hoarding of commissary items

• Increased levels of theft from the kitchen

• Mailing home of personal property items

- Cryptic warnings to staff to take a vacation or sick day

- Increased requests for antianxiety or anti-depression medication

- Increased requests to be put in the infirmary or an outside hospital

- Increased requests for protective custody status in the disciplinary unit

- Unexpected changes in seating arrangements in the dining hall or race-, ethnic-, or gang-designated territory in the recreation yards

- Unusual levels of silence at recreation, movies, meals, or other regularly scheduled inmate activities

- Increased numbers of anonymous warnings that "something is about to happen"

- Increased numbers of transfer requests

- Avoidance of staff with whom a friendly relationship previously had been advanced

- Increased numbers of calls from family and friends about conditions in the facility

- Increased smuggling of contraband by visitors

- Increased number of requests for cell changes

- Polarization of known inmate rivals

- Grievance flooding—an extremely sharp increase in formal complaints all focused on one specific subject, usually an unpopular change in policy

- Increased suicide attempts

Behavioral changes may be observed by any number and category of staff. Changes may be noted for one inmate, a group of inmates, or for the entire population. All staff should understand that changes of this nature are to be reported immediately to the Intelligence Unit for analysis. When an increase in any of the behavioral observation, or statistical data, categories is identified, especially if it is a sharp increase over a short period of time, the Intelligence Unit immediately should attempt to identify any underlying patterns that may be contributing to the increase. Patterns to look for include the following:

- A high frequency of involvement in violent incidents, or complaints, by a particular officer(s) or inmate(s)

- A commonly repeated complaint and/or any signs of coordination of complaint filing by specific inmates or groups

- Specific racial, ethnic, and gang involvement in a high percentage of incidents or complaints

- Specific locations in which a significant number of violent incidents are occurring

- Reaction to a planned, or implemented, policy change

- Significant changes in the inmate power structure

Once a pattern has been identified, staff can focus on that area and engage in appropriate level 2 mitigation activities.

The Use of Inmate Informants

Every good correctional officer has inmates who are willing to keep him or her informed of inmate activities and concerns. An effective Intelligence Unit also will make use of informants. Informants can provide advance warning of impending problems and suggest the need to take a closer look for changes in the categories previously discussed. Inmate informants are invaluable for providing the names of ringleaders, or potential ringleaders, because this may be the only way to identify inmates capable of organizing other inmates to engage in collective action against the facility once the statistical and behavioral observation changes have been detected and evaluated. However, informants should be used carefully, with every effort made to not compromise their security or allow them to manipulate staff and thus compromise facility security. The misuse of inmate informants can have tragic consequences, as was demonstrated at the Penitentiary of New Mexico in 1980, when a rage riot resulted in the butchering of thirty-three inmates identified as snitches. An intelligence system based exclusively on inmate informants is doomed to failure.

The Role of the Administrator in Level 2 Mitigation

Once the Intelligence Unit has collected data, analyzed them for trends, and developed a recommendation, it is imperative that the information go directly to the facility administrator. Moving this kind of information through the chain of command can cost valuable time and lead to delays that may prove to have unfortunate consequences. Once Intelligence Unit information has been received, the administrator should thoroughly assess the data and recommendations, confer with appropriate staff, and take any level 2 mitigation measures necessary to head off trouble. Thorough investigation of each report of potential trouble is critical, yet the temptation to overreact always must be kept in check. Any mitigation activity undertaken should be commensurate with the administrator's determination of the validity and the reliability of the information received:

However, it must be remembered that, in maximum security facilities, information regarding assaults, escape attempts, contraband, and the like, are transmitted on an almost daily basis . . . . Overreaction to reports of trouble can also place a correctional facility at risk. For example, ordering a lockdown to conduct a facility-wide search for weapons is a highly disruptive maneuver to normal operations and should only be done when truly warranted. Otherwise, the inmate population could react extremely negatively to such measures and conclude that they are being needlessly harassed (Coughlin 1991:49).

The administrator should depend on years of experience, and an Intelligence Unit composed of the best and brightest facility staff, to make the right decision. When the administrator receives information suggesting the strong probability of an inmate-precipitated disturbance, there are several possible level 2 mitigation activities to be considered:

• Continue to monitor the situation.

• If a policy change appears to be the cause of the discontent, discuss the policy with inmate leaders.

• Consider changing policies that are causing discontent, if this can be done without creating staff hostility or overempowerment of inmates.

• Transfer inmate ringleaders without advance warning.

- Have counseling staff talk to influential inmates in an effort to calm tensions.

- Cancel events that may provide the opportunity for disruptive inmate behavior.

- Increase administrative visibility within the facility so inmates have an informal opportunity to express concerns.

- Put the Corrections Emergency Response Team on standby in a public manner.

Level 2 mitigation activities that are least restrictive on normal inmate activities, but still address the problem, are probably the best course of action.

Chapter 8

Work Stoppages, Hunger Strikes, Escapes, and Walkaways

*B*ut in the past five years, according to research by Newhouse News Service, at least 117 killers have escaped. During that time, escapees have killed at least 25 people . . . . This year, if past figures are a guide, 11,000 inmates will escape in the United States—about one every 45 minutes (Patriot News 1995d:G2).

Inmate-precipitated emergencies may be viewed on a continuum of facility disruption, with work stoppages, hunger strikes, walkaways, and escapes falling on the low end of the continuum and gang-related emergencies and riots falling on the high end. Low-end emergencies may involve relatively small numbers of inmates and usually can be resolved through the use of internal resources. However, any inmate emergency has the potential of drawing in larger numbers of inmates and, in the worst case scenario, can trigger a riot that requires extensive external resources for response and recovery. Low-end emergencies rapidly can become high-end emergencies, regardless of original inmate intentions. For this reason, mitigation and preparedness and response activities are as important for low-end emergencies as they are for high-end emergencies.

Work Stoppages/ Hunger Strikes

Inmates may stop work as a protest, or go on a hunger strike, or combine the two actions, for a number of reasons. In general, they may be dissatisfied with specific work or facility conditions and believe a work stoppage or hunger strike is their only option to draw attention to their situation.

Level 2 Mitigation of Work Stoppages and Hunger Strikes

Close staff monitoring of the facility climate is the best means of reducing the probability of a work stoppage or hunger strike. These low-end emergencies usually involve a period of advance discussion and planning that allows time for the Intelligence Unit to identify the ringleaders. Level 2 mitigation activities may include segregating ringleaders to remove the leadership and discussing specific grievances in an attempt to resolve specific inmate concerns.

Preparedness/Response

If a work stoppage or hunger strike does occur, preparedness and response should emphasize using negotiation as the primary method of resolving the situation. Using force to resolve these situations is justifiable only if a striking inmate is attempting to assault a staff member or another inmate. As much as possible, the facility should continue routine operations during the work stoppage unless there is reason to believe that the work stoppage might escalate into violence that would spread to other inmates. Routinely locking down a facility because of an inmate work stoppage may fuel anger and resentment in inmates not already involved in the work stoppage. However, the area in which the striking inmates have positioned themselves should be secured, and the normal complement of officers reinforced.

If inmates are engaged in a hunger strike, it is likely that they have stockpiled commissary food items in their cells to prepare for the strike. Videotaping each cell will help record evidence of prior preparation as will reviewing commissary records. All records showing evidence of stockpiling purchases should be photocopied as documentation that inmates had access to food other than the meals they have been refusing.

Even if inmates have stockpiled food, medical staff should pay daily visits to the inmates on a hunger strike to assess any physical consequences of that strike. All inmates engaged in a hunger strike should be given a personal memo from the facility administrator that provides the following:

- A description of the medical risks associated with not eating for long periods of time

- Assurances that medical staff are available to respond to symptoms of starvation-related disorders

- Assurances that counseling staff are available to "talk out" any concerns

- Notification that if a state of starvation is attained, the facility will seek permission from a judge to begin intravenous feeding

- Notification that each inmate will be offered a meal in accordance with the regular dining schedule

- Notification that each refusal to eat will be documented for possible use at a subsequent disciplinary hearing

A daily medical report summarizing the overall medical status of the inmates should be provided to the facility administrator. In extreme cases, this documentation may be needed to secure the permission of a judge to intravenously feed any inmates truly committed to starving themselves. Such a situation is rare, but it does happen occasionally. Officers should not attempt to shakedown inmate cells to deprive them of stockpiled commissary food. Such activity has a high potential for violence.

Recovery

If inmates have engaged in a hunger strike, medical staff should examine all participants thoroughly to determine if any medical damage has been sustained. All findings should be recorded and highlighted on the

Photo courtesy Southern Ohio Correctional Facility

Inmates at the Southern Ohio Correctional facility started small fires in the recreation yard to keep warm, April 11. Yard was cleared at 2 A.M. April 12, with no activity.

medical record. All necessary medical treatment indicated by the initial post-hunger strike examination should be provided. Any subsequent complaints of medical symptoms should be responded to immediately and evaluated in terms of the probability that they represent a delayed response to the lack of regular meals. Appropriate disciplinary action also should be taken.

If inmates have engaged in a work stoppage, their individual suitability for return to their previous work assignments should be assessed by the classification committee after appropriate action by the disciplinary committee.

Escapes and Walkaways

Escape refers to unauthorized flight from the interior of a prison or jail. Walkaway refers to the unauthorized flight from a location outside of the perimeter of a prison or jail or from a community-based residential facility. Although preparedness and response for both events are similar, level 2 mitigation activities are different. To avoid confusion, the term "escapee" will refer to any inmate in an unauthorized flight status. Whether an inmate tunnels out of a maximum security prison or walks away from an outside work detail (as most do), unauthorized physical flight is a serious issue.

Level 2 Mitigation of Escapes

The barriers to escape from within a jail or prison are both physical and procedural. Physical barriers include a physically secure perimeter (wall or fence with razor ribbon) that includes motion-detection systems, video surveillance, mobile patrols (interior and exterior), and a clear line of sight in all directions. Procedural barriers include a formal count system; use of inmate passes; alert work supervisors; efficient, randomized patrol coverage of the perimeter; and permanent gate and visiting room officers who can visually identify any inmates attempting to exit through the gates with civilian visitors. Buildings close to a fence or wall should be inspected periodically to ensure inmates are not using the buildings as cover to tunnel out of the facility, as happened at a Florida prison in 1995.

The possibility of escape by helicopter should not be minimized in any facility where inmates have access to outdoor exercise yards with enough open space for a helicopter to land. Every federal institution and some states use poles with steel cable strung in between them in exercise yards as a form of mitigation. This has drawbacks, however. A helicopter hitting steel cables may crash, and if that crash is in a crowded exercise area, the number of casualties—of both staff and inmate—could eliminate any benefit derived from foiling the escape. For this reason, attempting to shoot down a helicopter attempting to extract an inmate also is not recommended. A helicopter crash can cause a high number of casualties in an area as confined as a prison. The best form of mitigation is Federal Aviation Administration posting of prison airspace as a no-fly zone. If this zone is breached, correctional staff can obtain the helicopter identification numbers, notify state police, and request they use their aircraft to investigate the situation. If an escape by helicopter has occurred, the state police will be in a position to pursue the escaping helicopter.

Level 2 Mitigation of Prison/Jail Walkaways

These situations usually involve inmates walking away from outside work details. The most effective approach to level 2 mitigation is a formal classification process that excludes inmates with any prior history of physical flight, including escaping, being absent without leave, jumping bail, not returning from furlough, or fleeing to avoid prosecution. This level of exclusion may not always be possible, but experience has shown that the best predictor of future behavior is past behavior. Inmates with one or more episodes of violence in their history, any psychiatric history, or any history of sexual aggressiveness should be carefully evaluated before placement outside the perimeter.

Level 3 Mitigation of Prison/Jail Walkaways

Even if all inmates with an escape risk factor in their history have been excluded from the work detail, policy should require all work detail supervisors to have a radio in any vehicle they are using, a hand-held radio, and a regular schedule for checking in with the command center on a periodic basis. Any failure of a supervisor to check in should be grounds to send officers out immediately to determine the status of the work detail. Reducing the time an inmate has before response is initiated can aid in capture and reduce the possibility of consequences, such as the escapee taking community hostages or engaging in property or assault crimes.

Level 2 Mitigation of Residential Facility Walkaways

The classification procedure that identifies inmates for residential placement should evaluate any prior incidents of physical flight seriously before a placement decision is made. Staff also should maintain contact with the inmate's family to determine any family changes in progress (such as divorce, death, or illness) that might motivate an inmate to not return. These individuals probably will be holding a community job or attending school. Periodic, random phone checks with supervisors and unannounced visits to the work or school site will let inmates know that strict monitoring of activities can detect unauthorized absence quickly.

Level 3 Mitigation of Residential Facility Walkaways

Level 3 mitigation includes a rigidly enforced log book procedure that documents when inmates leave the facility and when they are scheduled to return. Return times should be strictly enforced with minimal tolerance for late returns. There will be occasions when an inmate's return is delayed for reasons beyond his or her control, such as traffic jams or accidents, but staff should establish how much time will be allowed to pass before walkaway status is declared. A prompt declaration of walkaway status permits quick intervention by the police that will limit the walkaway's opportunities to commit new crimes.

Preparedness/Response for Escapes and Walkaways

These activities require formation of an Escapee Recovery Team. The prison or jail team will determine all possible escape routes from the facility, the most likely destination sites, places to hide along destination routes, and the search pattern that most effectively will allow coverage of routes, hiding places, and destination sites. The residential facility Escapee Recovery Team primarily will be used for surveillance of possible destinations. Regardless of the location from which flight has occurred, once the inmate has become an escapee, a standardized escapee information packet should be sent to local law enforcement agencies and the Federal Bureau of Investigation's fugitive task force.

While the search for an escapee is progressing, the inmate's counselor, or whoever is designated as most appropriate, should notify

---

The escapee information packet should contain:

- a recent photograph (all inmate photographs should be updated on a yearly basis) and notes on any recent grooming changes, such as the growing of a beard or mustache, or significant change in hair style

- a description of the clothing the inmate was last seen wearing

- a copy of the inmate's arrest history

- the names and addresses of all known friends and family

The classification summary and the inmate visiting list, respectively, are good sources for the last two items of information. The Intelligence Unit should question any inmates who are known friends or associates of the escapee to determine if any alteration of physical appearance has occurred before the escape, or if any specific destinations were discussed by the escapee during informal conversations. All new information should be sent immediately to the Escapee Recovery Team.

family members of the escape and ask for their assistance in persuading the escapee to surrender. In many cases, mothers, wives, and girlfriends, in particular, often are very concerned that the escapee will become involved in additional crimes or be harmed before a safe surrender can be arranged.

Any escapee recovery effort should include surveillance of, or periodic visits to, the escapee's home to determine if he or she has returned there. The value of this approach was demonstrated in Pennsylvania in August 1995. A convicted murderer who had escaped from Graterford Prison, a maximum security institution, and eluded capture for two weeks was found hiding underneath a bed in his mother's home in West Philadelphia.

Recovery

When the escapee is returned, receiving officers should carefully document and photograph any injuries. The source of the injuries should be elicited from both the escapee and staff and recorded. A standard procedure of written and photographic documentation reduces the chance of physical abuse. If abuse by correctional staff has occurred, the documentation will facilitate any departmental investigation of the situation. If abuse was inflicted by the police, the abuse documentation will provide a defense for correctional staff and administrators in any section 1983 litigation (42 U.S.C. 1983) of the Civil Rights Act, which declares that any person deprived of civil rights by persons acting under authority of law can sue for redress. All escapees should receive appropriate administrative disciplinary action and be prosecuted in court.

Chapter 9

Violence in Inmate-precipitated Emergencies: General Principles of Mitigation

W hen people think of prison violence, more often than not they think of a prison riot. Yet, prison riots are relatively rare events. More common are the day-to-day confrontations among inmates and between correctional officers and inmates. Many correctional administrators find this latter type of violence difficult to address (Stojkovic and Lovell 1992:330).

Causes of Prison Violence

Because many inmate-precipitated emergencies involve violence, this chapter briefly reviews the issue of prison violence in general before closely examining specific types of emergencies involving violence.

The research literature has identified three primary causes of prison violence: the violent inmate, a prison social climate that encourages and rewards violence, and prison crowding (Stojkovic and Lovell 1992:339).

The Violent Inmate

This model suggests that the roots of prison violence lie in community violence. Lockwood (1980:113) suggests that prison violence is a behavior that is learned on the street and then imported into the prison setting when the offender is incarcerated. Irwin (1970) and Abbott (1991) suggest that violence also can be learned in juvenile and adult correctional facilities. They identify many violent inmates as "state-raised" individuals who have spent years in state institutions, where learned violence is a form of adaptation that reinforces previous learning in urban environments where violence is an acceptable means of dispute resolution.

The Social Climate

Toch (1985:41-42) argues that the "contextual" environment of the prison can encourage violence in five ways by doing the following:

1. Providing "payoffs." Payoffs are the status the violent inmate earns through the respect

of other inmates and the fear such violence inspires in staff.

2. Providing immunity or protection. The code of silence may prevent inmates from reporting violence to staff. This silence provides immunity to the aggressor. However, some people believe that inmates tend to divulge information rather than conceal it if it is to their benefit.

3. Providing opportunities. The physical structure and staff routine that characterize the prison environment can provide many opportunities for those inmates who want to prey on other inmates.

4. Providing temptation, challenges, and provocations. The inmate social world is full of opportunities for inmates to test their manhood and challenge the manhood of other inmates and staff. Gangs, in particular, will emphasize the importance of proving manhood.

5. Providing justificatory premises. Some inmates, such as child molesters and snitches, are viewed as not deserving the respect of other inmates. This lack of worthiness can provide a justification for violence.

Crowding

Gaes and McGuire (1985:41-65), in a study of nineteen federal prisons in the United States, found that level of crowding was the strongest predictor of assaults in virtually every violent situation. Farrington and Nuttall (1985) also found violence to be strongly associated with crowding, although prison size was not.

Level 2 Violence Mitigation

Level 2 mitigation of prison violence can be discussed in terms of three models: institutional response, the environmental-change approach, and the societal-cultural model.

Institutional Response

DiIulio (1987) and Useem and Kimball (1989:227) suggest that poor management is the central cause of prison violence because controlling violence requires a strong central administration and well-run prison bureaucracy. They contend that prison violence is the result of weak administrators, lax rule systems, and inconsistent rule enforcement or poorly articulated rules. Therefore, the key to reducing the probability of violence includes the following:

• Tight formal controls in the hands of administrators

• Adequate levels of inmate programming

• Adequate work, cell, and recreational space for inmates

• Well-maintained physical security systems

• Coherent, written rules that are consistently enforced

The Environmental-Change Approach

Toch (1977), Bowker (1980), and Johnson (1987) suggest that the way to reduce prison violence is to modify the prison environment in ways that reduce the aspects of prison life that support and foster violence. Because aggressors need victims, level 2 mitigation activities should include the development of victimization data systems built into the classification system to identify the most aggressive inmates and those most likely to be victimized. Inmates with a high potential for victimization should be housed in areas of the facility with a low level of violence, if facility resources permit this type of space allocation.

Level 2 mitigation activities also should include using correctional ombudspersons to provide impartial decisions in staff-inmate disputes, holding face-to-face discussions with inmate grievance filers, increasing physical plant security, expanding visiting and visiting area improvements, and normalizing prison industries to make prison work correspond more closely to the free-world work experience and increasing work opportunities.

Toch (1985:43-45) has brought the police concept of "hot spots" (areas where there is a high concentration of crime) into the discussion of prison violence. Combining the concept of hot spots with the concept of environmental scanning leads to the suggestion that administrators can reduce the opportunity for prison violence by a systematic process of environmental scanning based on recognizing that every facility has hot spots where violence is most likely to occur and low-violence subenvironments where violence is rare. The Intelligence Unit can use the long-term statistical indicators discussed in chapter 7 to systematically identify violence hot spots and low-violence subenvironments. Once hot spots have been identified, the Intelligence Unit and the Post-traumatic Assessment Team can interview staff and inmates formally in high-violence areas to develop concrete plans of action to counteract facility conditions that support and condone violence in the hot spots. Then, support systems for victims of

violence and potential victims may be developed. In addition, although violent acts are still "hot," the Post-traumatic Assessment Team should come into the area to counsel the violent participants and attempt to eliminate any residual animosity that may spark another confrontation. This situation provides an example of recovery activities that also serves the goals of level 2 mitigation. All the information on violence gathered through this process of environmental scanning and program development should be used for two specific forms of level 2 mitigation: training staff and orienting inmates.

The Societal-Cultural Model

This model is the opposite of the institutional response model in that it argues that the roots of prison violence lie in community violence, and prison violence never will be reduced unless we as a society work to reduce violence in the communities from which prisons receive their inmates. Prison violence is a mirror image of the violence that exists in the community. Obviously, this approach is of little immediate or practical benefit to correctional administrators. However, it has generated a program—Alternatives to Violence—that may be of value to administrators (Lockwood 1980:150-54). Alternatives to Violence is designed to teach violent offenders that nonviolent methods are the most effective methods to resolve everyday conflict situations. There are four basic themes in Alternatives to Violence:

1. The importance of communication skills—listening, speaking, observing, and effective interacting—is stressed.

2. Cooperation and community building is stressed.

3. Self-esteem is developed.

4. Conflict situations are explored to identify creative solutions that can replace violence.

This is a transformation-of-values program. Although Lockwood (1980:153) admits that we may be asking too much from the Alternatives to Violence program when inmates are asked to respond nonviolently in an environment that so values violence, this program may offer at least a limited opportunity for violence mitigation. A similar program is the *Cage Your Rage* series available from the American Correctional Association and widely used in a variety of correctional settings (Cullen 1992).

Physical Plant Mitigation

Victimization rates are high in prison areas not open to the view of the staff. Violence can be mitigated by making prison space "defensible." For example, the roof of a covered walkway may be removed (or replaced with glass) so tower officers can observe inmate activity on the walkway. A cul-de-sac in a hallway that prevents staff observation can be walled off or monitored by a surveillance camera. New prison design should be done with the goal of maximizing defensible space. An example of this approach to level 2 mitigation is the Bayside State Prison in Leesburg, New Jersey. This facility is designed to house 500 men. All living units are constructed around landscaped open courts, with each of the four sides containing outside rooms built in two tiers. These self-contained rooms have secure, solid prison doors. Inside walls are glass from ceiling to floor, giving the impression of no walls at all (Nagel 1973:110). There is a greatly reduced opportunity for inmate victimization in this type of setting.

Training/Orientation Mitigation

All new staff should receive specific instruction concerning theories of violence, the concept of hot spots, the need to environmentally scan, and use of conflict resolution techniques when they see confrontation developing between inmates. It should be clearly communicated that staff are expected to play a proactive role in reducing prison violence through systematic mitigation. The most effective level 2 violence mitigation is well-trained line staff. An example of this type of communication can be seen in California where correctional officers are sent to conflict-resolution training to learn how to effectively handle tension that can build up in a facility. Training staff in conflict resolution methods promotes the idea that inmates and staff can find ways to work together to resolve officer-inmate and inmate-inmate grievances. Promotion of this idea can break down the barriers so conducive to violence (Weiner 1982:303).

New inmates also should receive information about the possibility of violence during their initial orientation. The negative administrative and personal consequences of violence should be emphasized along with the opportunity for violence-oriented treatment and victim-support programs if they exist.

Level 3 Mitigation— Using Technology to Reduce Consequences

The capability currently exists to provide correctional staff and inmates with wrist-worn bracelets with bar code locators that allow an individual being threatened with physical violence to transmit a distress signal to a control center. Technology options include radio-frequency, ultrasonic, and infrared sensors contained in wrist-worn bracelets, belt devices, and anklets that can identify location by specific areas (such as a cell) or quadrants of a large area and provide an automated headcount. This type of system can provide a computerized time-lagged listing of all individuals near the person under threat.

In addition to reducing the time it takes for other staff to come to the assistance of an officer, the information documented by the use of technology may be invaluable for prosecution or administrative hearings (Boyle and Ricketts 1992:78-80).

Chapter 10

Sexual Assaults and Suicide

*A*ny new person, they hollered obscenities at them and all sorts of names, and throwing things down from the galley and everything. They told me to walk down the middle of this line like I was on exhibition, and everybody started to throw things and everything, and I was shaking in my boots . . . . They were screaming things like, "That is for me" and "This one won't take long—he will be easy" and, "Look at his eyes" and "her eyes" or whatever, and making all kinds of remarks (Toch 1977:147-48).

Correctional emergencies involving violence also can be discussed in terms of a continuum based on the number of victims. At the low end of the continuum are emergencies involving a single victim. At the high end are emergencies involving large numbers of victims. Low-end emergencies include sexual assault and suicide.

Sexual Assault

Lockwood (1982:257) reports that violent sexual incidents among male inmates fall into two groups. The first group is the aggressors who use violence to coerce their targets into providing sexual privileges. The second group is the targets who react violently to sexual propositions they view as threatening. Toch (1965) notes that some targets will use violence against those who make sexual approaches to them to get the predators to leave them alone. Violence by a potential victim is clearly a conscious, deliberate activity with the specific goal of sexual assault mitigation.

Lockwood (1980) has identified certain characteristics specific to sexual victim and aggressor. The typical sexual target is a white male under the age of twenty-one, with a slender and attractive physical appearance (on average, fifteen pounds lighter than the aggressor). The victimization typically occurs within sixteen weeks of reception at the facility. Over half of the incidents take place in the housing units of the men involved. The victims generally are inexperienced and naive about their new environment (a situation that can be addressed at least partially by a proper reception orientation). The typical sexual predator is black (80 percent) and from an urban street subculture that emphasizes violence and male dominance.

Level 2 Sexual Assault Mitigation

The most effective methods of reducing the probability of sexual assault are as follows:

- Using a classification system that identifies potential targets and potential aggressors and prevents them from being housed together

- Identifying hot spots for sexual assault

- Placing additional staff in sexual assault hot spots

- Providing specific mitigation training to staff, especially those in hot spots

- Assigning victims or potential victims to special housing situations and supportive counseling programs

- Conducting training that sensitizes staff to the need to be alert to the possibility of sexual victimization

- Enforcing a policy of aggressive prosecution of sexual predators in the courts that is made known to all inmates

- Enforcing a policy of maximum periods of disciplinary segregation for sexual predators found guilty of sexual assault

- Establishing rape evidence procedures for medical staff that facilitate prosecuting the aggressor

- Implementing an Alternatives-to-Violence-type program

In addition, Nacci and Kane (1984:52) have proposed a "target hardening" approach in which staff teach potential victims about the realities of their new environment by warning them about possible mannerisms (attitudes, facial expressions, styles of clothing, and tones of speech) that attract sexual predators.

Preparedness/Response

Once a case of sexual assault is reported:

1. The Intelligence Unit interviews the victim in an attempt to gain the name(s) of the aggressor and any witnesses.

2. Medical staff treat any injuries while gathering and preserving physical evidence.

3. The Post-traumatic Assessment Team conducts an initial psychological evaluation to determine if medication or suicide-prevention interventions are needed.

4. The Criminal Prosecution Team attempts to build the case for both the internal administrative disciplinary hearing and court prosecution

Recovery

The effects of sexual victimization can be severe: feelings of helplessness and depression; fear of having contracted acquired immuno-deficiency syndrome; damaged self-esteem; possible self-destructive acts, such as self-mutilation or suicide; lowered social status; psychosomatic illnesses; increased difficulty in adjusting to life after release; and possibly increased risk of recidivism (Bowker 1982:64).

After a sexual assault victim has been identified, the Post-traumatic Assessment Team should provide supportive counseling, make referrals to more specialized treatment if necessary, and be alert to symptoms of post-traumatic stress disorder. Depending on post-assault adjustment, transferring the victim to another facility or placing him or her in protective custody may need to be considered. Notification of the family should be discussed with the victim—any notification should be the inmate's decision. If the victim does notify the family and reaction is negative, a member of the Post-traumatic Assessment Team may have to become involved in discussions between the inmate and family members. The possibility of suicide always should be kept in mind, and staff involved with the victim should be alert to any indications that suicide is being considered. In cases of extreme psychological reaction, medication and psychiatric intervention may be necessary.

Environmental scanning to identify sexual assault hot spots should be an ongoing recovery process, with appropriate mitigation measures taken as these areas are identified. Because sexual victimization always carries the possibility of litigation, any instances of sexual assault should be reported to the Litigation Response Team.

Suicide

Prison suicide is most common among young, unmarried white males (Hawkins and Alpert 1989: 295-96). Three types of inmates appear to be most likely to attempt suicide:

1. First-time offenders who deeply regret the shame and embarrassment their incarceration has brought to their family. These individuals usually attempt suicide early in confinement, often in the hours after reception.

2. Inmates who have been confined for a long time and have developed feelings of hopelessness and futility about the future

3. Antisocial inmates who attempt suicide, using a nonlethal method, to manipulate others into giving them privileges or opportunities they have not earned (Danto 1973:20-21)

The ecology of prison suicides has been fairly well established. Most suicides occur between 9 P.M. and 6 A.M. during the weekend, including Friday evening and most often when the inmate is in an isolation status, where there is minimal contact with both inmates and staff (Hayes and Rowan 1988).

Level 2 Suicide Mitigation

The most effective form of level 2 suicide mitigation is staff training that educates staff to the behavioral warning signs of impending suicide. This training should be a priority for all reception officers because suicide may occur shortly after reception in some cases, but every effort also should be made to acquaint the general population and the disciplinary unit staff with behavioral suicide warning signs. All staff should be alert to the following signs among inmates:

• Displaying a startling period of calm after expressions of depression, anxiety, fear, or unrest. This sudden calm may mean that the decision to commit suicide finally has been made and accepted.

• Giving away personal possessions to other inmates or sending personal possessions to family

• Calling family and friends to say good-bye (this often takes the form of an unexpected conversation expressing regret for "all the trouble I've caused")

• Withdrawing from the social group and normal activities

• Talking matter-of-factly about "how lucky the dead are"

• Developing lists of suicide methods, often hidden inside a personal Bible

- Exhibiting a sudden interest in reading about suicide or asking medical staff questions about suicide: "Does it hurt?"

- Suddenly lacking concern about future events or activities or troublesome situations

- Verbalizing a wish to be dead

- Making open statements about the intention to commit suicide. "I'm going to kill myself" statements never should be dismissed as "just talk"

- Having a sudden interest in religion and conversations with the chaplain about how happy the people with God must be

- Collecting newspaper and magazine articles about suicide methods and victims

Suicide mitigation requires a formal, standardized method of reporting symptoms of suicide to counseling staff. There should be at least one staff member with specialized training in counseling suicidal inmates who can assess the potential for suicide in inmates who display behavior changes in the ways noted earlier. This assessment may be supplemented with an objective suicide screening device of the type used by Jail Mental Health Service programs, which provide mental health coverage for the Custody Division of the Los Angeles Sheriff's Department (Kunzman 1995: 90-91). This screening device is used to document risk factors by focusing attention on the following:

- The gut feeling of the individual conducting the assessment—Gut feeling in many cases represents the accumulated wisdom from extensive experience.

- The history of the inmate—This includes prior criminal history; psychiatric history; the nature of the crime, particularly if it was shocking; previous suicide attempts; and drug or alcohol history. The absence of prior arrests may signal a first-timer whose shame about arrest, conviction, and incarceration may be overwhelming.

- Relationships—This includes relationships with family and friends, as well as significant losses through death, divorce, incarceration, or suicide.

- Current problems—These may include worrying about basic life issues; verbalizing thoughts of suicide; expressing feelings of hopelessness, depression, embarrassment, shame, anxiety, confusion, or anger; making strange comments or displaying strange behavior; and appearing to be incoherent, withdrawn, or mentally ill.

- Recent suicide attempts—Recent suicide attempts are reviewed and attempts are made to elicit the existence of a future, detailed suicide plan.

Scoring with this type of assessment is simple and provides an objective measure of suicide risk that can be used for referral and possibly psychiatric hospitalization. The most effective approach to level 2 suicide mitigation combines a formal screening process with a policy of not placing suicidal individuals in an isolated environment:

> *If the potentially suicidal inmate cannot have constant one-on-one supervision, housing detainees, arrestees or inmates in a group of two or more individuals with constant direct visual observation is the best advised housing*

arrangement. It will greatly decrease the possibility of a successful suicide (Kunzman 1995:94).

Preparedness/Response

When a suicide occurs, medical staff should provide prompt medical attention as the first priority, including transfer to an outside hospital if necessary. Full security precautions should be taken during transfer in case the suicide attempt is a means of gaining access to the community where escape may be more feasible. (This rule applies to any medical transfer of an inmate. Even inmates scheduled for surgery have been known to take advantage of the situation to escape).

Recovery

Once the physical wounds have been attended to, and the inmate has been returned to the facility, a period of observation in the prison infirmary, psychiatric/psychological assessment, and supportive counseling should be provided.

Chapter 11

Nongang-related Minor Disturbances and Gang-related Minor Disturbances

*W*hen you first arrive you are tested. We call that "getting your face." The first month I was here I had to physically defend myself. I didn't want to fight—I just wanted to do my number, but I had to fight in order to show that I couldn't be pushed around, and once I had shown that, I was left pretty much alone. There is a really strong protection racket here; if you let yourself be pushed around and don't defend yourself, you can get forced to pay for your own protection (Wright 1973:150).

Violent disturbances have a variety of causes: a prison gang seeking to achieve a specific goal by disrupting some aspect of facility operation; a quarrel between two inmates over a pack of cigarettes that leads to an assault or murder that draws in other inmates; or otherwise unorganized inmates briefly coming together to protest a common grievance. Disturbances can be the result of almost any inmate event, grievance, or activity. They can be minor or major, depending on the number of inmates involved. They can be gang-related or nongang-related.

Nongang-related Minor Disturbances

Mitigation

The level 2 and 3 activities noted in the discussion of mitigation of violence in general can be applied to this area. Of special importance in level 2 mitigation activity are the Intelligence Unit's efforts to constantly gather information on inmate disputes and identify developing conflict areas so that counseling or administrative interventions may be applied before a dispute erupts into violence.

Preparedness/Response

Minor disturbances do not involve the entire facility and, in fact, may be limited to one cellblock, building, or exercise area. In the event of a minor disturbance, correctional officers assigned to the area should seal off the area so other inmates cannot enter; evacuate the area until reinforcements arrive; and secure inmates who are not involved.

If the inmates stop the disturbance, but refuse to return to their cells unless their demands are met, the Hostage Negotiation Team should be brought in to persuade the inmates to relinquish control of the area and return to their cells. Calling in the Correctional Emergency Response Team when inmates have ended the disturbance should be done only if negotiations are not productive and there is a threat of loss of life or serious injury.

If inmates refuse to stop the disturbance, are destroying property, attempting to escape, attempting to take staff hostage, or otherwise representing an active threat to safety and security, calling on the Correctional Emergency Response Team to apply immediate force will be necessary.

Recovery

Once the minor disturbance has been quelled, the facility should not be designated secure until:

1. There has been a thorough shakedown to detect hidden contraband.

2. The Damage Assessment Team has inspected the site of the disturbance for sabotage of locking mechanisms, monitoring equipment, or perimeter security.

3. Damage Repair Teams have completed repairs and removed damaged property before inmates return to the area.

Inmates may use even a minor disturbance to justify instigating larger disturbances. Even if this does not occur, hard feelings may fuel future problems that could have been prevented. The Intelligence Unit should monitor the possibility of repercussions from the disturbance. The Criminal Prosecution Unit should gather the necessary information for administrative hearings and prosecution. The Post-traumatic Assessment Team should monitor the psychological status of disturbance participants and be alert to signs of inmate and staff post-traumatic stress disorder.

Gang-related Disturbances

A growing problem for prison administrators is the increase in gang activity within correctional facilities. Gangs are becoming an increasing problem in many prisons and jails, although some researchers suggest there is administrative denial in some parts of the country that the problem is serious (Baugh 1992:82). The seriousness of the gang problem can be seen in a national survey conducted in 1992 that indicates that 47,445 inmates throughout the country are members of 755 security threat groups operating within prisons throughout the United States, especially in California, Illinois, New York, and Texas (American Correctional Association 1993:4). The presence of gangs appears to increase the probability of violence. In 1984 and 1985, the Texas Department of Criminal Justice witnessed 52 inmate homicides and more than 7,000 inmate and staff assaults, with 92 percent of the homicides and 80 percent of the assaults attributed to gang-related activities (Buentello 1992:58). One prison gang, the

Aryan Brotherhood, was responsible for 18 percent of all homicides in the Federal Bureau of Prisons between 1982 and 1992 (Trout 1992:62). Most prison gangs have street gang origins and are racial and ethnic in nature, grouping together for power and protection. "All prison gangs are organized strictly to take part in only antisocial and criminal behavior" (Allen and Simonsen 1995:524). The Washington Department of Corrections defines a prison gang as:

> *An exclusive and clandestine group of disruptive inmates involved in the mutual caretaking of each other. Methods used to maintain their identity are most often illegal and counterproductive to the best interest of the prison administration* (Riley 1992:70).

Gang members individually can engage in a wide range of illegal behaviors that may not be connected with the gang, but correctional administrators have special reason to be concerned about organized gang behavior:

> *. . . [A]side from their strong-arm tactics and corrupt activities, one of the greatest threats of gangs to institutional security is their ability to unite the inmate population into polarized groups prepared for collective violence* (Fox and Stinchcomb 1994:400).

The ability of the prison gang to initiate and direct organized violence constitutes an emergency, particularly as crowding and inmate anger and frustration increase.

Level 2 Mitigation

Sergeant William Riley (1992:68-71) reports that the Washington State Penitentiary in Walla Walla uses level 2 gang mitigation that involves two activities based on staff being "gang conscious": having the awareness that any inmate may be a member of a gang capable of causing disruption.

The first activity is identifying gang members during the intake process. New inmates are screened by an intake committee that examines the inmate for tattoos and scars indicative of gang affiliation; the inmates are asked if they are gang members; and, if the answer is yes, the intake officer asks if separation from members of other gangs is necessary. Facilities interested in developing classification criteria for identifying gang members can learn from the Salt Lake Area Gang Project criteria:

> *An individual is considered a gang member if he or she admits to being a member or has tattoos or clothing exclusively associated with certain gangs. Other indicators include use of the gang's hand signals, an arrest while committing a crime with known gang members and confirmation of close association with known gang members from a reliable informant* (Mendez 1992:75).

The second activity is physical separation of rival gang members through a process of dividing the facility into three sections, restricting movement, and monitoring inmate traffic as part of a strategy to ensure housing units are not dominated by a particular gang. An inmate's gang status is verified through a process of cell searches, routine observation of inmate activity, and information received on inmates about to be received. Gang status reports are maintained and used to prevent any gang from achieving numerical superiority in a housing unit. Preventive intelligence gathering coordinated by a disruptive groups information analyst is used to determine the percentage of gang members in each housing area and to identify leaders.

Washington State Penitentiary emphasizes the role of staff training in level 2 mitigation. Staff are taught the value of close observation and the need for the development of inmate information sources. Information from line staff allows administrators to track the emergence of new gangs and develop effective interventions:

> *New information and updates of old information are often relayed during training sessions. Line staff have been and always will be the eyes and ears to detect changes in inmate behavior. Inmates who see that staff are successfully dealing with problems caused by gang members realize they do not require a gang to ensure their needs are being met* (Wiley 1992:71).

Buentello (1992:58-60) reports that the Texas Department of Criminal Justice has introduced a number of level 2 mitigation activities to reduce the impact of gangs:

• **Staff Training.** A program of increased in-service and preservice training to focus staff attention on the nature of inmate gangs has been implemented. Many individuals new to corrections have little or no experience with gangs, their organizational structure, and

their rules. All new staff should be educated about the types of gangs operating in the community and prison and their philosophy, membership requirements, crime preferences, language, and codes—verbal and visual. Also, additional new staff have been hired and trained in this way.

Although Buentello did not reference female gang members in his discussion, it is likely that gang identification and suppression policies applied to male gang members may be applied, with some modification, to female gang members.

• **Policy Initiatives.** The Texas Department of Criminal Justice has designated gang intelligence officers for each Texas facility to gather information about gang activities and identify gang members in the general population. These staff have established a process of active communications with state and federal law enforcement agencies to share information useful for disrupting community gang activity and aiding federal-level criminal prosecution. Once a gang member has been identified, he or she is removed from the general population and placed in administrative segregation. Doing so reduces inmate fear and anxiety, as seen in a reduction in the number of inmates requesting protection status and transfer. The policy of isolating identified gang members from general population has proven to be particularly effective in frustrating gang leader's attempts to recruit and organize:

> *It became apparent gangs were having a difficult time recruiting and carrying out illegal activities from administrative segregation status. They became increasingly*

frustrated, which in turn lessened their effectiveness. As new facilities opened, gang members were housed in a manner that precluded them from having physical contact with inmates in the general population (Buentello 1992:60).

Level 2 mitigation efforts may emphasize a systemwide classification of gang membership identification to ensure minimal concentration of gangs at any given facility. Gang intelligence officers aggressively should focus on gang members and all gang-related activities, no matter how legitimate they appear to be. Members of this unit should receive special training in providing court testimony, the rules of evidence, and chain-of-custody evidence procedures.

The Federal Bureau of Prisons practiced level 2 mitigation in the form of identifying and separating gang members until the latter part of the 1980s. Because of the changing nature of street and prison gangs, and the threat presented by members of drug cartels who have been incarcerated, the Bureau of Prisons has moved to a mitigation strategy of tracking "security threat groups." These are groups that appear to present a compelling potential threat, even though they do not meet the traditional definition of a prison gang:

Example profiles might include a history of assaulting or murdering officers, a history of escape, particularly helicopter escapes and plots, a history of rape, and a history of leading food strikes or work stoppages. Skills of specific concern in the prison environment might

include locksmiths, gunsmiths, security electronic experts, explosives experts and computer hackers (Trout 1992:66).

The Bureau of Prisons also uses a formal threat assessment process that establishes links between documented threat activity and the best methods for mitigating that group:

For example, mandatory urine testing can be limited to only those groups documented as having involvement in drug activities, which can be partially determined through the use of less expensive random urine testing (Trout 1992:66).

Once threat assessment data no longer support the security threat group designation, mitigation initiatives and resources targeting that particular security threat group can be concentrated elsewhere.

Preparedness/Response

When gang violence does erupt, staff response should be along the lines discussed for nongang-related minor disturbances. If violence escalates to the level of a riot, response should be in accordance with the discussion detailed in chapter 12.

Recovery

Recovery efforts should be the same as those discussed for nongang-related minor disturbances. However, recovery may be assisted by legislative awareness of the problems presented by prison gangs. In Texas, the legislative contribution to recovery was to provide funding of a special prosecutor to focus on prison gang activities and to pass two inmate-specific statutes. The first statute made it a felony for any inmate to possess a weapon. The second statute stipulated that any inmate convicted of a crime while incarcerated would serve that sentence consecutively. The Texas Department of Criminal Justice has made use of these statutes to actively prosecute cases of gang violence.

The aggressive use of the special prosecutor and gang-related statutes in Texas during recovery clearly produces a powerful level 2 mitigation effect. As gang solidarity breaks down, the organized threat to the facility that gangs represent decreases. Many inmates have defected from gangs, which have experienced an increased level of intragang fighting. New factions have formed as distrust increased and defectors were used more frequently as state

witnesses against the gangs. There has been an increase in gang members willing to turn informant, and this has further fragmented gang solidarity. Fearing prosecution, these informants warn of impending gang violence in time for correctional staff to intervene (Buentello 1992:60).

If a state does not have gang-specific legislation, correctional administrators still should pursue an aggressive policy of prosecution of gang-related disturbances as a means of breaking down gang solidarity. A special emphasis on identifying the leadership of gangs involved in the disturbance, placing them in disciplinary segregation, and transferring them from the facility as quickly as possible also will help break down solidarity—as long as the receiving facility has the same effective approach.

Chapter 12

Riots and Hostages

*T*he watershed riot at the New Mexico State Prison in Santa Fe began shortly after midnight on Saturday, February 2, 1980. Curiously, the impregnable control room was readily breached; the shatter-proof glass, shattered . . . interior guards were soon captives; the tower guards powerless to report the riot since all phone lines were cut . . . . The carnage began . . . . In uncontrollable frenzy, using [a portable acetylene tank and cutting torch], and an assortment of prison-fashioned and smuggled weapons, 12 snitches were burned, decapitated, castrated, and eviscerated . . . many in the protective custody unit were beyond physical identification (Dinitz 1981:3-4).

There have been four prison riot "epidemics" in this century. The first wave took place at the time of World War I. The second wave took place in 1929-1930, during the time of the Great Depression. The third wave took place in 1950-1966, when more than a hundred riots and major disturbances occurred. The fourth wave began in the 1960s and continues to the present. Since 1951, there have been an average of ten prison riots per year (Bartollas and Conrad 1992:424-25).

Riots may be classified as expressive (spontaneous) or instrumental (planned with some goal in mind) (Hawkins and Alpert 1989:254). If a facility has a high degree of inmate solidarity, a riot may be planned. However, in facilities where inmates are disorganized, without effective leaders, and fragmented into numerous groups, the riot is likely to be spontaneous and extremely violent. Unfortunately, riots are not as rare as administrators would like to think. The first recorded riot occurred in 1774 at the Newgate Prison in Simsbury, Connecticut:

> Since then, correctional institutions throughout the country have been plagued by hundreds of riots and countless less serious disturbances (Fox and Stinchcomb 1994:402).

It is the rare prison that is not vulnerable to a riot. As one inmate gang leader stated:

> "We're in control around here. If we wanted to, we could take the prison apart, but we choose not to. We've too much to lose" (Bartollas and Conrad 1992:425).

Riot at the Southern Ohio Correctional Facility, April 1993. Inmates placed barricades in the cell blocks to inhibit a tactical assault.

Riots and hostage situations are discussed together because the riot is the inmate-precipitated emergency that has the highest probability of involving hostages.

Mitigation

The level 2 and 3 mitigation activities discussed in chapter 7 apply particularly well to riots. However, with riots, another dimension is added to mitigation. Up to this point, mitigation has been presented as an activity that occurs before an emergency. Yet, mitigation activities also may be undertaken during recovery. The discussion of the riot recovery phase illustrates the value of specific recovery

activities to achieve level 2 mitigation of future inmate-precipitated emergencies.

Preparedness and Response

Preparedness and response activities are designed to achieve three specific goals: containing the disturbance, freeing hostages, and retaking the facility.

Containing the Disturbance

Whether a riot is planned or unplanned, immediate containment is essential:

> *The theory of containment is a variation of the "divide and conquer" theory . . . . By restricting*

movement in the institution from one zone to another, rioters will be limited in their ability to spread the disturbance directly. Except in those instances where pre-disturbance planning on the part of the rioters results in simultaneous takeovers of various parts of the institution, the containment strategy should be useful in stopping a small disturbance from spreading (Henderson 1990:49).

The heart of containment is the controlled lockdown of all areas inside the facility, a process that maximizes the use of existing physical barriers. Strategic planning should clearly designate staff responsible for securing all gates, grilles, doors, cell doors, and nonrioting inmates; sealing off those areas of the facility under staff control; and locking up tools and hazardous materials. Tower and perimeter patrol officers should maintain the integrity of the perimeter by maximizing their visibility through a show of weapons intended to keep rioting inmates from rushing the perimeter. Any use of lethal force should be permitted specifically by the emergency plan. The external perimeter should be secured by law enforcement personnel.

Once the riot is contained, an interior perimeter of armed Correctional Emergency Response Team members and law enforcement officers should be established to guarantee staff control of critical areas, such as the infirmary drug room, food storage and preparation areas, shop, factory, warehouse areas where tools and hazardous/flammable substances are stored, and any administrative areas where inmate or confidential staff records are stored. It is important to remember that during a riot,

nonparticipating inmates should continue to be provided with such things as food and showers. In past riots, some institutions have ignored nonparticipating inmates.

Freeing Hostages

Riots virtually guarantee a hostage situation. This goal of freeing hostages requires the coordinated activities of the Correctional Emergency Response Team and the Hostage Negotiation Team. The goal of resolving the riot with minimum injury and loss of life and securing the release of all hostages is the same for both teams, but activities to achieve the goal are different. The Hostage Negotiation Team emphasizes communications, psychology, and persuasion as the chief tools of conflict resolution. The two cardinal rules of correctional hostage negotiation are (1) the safety of hostages is the highest priority and (2) never promise inmates their freedom or immunity from prosecution. The delicate balance between these two conflicting rules must be maintained at all times.

Ideally, the corrections Hostage Negotiation Team will have trained with local law enforcement negotiation teams. Shared training allows team members to get to know each other and determine the depth of experience and skill available in an emergency. The act of training together as a confidence builder is important because, during an actual hostage situation, it may be necessary, or advisable, to allow a law enforcement team to conduct the negotiations, especially if it has more real-life experience than the corrections team. Pride should not influence the decision as to which team does the negotiating. During the second riot at Camp Hill, the state police negotiation team conducted the negotiations with inmate

Plan of Action

No matter how great the pressure to "just do something, for God's sake," there should be a plan of action before additional staff are placed at risk. The first two rules were successfully applied the second night of the Camp Hill riots. The plan of action to retake the institution consisted of three primary elements. The first element involved hundreds of state police officers entering through the main gate, covered by officers with rifles on the main gate catwalk. Once inside the institution, commanders organized double skirmish lines of armed troopers in full riot gear in front of the Group I complex to provide cover for a smaller group of troopers and correctional officers who escorted fire trucks into position in front of the burning command post in Group I. These officers and firefighters quickly were able to effect the rescue of the trapped staff and take them outside the institution to a medical triage area.

The second element involved using the double skirmish lines in a pincer movement (one pincer in front of the Education Building, the other pincer sweeping up behind Kitchen 2) to drive inmates back into the area of Group II and III. This area is so small that inmates were forced to retreat into the cellblocks. State police secured all buildings along their route to protect against inmates hiding and attacking from behind.

The third element was to surround the Group II and III cell blocks, demand the surrender of all inmates, and provide such a show of firepower that the Hostage Negotiating Team had a relatively easy time persuading the inmates to surrender. As inmates surrendered, they were handcuffed and led in groups to the main stockade field. As each cellblock cleared out, squads of troopers entered to search for inmates hiding in the debris.

ringleaders who had refused to talk to the members of the corrections team.

The Correctional Emergency Response Team emphasizes proficiency in assault techniques, including using firearms, batons, and chemical agents as the chief tools of conflict resolution. A general rule of thumb is to negotiate unless there is a significant risk to the lives of hostages, or if a life actually has been taken. Even if a life is taken, there should be a reasoned assessment of the danger to the remaining hostages. There are no rigid rules for determining when an assault replaces negotiations. Once the decision has been made to assault, the primary responsibility of the Correctional Emergency Response Team will be the rapid, safe removal of hostages.

Retaking the Facility

The emotional need to do something when a riot has started is powerful, especially if staff are in danger. Staff often express the desire to rush into the riot as soon as they learn their co-workers and friends are in trouble. A pell-mell rush into a riot violates three critical principles:

1. Never take action when you're angry.

2. Don't rush into a situation where you're outnumbered.

3. Don't act without a detailed plan of action.

Staff not trained in special crisis management tactics, motivated only by the thought of what the inmates are doing, will not be able to respond effectively. Driven by anger and fear, these staff are at high risk of making fatal errors, as witnessed by the deaths of thirty-nine staff and inmates during the retaking of Attica in 1971 (Winfree 1996:45). In addition, they are likely to engage in acts of retaliation that will plant the seeds for future problems. At the very least, untrained staff will make the Correctional Emergency Response Team's job more difficult by getting in the way.

Retaking a facility should be guided by five rules:

1. The number of staff entering the riot area should be as large and as well trained as resources permit, even if this means waiting for the arrival of officers from other correctional facilities or law enforcement agencies.

2. There should be a well-developed plan of action thoroughly understood by the chain of command of all the agencies actively involved in the retaking of the facility.

3. Strict fire discipline should be maintained at all times during the retaking of a facility. Inmates often exchange clothing with facility personnel, and armed staff too ready to fire on inmates may kill staff, as happened at Attica in 1971. Personnel should fire their weapons only when their safety—or the safety of hostages, assault personnel, or nonrioting inmates—is at risk. All staff permitted to carry firearms should thoroughly understand their department's policy governing the circumstances under which lethal force may be used. Policy concerning the firing of warning shots should clearly establish when the use of lethal force may replace the warning shot. Firing always should be at a specific target, never indiscriminate.

The use of weapons always should be in accordance with legal statutes. In Pennsylvania, for example, correctional staff may use only the weapons the department has certified them as trained to use. Use of a firearm not authorized by the department, or a firearm authorized, but which the officer is not qualified to use, leaves the officer and the department open to legal liability if an inmate is killed or wounded by that officer. Supervisors should ensure that correctional officers are not carrying unauthorized firearms into the institution and that armed noncorrectional officer staff are not entering the institution.

4. Clear visibility and open lines of communication for assault personnel are vital. There should be a sufficient number of fully charged hand-held radios for communications with the command post and along the skirmish lines. There should be no dropping of tear gas into the facility unless this serves a vital function. If tear gas is used, all personnel should be equipped with modern tear gas masks, because a wind shift may blow tear gas into the ranks of personnel. Even if the tear gas does not blow into the faces of the assault force, it can contribute to the lack of visibility already created by the smoke and ash coming from burning buildings. Helicopters should not be used in the immediate vicinity of personnel because the rotor noise may disrupt communications. Any disruption in communications may lead to panic and confusion, both of which may be fatal in a retaking operation, especially if the action is being taken at night.

All personnel participating in retaking a facility should be thoroughly briefed and under the command of supervisors with whom they have trained. If a mixed assault force of correctional officers and law enforcement is being used, it is imperative that each group be under the command of the supervisor who trained them, and the supervisors from both agencies be in complete agreement about their roles in the operation before the first officer sets foot inside the facility. Ideally, members of the assault force will have trained together.

5. The inmate surrender should be tightly controlled. All surrendering inmates should be shaken down for contraband and immediately escorted to an open area as far away from the rioters as possible. A sufficient supply of hand-cuffs should be on hand. All inmates who surrender should be maintained under conditions of maximum security until their role, or lack of a role, in the riot has been firmly established. Even inmates who surren-der at the beginning of the riot, or at some point before the riot has been managed, should be subjected to close supervision until it has been established by the Criminal Prosecution Team that they were not involved in planning the riot. Cuffing should be behind the back, with leg shackles applied as soon as possible. All movement of inmates should be under the command of a commissioned officer to ensure no retaliation is taken against the inmates. Any sign of inmate injury or illness should be reported immediately to the Medical Response Team.

If at all possible, one of the conditions of surrender should be the immediate release of all hostages before the first inmate is taken into custody. Hostages should be escorted to med-ical staff for examination immediately after release. If the inmates surrender before all hostages have been released, Correctional Emergency Response Team members should locate the hostages as soon as it has been determined that there are no inmates waiting in ambush.

Recovery

The recovery phase may be particularly dif-ficult because of trauma staff experience dur-ing a riot. There are five recovery activities of particular importance: clearing the count, shaking down the facility, assessing facility security status, evacuating, and mitigating staff retaliation.

Clearing the Count

As soon as it is safe to enter the facility, two teams of staff should be assigned to account for all staff and inmates. One team should be a staff count team; the other team should be an inmate count team. The staff count team should work from a staff roster, checking off names as they locate staff at the facility, in local hospitals, or at home. The team also might check the names of those whose identification badges have not been returned. The inmate count team also should work off of a roster that is updated daily. Inmates should be either in the facility or at a local hospital. If they are not in either location, then the possibility of escape during the riot should be considered. This possibility may be confirmed only after the entire facility has been searched.

Establishing the count can be a very com-plicated job. At Camp Hill, several days passed before officials were confident there were no bodies hidden in the ashes of the burned-out buildings, a process given urgency by rumors that a modular unit officer had been hand-cuffed to his desk and left to burn to death during the riots. The only way to refute such rumors is to physically account for every inmate and staff member. Count should clear before any inmate evacuation occurs unless there is a compelling security reason for immediate transfer, in which case, the inmate count team should be notified of the names of those transferred. Otherwise, clearing the count will become a nightmare.

Shaking Down the Facility

It is a given that a shakedown of the facility is mandatory after response. But this process may be quite difficult. At Camp Hill, there were fifty-two acres inside the fence and tens of thousands of square feet inside of buildings that had to be searched. An effective search of a large facility takes time and personnel. Strategic planning should establish the number of personnel needed to search the entire facility, including tunnels and basements; the most effective search pattern; and the need to consider a preshakedown cooling-off period.

A thorough shakedown is necessary because inmates may use a riot as an opportunity to hide contraband. Depending on the length of the riot, inmates may have time to create hiding places in walls, ceilings, floors, toilets, mattresses, and other areas where a routine search may not locate the contraband. The search should be systematic and conducted by officers who are not traumatized or fatigued. The recommended search pattern is to establish the housing units, or the location where the inmates are to be temporarily kept, as the center of the search pattern and move out in a concentric circle pattern until the team has searched all areas of the facility. Every area of the facility, including steam tunnels, or any

pipe large enough for the smallest inmate to hide in, must be inspected. The initial shakedown should not be considered the only shakedown needed. Testimony of Camp Hill staff in federal court established that correctional officers still were discovering riot-related contraband nine months after the riot.

The timing of the shakedown is critical. Sending tired, angry officers into a cell block still housing frightened inmates to conduct a search carries a high potential for physical conflict and the type of retaliation administrators

Photo courtesy Allied Pix Service Inc., State Correctional Institution, Camp Hill, PA

Inmates destroyed 15 of Camp Hill's 31 buildings during the riots of October 25, 1989, forcing the Department of Corrections to build new cell blocks and upgrade existing ones.

fear. The volatility of inmates who anticipate staff retaliation always is a risk during a shakedown of occupied housing units. Inmates refusing to leave a cell should be removed by Correctional Emergency Response Team officers trained in professional cell-extraction procedures.

Assessing Facility Security Status

As the shakedown proceeds, the Damage Assessment Team should be assessing the integrity of the physical plant to determine if the physical control of inmates has been compromised during the riot. If a cooling down period before a shakedown is determined to be the best course of action, the Damage Assessment Team still should enter the housing units to immediately determine the status of cell door locking devices. Failure to do this may leave the facility vulnerable to a second riot, as happened at Camp Hill.

Evacuating

Evacuating large numbers of inmates should be considered only if there has been a significant loss of housing units. Total population evacuation is dangerous (because of the complexity of this activity, it will be discussed in detail in Chapter 18). However, identified ringleaders should be transferred to a maximum security facility as quickly as possible during recovery as a level 2 mitigation activity. A written status report and complete classification file should accompany each ringleader. Verbal contact with the receiving facility before transfer will permit a discussion that may prepare receiving staff to better handle inmates who still may be disruptive.

Mitigating Staff Retaliation

The potential for staff and law enforcement retaliation against inmates, even those who did not participate in the riot, should not be underestimated. After the 1971 Attica riot, 45 percent of the inmates who had been in D Yard during the riot suffered bruises, lacerations, abrasions, and broken bones at the hands of correctional officers:

> The tragedy of Attica did not end when the shooting stopped. Despite promises of no reprisals, inmates continued to be kicked, prodded, beaten, and subjected to verbal abuse after the revolt was crushed. This abuse was still evident when the Attica Commission completed its investigation and held public hearings five months after the riot (Silverman and Vega 1996:171).

In the aftermath of the 1979 riot at the West Virginia Penitentiary, inmates alleged that in addition to being harassed and denied medical treatment:

> The state police came in and just brutally intimidated us. They singled out for beatings inmates that sort of had it coming, if you accept that. And the other inmates, they just made it known that each minute was a potential for beatings, if you even thought of getting out of line (Useem and Kimball 1989:167).

Inmates at Camp Hill alleged a similar pattern of beatings after a 1983 attack on a correctional officer as well as during recovery from the 1989 riots. Staff retaliation may be addressed with specific level 2 mitigation activities:

Preriot Commitment to Professional Behavior—Administrators may significantly mitigate inappropriate staff behavior long before a riot by developing an institutional climate in which staff brutality is not tolerated. Such a climate is established by (1) implementing a rigid policy of consistently and thoroughly investigating all complaints of staff brutality during the routine operation of the facility and (2) imposing firm discipline, including dismissal, against all staff found guilty of brutality or other acts that involve the misuse of authority. An essential element of such a policy is holding supervisors accountable for the actions of their subordinates. Discipline of supervisors for the failure to hold subordinates accountable to a professional model of behavior can send an important signal to staff and inmates alike.

Staff Behavior Control Activities— Routine, systematic videotaping of staff-inmate contact in the immediate aftermath of a riot, especially during line movements, may deter staff brutality. Inmates being moved should not be run through a gauntlet because this may invite unprovoked violence against inmates. If law enforcement agencies use mounted officers to help manage inmates, the horses should be kept at least eight to ten feet from the inmates so there is minimal chance of a horse inflicting inmate injury.

Supervision in the Disciplinary Unit— The Disciplinary Unit has an extremely high potential for abuse. Inmates viewed as particularly dangerous will be moved into this unit as soon after the riot as possible. The fact that

these inmates now are out of public view, often are angry and agitated, and have been identified, rightly or wrongly, as key participants in the riot creates an environment in which staff anger and resentment may be released easily. Staff who lose control of their emotions are most likely to lose them in the Disciplinary Unit, particularly during the initial strip search. A senior supervisor of proven stability should be physically in charge of this highly volatile area as soon as the first inmate arrives. All movements into, out of, and within the block should be videotaped, with the commissioned officer submitting a written daily report to the facility administrator describing staff and inmate behavior.

Policy Establishing Guidelines for Inmate Property—Staff also may retaliate by destroying inmate cell property and personal property. After the May 22, 1981, riot at Southern Michigan's Northside complex, inmates reported:

> *During the lockdown there was a lot of things [the guards] did that prompted guys to want to do something. They'd come in your house, handcuff you to the end of the gallery, and throw your stuff out on the base [that is, they would throw it over the railing and let it crash on the floor of the lowest tier]. They'd say, "that's not your number" [engraved on the item], or "It's contraband." A lot of stuff I bought through the store, they threw away—guys' typewriters, TVs. I guess they called that getting revenge* (Useem and Kimball 1989:138).

Lawsuits filed by Camp Hill inmates after the 1989 riots frequently included allegations of retaliatory staff destruction of both cell property and personal property. Preparedness should include plans for management, and storage if necessary, of all inmate property not damaged in the riots. Specific staff should be assigned to this task and held strictly accountable.

Environmental Scanning for Psychological Abuse—Staff retaliation also may be psychological. Camp Hill inmates alleged numerous acts of psychological torture during recovery that included state troopers pulling the triggers of unloaded shotguns held to the heads of inmates; an inmate being made to kiss the rear end of a state trooper's horse, and various threats of impending physical violence, intimidating abusive language, and denial of the use of toilet facilities for such long periods of time that soiling occurred.

The Post-traumatic Assessment Team may play a valuable psychological triage role by circulating throughout the facility during recovery, talking to staff and inmates, carefully observing staff behavior and attitudes, and helping supervisors determine which staff are not under sufficient emotional control. The retaliatory beating and psychological abuse of inmates serves no legal or penological purpose. Inmates brutalized by staff may be temporarily subdued, but the seeds of revenge have been planted and at a later date they may retaliate against other staff or inmates or, ultimately, citizens in the community to which they have been released. Staff identified as too traumatized to work effectively with inmates should be sent home and given written referrals for follow-up counseling and support services.

Supervision of Outside Correctional Officers—Because it is likely that correctional officers will be brought in from other facilities, it is important that these officers be under the direct command of supervisors assigned to the facility experiencing the riot. Otherwise, there may be a serious loss of control and accountability that results in retaliation and subsequent litigation directed at officers the inmates know, not officers from the other facilities who may have been the ones engaged in retaliation.

Monitoring of Noncorrectional Officer Staff—Strategic planning always should consider the fact that it is not just correctional officers who may be tempted to retaliate against inmates: teachers returning to find their classroom burned out; maintenance staff finding their shops destroyed; food service supervisors finding their kitchens looted and burned; and counselors finding their offices, which once contained personal pictures of the family and mementos of personal achievements, looted, burned, or otherwise desecrated. They may become angry enough to act irrationally, especially if they are in contact with inmates who appear to be gloating about the destruction wrought by the rioters.

During the early hours of recovery after the second Camp Hill riot, it was reported that a member of the maintenance staff was livid with rage, vowing to beat "with a club" the first inmates he could get his hands on, because his beloved shop had been burned out during the riot. The report turned out to be without foundation, but several valuable hours were spent establishing that fact. For this reason, only staff with specific assignments and responsibilities should be allowed to enter the facility during recovery.

High Management Visibility—The final level 2 mitigation activity is the high-profile presence of senior management staff during recovery. Senior staff working separate twelve-hour shifts who are alert to any hint of inmate abuse should provide high visibility twenty-four hours a day. Their presence, attitude, and personal display of restraint during a highly stressful time sends a strong signal that professional behavior is expected.

The Brutality Ripple Effect

It is not only the administrators of the facility where the riot has occurred who have to be concerned about the possibility of staff retaliation. The power of rumors to inflame the emotions of staff hundreds of miles from the riot should not be discounted.

Administrators of facilities receiving inmates from the stricken facility also should be aware that their staff, inflamed by news coverage of the riot and rumors of violence against hostages, may retaliate. In the aftermath of the 1989 Camp Hill riots, inmates transferred to the State Correctional Institution at Graterford alleged that the receiving correctional officers beat them. A subsequent, highly public investigation resulted in staff disciplinary action and adverse media attention. Various Camp Hill litigants also accused superintendents of other receiving institutions of allowing their staff to retaliate.

Administrators at facilities receiving inmates from riot-stricken facilities also should be prepared to implement the mitigation of staff activities discussed in this chapter.

Chapter 13

The Rumblings of Staff Discontent: Early Warning Signs

*B*ut when the riots came, erupting one after the other like a string of firecrackers in the last days of May 1981, they did not come as one might expect—as the spontaneous reaction of inmates, aggrieved by overcrowded and unsanitary accommodations. No, the catalyst was a mutiny of the guards themselves, an organized takeover of the State Prison of Southern Michigan (SPSM), the largest prison in the world (Useem and Kimball 1989:114).

Chapter 7 introduced the concept of environmental scanning of inmate behavior as an effective level 2 mitigation activity because conventional planning traditionally views inmate-precipitated emergencies solely in terms of inmate behavior. However, staff discontent can create a climate that encourages or actually permits inmate-precipitated emergencies, as happened in Michigan in 1981. For this reason, strategic planning requires that staff behavior be routinely subjected to environmental scanning. Of specific interest are indications that staff are losing their loyalty, sense of professionalism, and commitment to organizational goals. When this occurs, work performance may become so sloppy that

inmates are motivated to take advantage of the situation and create problems. The warning signs of staff discontent may be found in three major areas: the quality of work performance, the labor relations climate, and statistical data.

Quality of Work Performance

Each facility should have a system of formal, documented monthly inspections of the facility by administrative staff, including the facility administrator. These inspections provide an opportunity to assess the overall level of staff cleanliness and sanitation standards. High standards reflect the pride and professionalism of a staff working together to achieve common goals. Low standards reflect the lack of pride and professionalism typical of an institution where staff no longer believe they are important and feel no pride in their job:

> . . . *substandard conditions of sanitation—dirt and grime in the corners of rooms, cockroaches scampering beneath kitchen equipment, and leaky sewage*

pipes. Hallways may be dank and dark, with walls in need of painting and floors not recently shined. In poorly run prisons, inmates mill around with no particular destination or work to do. You hear shouts, insults, and incessant testing of one another. Violence occurs routinely and inmates easily acquire drugs and alcohol (Wright 1994:6).

The appearance of graffiti, especially in areas open to staff and public view, is another sign of low staff pride. A change in the quality of work performance, especially if the change is sudden and occurs simultaneously with other signs of staff discontent, should be a warning that the facility may be moving into a dangerous state of staff discontent.

Negative changes in staff performance are not limited to the physical plant. Changes in the quality of the directives for written policies and procedures and public documents, such as annual reports and press releases, can signal a warning that facility staff are focused on issues other than professionalism. The quality of written documents disseminated by the central office of a correctional system can serve as a barometer of the degree of staff morale within the entire system. Slippages in the quality of public documents, as evidenced by typos, general sloppiness, and a lack of attention to detail at both the facility and central office level are warning indicators, especially if they occur during a period of leadership or philosophical transition.

Any significant decline in staff performance should be investigated to determine if it is a symptom of a larger problem that needs to be addressed immediately. When staff lose pride in what they do, their lack of attention to detail and indifference to the general environment of the facility may encourage inmates to take part in collective action against a staff person seen as unable to respond effectively to their challenge. This action may not be violent; it may take the form of class action litigation or work stoppages. However, staff indifference can lay the groundwork for inmate-precipitated emergencies by encouraging inmates to believe that they are in a position to be manipulative.

Labor Relations Climate

A vast majority of correctional staff have won the right to unionize (American Correctional Association 1991:57), and correctional officer unions traditionally have been strong. Because most correctional officers are represented by a union, the relationship between union and management can be a significant indicator of staff morale. If the relationship is open and trusting enough to permit informal resolution of grievances and hallway discussion of topics of interest, staff morale tends to be high. If relationships are rigidly formal and discussions confined to the antagonistic arena of the meet and discuss and arbitration hearing, staff morale tends to be low. When morale is low, sloppy work performance may become a significant problem as staff focus on their problems with each other instead of concentrating on inmates. Statistical indicators that suggest low staff morale include steady increases in the number of:

• Formal grievances filed

• Unresolved grievances at the local level that have to be resolved at the state or arbitration level

- Items on the local meet and discuss agenda

- Items continually appearing on the local meet and discuss agenda regardless of the length of previous discussion they received

- Disputes taken to arbitration despite management offers of settlement

- Allegations of management harassment of union officials

- Unfair labor practice charges filed

In addition to these, there may be requests by state labor leadership for personal meetings with the system administrator to discuss a particular facility as well as notification that state leaders plan to attend all local meet and discuss sessions and would like the facility administrator to be present. This type of climate may lead to demands that minutes be taken for each meet and discuss session, but that these minutes will not be considered official unless the union has read them before dissemination. In a worst case scenario, labor and management may find themselves arguing over whether the person taking the minutes is union or management.

The quality of labor grievances filed also should be considered. When an extremely experienced correctional officer files a grievance asking, Is it okay if inmates do chin-ups from the tops of the recreation cages in the disciplinary unit?, this is a sign that staff discontent has reached the point of formally asking questions that would not be asked if morale were high and management were trusted.

Staff who have come to believe, for whatever reason, that they are no longer respected as members of the team may display passive aggression in the form of repeatedly asking questions to which they already know the answer and constantly challenging every rule and policy applied to their work performance, all within a formal framework that says because they no longer trust management they want every issue on the record.

Statistical Data

The information routinely compiled by personnel officers is invaluable in staff environmental scanning. Every facility should have a standardized data collection system that permits the recording and retrieval of the level of staff overtime, workers' compensation claims, use of earned leave (sick, vacation, and personal), number of staff who have formally requested transfer to another facility, and number of resignations. Comparison of this information on a month-to-month and year-to-year basis can alert both the facility administrator and the agency administrator to negative staff trends.

Such trends are found in an analysis of personnel information for New York's Southport Correctional Facility, which notes that although there was no significant increase in injuries reported by Southport staff before a 1991 hostage-taking incident, workers' compensation claims increased from 672 calendar days in the first five months of 1990 to 1,604 calendar days in the first five months of 1991. During the same period, overtime increased from 4,739 hours to 16,618 hours. And the hours lost per pay period to workers' compensation increased from 42 hours in an April 1990 biweekly payroll to 721 in April 1991, an increase of 2,000 percent that accounted for all except 3,786 overtime hours (Coughlin 1991:34-35).

Staff who no longer perceive themselves to be part of the team may begin to engage in a practice of systematic work avoidance. The use of earned leave may increase dramatically, with some staff taking days as soon as they are earned. More and more staff take "mental health" days as the emotional environment deteriorates. However, it's not just the number of days missed that is important. The explanations provided for missing work can be very suggestive. For example, an analysis of seventy-seven pending workers' compensation claims at Southport Correctional Facility revealed the following causes for claims:

19 for injuries sustained in actual contact with inmates, either because officers were physically attacked, were attempting to restrain an inmate or were attempting to break up a fight among or between inmates.

23 because of inmates throwing solids and liquids, mostly feces and urine.

Stairs and steps drew these individual explanations for claims: fell on stairwell, lost footing/slid down stairs, slipped on stairs, fell walking up stairs, fell walking up circular stairwell, slipped off garbage truck step, caught heel on step, slipped on stairway, fell down steps.

Floors and grounds led to several individual claims, with one claim each for having slipped on mud, fell backwards on ice, slipped on water, slipped on wet floor, slipped and fell on wet floor, slipped on greasy kitchen floor and fell in parking lot.

An officer who claimed to have been "smashed between wall and inmate" went out for exactly seven days—with his return day coinciding with his previously scheduled vacation (Coughlin 1991:35-36).

As morale dives lower and lower, the number of staff formally requesting transfer, or resigning, tends to increase. An analysis of the 1980 riot at the Penitentiary of New Mexico noted that between 1974 and 1975 the yearly officer turnover rate increased from 24 percent to 44 percent and reached a staggering 80 percent in 1978. One year before the riot, the yearly turnover rate stood at 76 percent (Mays and Taggart 1985:45). This level of staff turnover makes it impossible to maintain continuity in policy implementation and staff professional development.

Once it is determined that staff morale is deteriorating, it is imperative that both the facility administrator and the agency administrator work together to identify the sources of the deterioration and the remedies necessary to prevent further deterioration. This may necessitate some difficult and painful personnel decisions.

Union leaders and local management should be encouraged to work together to find mutually acceptable solutions. If no action is taken to restore staff morale and trust, then the probability of inmate-precipitated emergencies becomes very high. As DiIulio (1987:255) notes: ". . . prison management may be the single most important determinant of the quality of prison life . . . ."

The Staff Strike

The most obvious indicator of staff discontent is use of the strike. Although correctional officer strikes are illegal in most states, a sharp decline in staff morale and increase in tension between labor and management contain the potential for motivating correctional officers to call an illegal strike or engage in the "blue flu."

Level 2 Strike Mitigation

The most effective level 2 mitigation is:

1. Legislation that bans strikes by correctional officers and provides severe penalties for illegal strikes

2. Managers and union leaders who truly have the best interests of the facility at heart and are willing to work hard to maintain open lines of communication

It's beyond the scope of this chapter to discuss leadership and management theory, but a comprehensive discussion of these critical areas can be found in many of the references provided in the reference section.

Level 3 Mitigation

The most effective method of reducing the negative consequences of a staff strike is a Memorandum of Agreement with law enforcement agencies and commercial vendors. The Memorandum of Agreement with the state police should indicate that police will provide perimeter security, enforce laws regarding the number and location of pickets at a correctional facility, ensure the delivery of medications and other vital supplies necessary for maintaining the health of the inmates, and safeguard the entrance and exit of staff not participating in the job action. Memoranda with commercial vendors should provide for delivery of all scheduled products and services with no honoring of any picket lines.

Preparedness/Response

Unfortunately, even if legislation bans strikes, staff may engage in a "blue flu" where large numbers of staff members call in sick or actually take to the picket lines. Response should entail activation of the communications tree to call in all administrative and supervisory staff to staff preassigned strike posts on a twelve-hour shift basis. The goal should be to maintain as normal a state of facility operations as possible. It may be necessary to suspend some facility programs, but careful thought must be given as to which programs. Inmates may react negatively to the loss of programming activities. Staff can be brought in from central office, but this action should be limited to those staff who have previous facility experience. Supervisors also may be brought in from other correctional facilities. The facility administrator immediately should request a court injunction to stop the strike. If the strike is a "blue flu" situation, sick slip procedures should be strictly enforced. A strong law enforcement presence on the perimeter, within view of the inmates, can provide the incentive to maintain order.

Critical to the ability to maintain normal operations is the training of supervisors and administrators in the specific strike assignments they will receive. If this is not done, supervisors unfamiliar with the requirements of their strike post may give inmates the opportunity to be disruptive.

Recovery

A staff strike can create a highly emotional negative climate. Staff and administrators, as well as inmates whose freedom and privileges may have been curtailed during the strike, often feel that they have been unfairly treated. Negative emotions experienced by striking staff may be increased if there are staff who have chosen to work instead of strike. During recovery, it is imperative that administrators maintain high visibility within the facility and a willingness to openly and candidly talk to staff and inmates about any negative emotions and attitudes generated by the strike. The healing plan of action presented in chapter 25 can be very useful during recovery from a staff strike.

Chapter 14

Facility Fires and Technological Emergencies

*F*ire is the most common of all the haz- *ards. Every year fires cause thousands of deaths and injuries and billions of dollars in property damage* (Federal Emergency Management Agency 1993:51).

Facility fires can result from any form of inmate-precipitated disturbance; staff and inmate carelessness with tobacco products, matches, and lighters; sabotage; lightning; electrical wires shorting out; staff or inmate accident; or an unknown origin. Technological emergencies may occur independently or as one of the consequences of a riot, flood, hurricane, earthquake, illegal staff strike, or terrorist activity.

Facility Fires

Fires are particularly dangerous in the correctional setting because they may occur when inmates are locked in their cells or in a secured building from which escape is not possible without staff assistance. Housing units, especially those that are climate controlled, can become deathtraps if heavy smoke accompanies a fire. Strategic planning for facility fires centers around the fire safety officer and the Fire Safety Team.

The Fire Safety Officer/ Fire Safety Team

The Fire Safety Team should be trained in the emergency life cycle of a wide range of fires and be led by a fire safety officer. If the facility is large, the position of fire safety officer should be full time. Regardless of size, this team leader should report directly to the deputy superintendent for operations. Volunteer fire personnel generally make excellent team members. Team members not only respond to a fire, they are responsible for level 2 mitigation and preparedness activities involving other staff and community fire personnel. This responsibility requires them to maintain a close working relationship with the nearest community fire department. Team members should know the exact capability of every fire department within the area. Local fire chiefs should have a working familiarity with the facility, its entrances and exits, evacuation routes, locations of readily accessible water, and facility fire fighting capability.

In addition, even if a correctional facility is not required by the state to be operated in accordance with the fire codes that regulate building operation in the community, team knowledge of community codes and regulations can be invaluable during mitigation and preparedness.

Level 2 Mitigation

Reducing the probability of a facility fire involves formulating specific policy and physical plant characteristics.

Policy—Policy designed to achieve level 2 mitigation should:

1. Establish procedures for the safe handling and storage of all flammable liquids and gases and the prevention of accumulation of combustible materials, especially in shops and other work areas.

Flammable substances should be stored in a secure location outside the facility in approved metal containers with tight-fitting caps. The staff/inmate tendency to create makeshift containers out of plastic gallon milk containers and other types of containers should be prohibited. Makeshift containers can be easily breached, burned, or otherwise damaged in ways that can create a fire hazard. All containers should have a permanent label that clearly identifies the contents. Containers should be dedicated to the substance on the label: gasoline containers should contain only gasoline; kerosene containers should contain only kerosene; oil containers should contain only oil; containers for liquids used for paint removal should contain only those liquids. A flammable substances inventory control system and regulations limiting the amount of combustible material in any building should be strictly enforced.

Policy should restrict the amount of combustible materials permitted in housing units. Many inmates build up supplies of magazines, newspapers, and books that can be a ready source of fire if the quantity of inmate combustible material is not rigidly regulated.

2. Establish a preventative maintenance schedule to keep all mechanical equipment in proper operating condition.

3. Develop a fire safety educational program available to both staff and inmates that includes a comprehensive set of fire prevention practices.

4. Mandate monthly fire safety inspections of the entire facility to ensure that:

   • Fire doors are closed at all times.

   • Flammable substances storage and handling procedures are followed to the letter, regardless of inconvenience to staff and inmate workers.

   • All smoking materials are safely disposed of in proper fire-resistant receptacles.

   • The preventive maintenance schedule is being followed, with all repairs immediately made.

   • The facility is in compliance with all applicable fire codes and regulations.

   • Changes in material use or procedures that could cause or support a fire or contaminate the environment in the event of a fire are identified.

   • Emergency generators are tested on a biweekly basis.

In addition, the fire safety officer should be required to participate in the design and construction phase of any facility renovation projects, recommend fire mitigation projects for budget submission, and conduct ongoing fire vulnerability analysis to identify areas newly vulnerable to a specific type of fire.

Physical Plant—Physical plant characteristics essential to level 2 mitigation include fire-resistant walls and doors; concrete and steel housing units; the avoidance of wooden-frame modular housing units; and the avoidance of any materials, including mattresses, that can be set on fire easily.

Level 3 Mitigation

Reducing the consequences of a facility fire also involves policy formulation and physical plant characteristics:

Policy—The policy for monthly fire safety inspections should include a provision that staff be educated concerning fire reporting procedures, containment techniques, and evacuation routes and procedures. Safety inspections should ensure all evacuation routes are clear of debris and clearly identified, all fire extinguishers are fully charged, smoke detectors are functioning properly, smoke detector batteries are changed annually, and the inmate combustibles policy is strictly enforced.

Evacuation routes should be identified with brightly colored, prominently displayed, permanently mounted fire evacuation route maps on each floor of every building. If the facility has towers, appropriate fire evacuation procedures for these buildings should be displayed. Towers often are overlooked in planning for fires, because they generally have only one officer and no inmates are involved.

Physical Plant—Physical plant characteristics useful in level 3 mitigation include:

1. An automatic sprinkler system (out of reach of inmates)

2. Fire hoses and an internal and external supply of readily accessible water

3. An emergency cell access system that can open all cell doors simultaneously

4. A fire alarm system that will automatically notify the nearest fire department.

5. Battery-operated smoke detectors

6. Maps of evacuation routes on each floor of every building.

7. Lighted exit signs above every exit

8. An outside-of-perimeter source of water readily accessible by community fire departments

9. Identification of all electrical, power, gas, or water shutoffs for rapid utilities shut-off

10. A fire-resistant flammable substances storage area outside of the facility

11. Designated evacuation sites where inmate control can be readily maintained during response and recovery

12. Designated, and separate, evacuation sites for civilians, nonuniformed staff, and inmate visitors during response and recovery

13. High-security fenced areas near disciplinary units for disciplinary inmates

14. Sallyports or gates large enough to accommodate the largest piece of community fire fighting equipment

15. Emergency equipment for removal of smoke from enclosed areas and portable emergency lighting systems

Preparedness/Response

Fires can spread rapidly in a correctional facility. Because fires often are a result of inmate-precipitated emergencies, response policy should mandate that no attempt to fight a fire will be made while inmates are unsecured in the area where the fire is located. If there are staff and inmates trapped in burning buildings and fire fighting personnel are needed to effect a rescue, response should involve a significant show of force to convince inmates to not attack rescue personnel. Civilian rescue personnel should not be permitted inside a correctional facility unless they are accompanied by correctional officers who can provide protection and advice about the buildings and staff under threat.

In the event of a fire, immediate and effective response is the goal. The Fire Safety Team should:

- Train all staff in the proper use of fire equipment.

- Conduct quarterly, unannounced fire drills, timed with a stopwatch, with results reported to the facility administrator.

- Coordinate all facility fire fighting response with community fire officials.

- Help medical staff develop procedures for the medical management of injuries.

- Establish with the facility administrator the level of fire response a facility is equipped to initiate.

The facility level of fire response is independent of the assistance that would be received by community fire departments. There are five possible levels:

Level 1—No staff attempt to fight the fire. Staff response is limited to evacuation.

Level 2—All staff are trained in fire extinguisher use. Staff in the immediate area of a fire attempt to control it. If they cannot, the fire alarm is sounded and all staff evacuate.

Level 3—Only designated staff are trained in fire extinguisher use.

Level 4—A fire team is trained to fight incipient-stage fires that can be controlled without protective equipment or breathing apparatus. Beyond this level of fire, the team evacuates.

Level 5—A fire team is trained and equipped to fight structural fires using protective equipment and breathing apparatus (Federal Emergency Management Agency 1993:52).

Once the level of response capability has been selected, all staff should receive written notification of the role they are expected to play in fire response. Training should be appropriate to the expected role. For example, a facility with a Level 2 or 3 response capability should train all staff to attempt to fight only those fires small enough to be handled by a fire extinguisher. Staff authorized to use fire extinguishers should know, at a minimum, the following information:

1. **Classes of Fires.** There are four classes of fires. Class A fires involve ordinary combustibles, such as wood, cloth, and paper. Class B fires involve flammable liquids, such as gasoline, oil, and oil-based paint. Class C fires involve energized electrical equipment, such as wiring, fuse boxes, circuit breakers, machinery, and appliances. Class D fires involve combustible metals, such as magnesium and

sodium (National Fire Protection Association 1995).

2. Types of Portable Fire Extinguishers.

Each class of fire, if small enough, can be extinguished by proper use of a fire extinguisher. Each class of fire has characteristics that require knowledge of the different types of fire extinguishers. Pressurized water models are appropriate for use on Class A fires only. They should not be used on electrical or flammable-liquid (oil, grease) fires. Carbon dioxide fire extinguishers contain pressurized liquid carbon dioxide, which turns to a gas when expelled from its container. Because carbon dioxide does not react with water or conduct electricity, these fire extinguishers are rated for Class B and C fires, but also can be safely used for Class A fires. Dry-chemical extinguishers blanket burning materials with powdered chemicals that are corrosive. Sodium bicarbonate extinguishers are appropriate for Class B and C fires and are the preferred extinguisher for fighting grease fires. Grease fires require specialized training beyond the capability of untrained inmates or untrained staff. Potassium bicarbonate, urea-based potassium bicarbonate, and potassium chloride extinguishers can extinguish bigger fires than sodium bicarbonate extinguishers can, but leave a powdered chemical residue that can damage electrical equipment. Foam extinguishers coat the surface of a burning flammable liquid with a chemical foam to lower the temperature of the liquid or cut off oxygen to the fire. The foam contains water, which conducts electricity; therefore, foam extinguishers should not be used on electrical fires (National Fire Protection Association 1995).

The National Fire Protection Association (1995) provides guidelines for use of the different types of fire extinguishers. All fire extinguishers are labeled using standard symbols for the classes of fires they are designed to fight. A red slash through any of the symbols indicates that the fire extinguisher should not be used on that class of fire. An extinguisher with no symbol indicates that it has not been tested for a given class of fire, but may be used provided an extinguisher with the rating of the fire is not available. Portable fire extinguishers are rated for the size of fire they are designed to handle. The rating is expressed as a number from 1 to 40 for Class A fires and 1 to 640 for Class B fires. This rating appears on the label of Class A and B portable extinguishers. The larger the numbers, the larger the fire that can be fought. No number accompanies a C rating or a D rating. The C rating on a fire extinguisher indicates only that it is appropriate for fighting an electrical fire. Extinguishers for Class D fires should match the type of metal that is burning; extinguishers appropriate for Class D fires are labeled with a list of the metals matching the extinguisher's extinguishing agent.

Level 2 and 3 response staff also should be familiar with all available escape routes in the event the fire cannot be contained without assistance and to close all fire doors when evacuating.

A facility with a Level 4 and 5 response capability should ensure all staff know the appropriate evacuation routes and destination sites and the fire team is trained to respond as rapidly as possible to the scene of the fire, prepared to use the same equipment and techniques the local community fire department will use when it arrives on the scene.

Evacuation of Staff and Inmates

The most complicated fire evacuation involves the housing unit. Drills for housing unit staff readiness for evacuation should focus on establishing specific skills. Housing unit officers should be able to efficiently operate both electric and manual locking systems under conditions of heavy smoke and danger. They should be able to identify and use all security door keys under these same conditions. Specialized knowledge includes all procedures for sounding the fire alarm and immediate activation of the emergency plan. It should be clear who has the authority to order an evacuation.

When a fire occurs, housing unit staff should be prepared to direct the orderly evacuation of inmates from every building on facility property to their designated evacuation site. This process includes removing inmate personal property, which should be limited to the clothes being worn, and a coat if the weather requires. All keys, weapons, ammunition, security control devices, log books, security records, computer disks, and documents should be removed, if this can be safely accomplished, from buildings involved in the fire. The count must be cleared before a building is declared officially evacuated. Evacuated inmates should be closely monitored for signs of injury by the Medical Response Team. The Correctional Emergency Response Team should be on alert to reduce the opportunity for inmate acting-out.

All visitors should be evacuated from the facility as soon as the fire alarm is sounded. Visitors can get in the way, especially if they are concerned about loved ones.

Recovery

Once response has been effective, recovery priorities should be to use established criteria to determine whether the fire has been completely extinguished and evacuated buildings are safe for habitation. Fire-involved building status should be determined by the Damage Assessment Team, with the Damage Repair Team performing any repairs that can be done immediately. If fire damage is massive, the Stepdown Committee should become involved. Staff performance should be critiqued immediately by facility and community fire personnel, with any recommendations for correction of deficiencies included in the annual contingency plan review. The Post-traumatic Assessment Team should monitor the emotional status of staff and inmates.

Technological Emergencies

A technological emergency involves the disruption of any life support or security system necessary to maintain facility operation: electrical; power; heating; water; plumbing; air conditioning; ventilation; lighting; waste water treatment; security; surveillance; alarm; and communications systems, including telephone, radio, and computer networks.

Level 2 Mitigation

Mitigation consists of four activities:

1. Methodical evaluation of all life support and security systems to determine the potential for system disruption

2. Development of a comprehensive preventive maintenance schedule that maintenance personnel rigorously follow

3. A monthly report system that documents system deficiencies and recommended corrections

4. A system of prioritizing the work orders submitted when system deficiencies are discovered

Level 3 Mitigation

Systematic evaluation of the potential for system disruption should determine the need for backup systems and provide justification for funding the installation of backup systems with an appropriate preventative maintenance schedule. Backup systems are critical in reducing the consequences of a technological failure.

Preparedness/Response

All maintenance staff should be thoroughly trained to immediately respond to any disruption in a life support or security system by participating in periodic drills. Response effectiveness is increased by developing and maintaining on-hand inventories of essential tools, materials, and supplies that can be reasonably expected to be useful in the event of a technological emergency. If these items are not immediately available, preparedness should include developing a list of vendors who can respond quickly.

Recovery

The primary goal of recovery is to ensure that response has corrected the deficiencies creating the emergency. The Damage Assessment Team should use a checklist system to ensure every element of the defective system has been thoroughly evaluated and appropriate corrective actions taken. Within a month of the final corrective action, the system should be thoroughly reevaluated. Adjustments to the preventative maintenance system, if necessary, should be made.

A facility fire or technological emergency can provide the opportunity for inmate-precipitated emergencies. If the security system fails, inmates who know of this failure may be tempted to escape. The failure of air conditioning systems or plumbing systems during hot summer months may trigger inmate disturbances, especially if they believe staff are deliberately not fixing the problem. A fire in a cellblock and subsequent evacuation may be viewed as an opportunity to attempt an escape, settle old scores, or engage in disruptive behavior. To minimize the possibility of such events, response should provide for:

1. Additional perimeter patrols, mobile and foot, consisting of armed correctional officers with highly visible backup provided by law enforcement, if necessary. Armed tower officers should be visible during response.

2. Procedures for returning all inmates to their housing units if those areas are not affected by the emergency

3. A policy defining the degree of force to be used on any inmate resisting evacuation, endangering staff, or attempting to escape

4. A secure area in which unruly inmates can be housed if there is no room in the disciplinary housing unit

The potential in a fire or technological emergency for inmate-precipitated emergencies always should be considered.

Chapter 15

Floods, Hurricanes, and Tornadoes

Of course, we cannot control "acts of God".... We can, however, plan for such occurrences by developing and practicing ways to respond better to these circumstances. While you may not be subject to earthquakes if you live in Maine, you should have contingency plans for responding to all types of disasters—both natural calamities and crises such as riots and hostage incidents. All too often, these plans become a low priority, particularly during these tough financial times (Gondles 1992:6).

The natural and human emergencies discussed in chapters 15 through 17 differ from inmate-precipitated emergencies, facility fires, and technological emergencies in a number of significant ways: source of the emergency; magnitude of the emergency; the nature of fear; inmate assistance; personal, family, and community consequences; and recovery.

Source of the Emergency

The source of the emergencies discussed up to this point are located, with rare exception, located within the facility. Their probability of occurrence can be reduced only through appropriate level 2 mitigation activities. However, the source of natural and human emergencies is located in the environment outside of the facility. Some of these emergencies are the result of forces and events that may be avoided through appropriate level 1 mitigation activities. Although the actual emergency may not be preventable, all three levels of mitigation activity should be considered in strategic planning. The lack of appropriate mitigation activities can be more devastating than the emergency itself:

> *Allowing high density population concentrations in flood plains, having poor or unenforced earthquake building codes for structures . . . providing inadequate warnings . . . for example, are far more important than the disaster agent itself in creating the casualties, property and economic losses, psychological stresses, and disruptions of everyday routines that are the essence of disasters* (Quarantelli 1990:18).

Magnitude of the Emergency

These types of emergencies contain the potential to threaten the entire physical plant, staff, and inmate population. Response and recovery may involve the full range of local, state, and national medical, emergency response, and law enforcement resources outlined in chapter 3.

The Nature of Fear

Staff and inmates can be expected to experience some degree of fear in most serious inmate-precipitated emergencies, or facility fire, but that fear is different from the fear experienced in natural and human emergencies. Inmate-precipitated emergencies and facility fires may have no warning—no time for a build-up of anticipatory fear. The event occurs suddenly, and staff and inmates experience fear as they abruptly confront the threat.

In natural and human emergencies, there may be a period of waiting between warning and event that can arouse extremely high levels of anticipatory fear and anxiety in the most courageous individuals. The fears of these inmates and staff are not just for themselves—they also may be frightened by the potential impact of the emergency on their loved ones in the community. This fear can increase through the long days of recovery if they are unable to communicate with family and friends because of a disruption of communications.

Inmate fear is unavoidable, but the potential consequences of this fear, in the form of acting-out behavior, can be reduced through level 3 mitigation activities:

- **Notification.** Inmates should be told that there are warnings of an impending emergency and informed of the actions being

Flood of 1993. Interior view of Renz Prison dorm built on high ground. Note water mark on back wall. Structure had to be torn down.

Debris left at Renz Prison after flood of 1993. Foreground shows a twisted frame of mobile home.

taken to provide for their safety. Any danger from alerting inmates to a potential emergency is outweighed by the danger presented by rumors that go unchallenged. Officers should be quick to reassure panicky inmates that precautions are being taken.

- **Monitoring.** The Post-traumatic Assessment Team should monitor fear levels among both staff and inmates, providing supportive interventions whenever signs of panic are identified.

- **Security Measures.** Correctional Emergency Response Team members should be placed on alert with the facility in a lockdown status. The fears of staff can be mitigated through their active involvement in the duties assigned them by the emergency plan.

- **Inmate Assistance.** Because natural and human emergencies are not caused by inmates, it may be argued that inmates and staff are literally in the same boat when these events occurs. Fear and the need to be safe can be powerful motivators for inmates to help out as much as possible during response. In 1992, as Hurricane Andrew approached the Metropolitan Correctional Center in Miami:

> *MCC-Miami staff and inmates worked all day and into the night to fortify the buildings on the prison compound. The buildings' reinforced walls were expected to provide substantial protection from winds, but windows and other design features appeared potentially vulnerable and were reinforced with plywood* (Samples 1992:109).

Inmates also may assist in recovery, as occurred in the aftermath of the 1993 Midwest floods:

> *Many Illinois, Wisconsin, Iowa and Missouri inmates contributed to their local communities by filling sandbags, shoring up and repairing levees, and cleaning up. The Minnesota Department of Corrections also contributed to the effort by sending offenders in its Sentencing to Service Program to help* (Spertzel 1993:160).

Personal, Family, and Community Consequences

Because staff work in the facility, and inmates are confined there, does not mean they are immune to the community consequences of these types of emergencies. Stress may be increased when homes and personal property of staff or inmates are destroyed, friends and family suffer injury or death, and and staff find they cannot make it to work because of the damage done to their normal route of travel. Recovery planning should include help to staff experiencing the community consequences of natural or human emergencies. Because inmates may become panicky at reports of their communities being devastated and fearful about what has happened to their families, efforts to reestablish inmate contact with their families should be a priority.

Recovery

Recovery activities for inmate-precipitated emergencies, facility fires, and technological failures vary depending on the nature of the event. Recovery activities in the case of an inmate suicide bear little resemblance to recovery activities for failure of a plumbing system. Yet, natural and human emergency recovery activities share so many features in common that they may be discussed in terms of a standard recovery protocol. This protocol has the overall goal of efficiently returning the facility to a normal state of operation through Stepdown Committee oversight of the following activities:

- Assessing the structural integrity of all physical plant structures and all systems by the Damage Assessment and Architectural Review Teams

- Repairing damaged structures and systems by the Damage Repair Team and/or coordinating repairs with community contractors

- Reestablishing communications and travel with the community

- Evacuating if physical plant damage is too extensive for housing and maintaining inmates

- Establishing a triage system, treating and monitoring injuries by the Medical Response Team

- Post-traumatic Assessment Team monitoring of staff and inmates for symptoms of post-traumatic stress disorder

- Maintaining a high level of inmate security by Correctional Emergency Response Team members and the Intelligence Unit, with appropriate assistance from law enforcement, as needed

- Clearing count and periodic inmate/physical plant shakedowns for contraband

• Subsequently modifying strategic planning using information gained from the emergency

The discussion of recovery activities in the chapters to follow are in terms of any activity other than those in the standard recovery protocol that is unique to a specific type of emergency, or that needs to be emphasized.

Natural Emergencies

Floods

A flood can be a powerful force capable of inflicting devastation:

In my 27 years in the criminal justice field . . . . I have seen several major floods along the Missouri River. None, however, in our lifetime or that of our parents, grandparents, or even great grandparents, can compare to the Great Flood of 1993. The flood had an effect on 112 of 114 counties in Missouri. Both the Missouri and Mississippi Rivers ran wild. In Jefferson City, transportation was shut down for several days—air, train and highway. A gas line *broke under the Missouri River. Propane and storage tanks hit the Missouri River bridge. Train tracks washed away. Cemeteries, including over 700 graves at Hardin, were exposed or totally washed away. Sand and mud were several feet thick. Highways buckled. Drinking water and sewage were effected. Insects, animals, snakes, etc., were driven into areas where they normally would not be seen. Property loss and crop loss was tremendous. Its effects will be felt for years. Some farmland will not recover in our lifetime* (Schreiber 1995:2).

Photo courtesy of Mark S. Schreiber, Missouri Dept. of Correction

Main entrance to Renz Prison during flood of 1993. Sign later washed away.

Despite its vast destructive power, flooding is a potential problem that has been traditionally ignored in correctional design and construction. Correctional facilities are not immune to this type of emergency, as dramatically demonstrated in 1993 when the Missouri River flooded and flowed into Missouri's Renz Correctional Center, a maximum security women's prison:

> . . . destroying the prison's electronic security system and nearly three miles of perimeter fence. Inside the facility's buildings, flood waters dislodged large freezers and other appliances, destroyed desks and office equipment and soaked everything below top-bunk level. A concrete block maintenance building was hollowed out by the water and resembled a muddy carport after the waters receded . . . . Damage estimates are between $8 and $9 million (Spertzel 1993:159).

In addition to the Renz Correctional Center, flood waters damaged correctional facilities in Illinois, Iowa, Minnesota, and Wisconsin.

Flood classification recognizes three distinct types:

1. Slow-Onset Floods. These occur on flood plains and develop slowly over a period of days as the result of continuous, or near-continuous, heavy rainfall. This type of flood provides sufficient time for emergency measures, including evacuation.

2. Combination Floods. In this situation, rivers also are overflowing their banks with heavy rainfall or coastal storms. This type of flooding can be more devastating than ordinary slow-onset flooding, but there usually is time for emergency measures.

3. Rapid-Onset Floods. This type of flood may generate a substantial number of casualties because there may be little warning of the impending event. Rapid-onset floods include flash floods associated with hurricanes, tidal waves (tsunamis) caused by undersea earthquake, landslides, or volcanic activity, or dam collapse (Blaikie *et al.* 1994:126-27).

Level 1 Mitigation. Floods can be avoided if facilities are constructed as far away from the nearest flood plain as possible and as high above the surrounding area as possible.

Level 2 Mitigation. If facilities are to be built on, or near, a flood plain, site analysis of the flood plain should involve local emergency management officials and concentrate on determining the part of the flood plain that either has a long-standing history of being the least vulnerable to flooding or is protected by the type of flood-control projects in which the Army Corps of Engineers specializes, or both.

Level 3 Mitigation. If a facility already exists on a flood plain, mitigation involves both the physical plant and policy formulation:

Physical Plant. The most important element of level 3 flood mitigation in a high-risk area consists of systematic efforts to reduce the amount of water that can invade the housing units and other structures within the perimeter. The least expensive approach to level 3 mitigation occurs in the design and construction phase of a new facility, although many of the suggestions to follow can be added through renovation projects (Federal Emergency Management Agency 1993:56):

- Installing check valves to prevent water from entering where utility and sewer lines enter the facility

- Reinforcing walls to resist water pressure

- Sealing walls to prevent or reduce seepage

- Building watertight walls around equipment or work areas within the facility particularly susceptible to flood damage

- Constructing floodwalls or levees outside the facility to keep flood waters away

- Elevating the facility on walls, columns, or compacted fill. This approach is most applicable to new construction, though many types of buildings can be elevated

- Installing watertight barriers, called flood shields, to prevent water passing through doors, windows, ventilation shafts, or other openings

- Installing permanent watertight doors

- Constructing movable floodwalls

- Installing permanent pumps to remove flood waters

Many communities in Pennsylvania have reacted to recent flooding by adopting building codes that require the lowest floor in a building being constructed in high-risk flood areas to be at least one foot above the base-flood elevation (Pennsylvania Emergency Management Agency 1996:1), a height determined by examining the area's flood history.

Minimizing the number of doors and windows that can be breached by flood waters also can be of value. The use of skylights as a source of natural light, instead of windows set low to the ground where they can be reached by rising waters, for example, can reduce the probability of flood waters entering a building and doing massive damage. External doors with waterproof seals also can help mitigation.

Photo courtesy Federal Bureau of Prisons

Metropolitan Correctional Center, Miami. Aerial view of damage from Hurricane Andrew, 1992

Physical plant mitigation activities also should include on-site backup systems: portable pumps to remove flood water; alternate power sources, such as generators or gasoline-powered pumps; and battery-powered emergency lighting (Federal Emergency Management Agency 1993:56).

In the event of a flood, valuable records and electronic equipment may be lost. Waterproof rooms for emergency storage of items too bulky for easy transportation from the facility should be included in flood mitigation.

Policy Issues. Level 3 mitigation should stress the importance of providing as much advance warning as possible:

> *Mitigation policies can save lives and protect property . . . . The most conventional of such preparatory methods is flood warning systems, the effectiveness of which has been shown in a range of countries* (Blaikie et al. 1994:145).

Communication is critical and begins with the ability to alert staff and inmates to the impending emergency. A National Oceanic and Atmospheric Agency weather radio, with a warning alarm tone and battery backup, maintained and monitored by a staff member will help to begin the flood warning communication process quickly. The availability of advanced warning can be increased by correctional administrators working with state and federal authorities to gain direct access to advanced technology systems, such as satellites designed to function as early warning systems for severe natural emergencies.

Preparedness/Response. Once warning of a flood has been received, staff activities should attempt to reinforce the effectiveness of level 3 mitigation efforts through such actions as building walls with layers of sandbags, constructing a double row of walls with boards and posts to create a "crib" that is filled with packed soil, and constructing a single wall by stacking small beams or planks on top of each other, leaving as little gap between planks as possible (Federal Emergency Management Agency 1993:56).

Flood drills always should be incorporated into the facility emergency plan testing program. Strategic planning for floods always should anticipate the possibility of having to evacuate the facility. If evacuation becomes necessary, it should be undertaken in accordance with the process outlined in Chapter 18.

Recovery. In addition to the activities noted in the standard recovery protocol, the Medical Response Team should pay particular attention to the possibility of water-borne diseases brought into the facility by the flood. Public health evaluation of the facility's source of potable water should be a priority. Inmates and staff engaged in recovery activities should be provided with appropriate gloves, clothing, and boots to prevent injury and contamination of sores or wounds by polluted water. Because of the inherent risk of electrocution, utility turn-on should be left to skilled electricians or utility company representatives.

Hurricanes

The damage potential presented by a hurricane should not be underestimated. Hurricane winds can reach 160 miles per hour and extend inland for hundreds of miles. A fully developed hurricane releases the energy

Metropolitan Correctional Center, Miami. Collapsed warehouse caused by Hurricane Andrew, 1992.

equivalent of "many Hiroshima-sized atom bombs" (Milne 1986:71). It has been estimated that an extreme Camille-sized hurricane hitting Dade County, Florida, (near Miami) would destroy an estimated 18 percent of the coastal structures and up to 7 percent of the structures within a hundred-mile radius of the coast (Cochrane 1975:19). When Hurricane Andrew struck the Federal Prison Camp on Homestead Air Force Base and the Metropolitan Correctional Center in Miami in 1992, it caused significant damage. At the Metropolitan Correctional Center-Miami, high winds leveled the prison's two perimeter fences, destroying the perimeter detection system, and seriously damaging the food and health services areas and the warehouse. Flying debris destroyed nonballistics-resistant glazing, and major security features were knocked out. Water, electricity, and phone systems were

damaged so badly that the facility was in total darkness, and sewage backed up in the buildings. Roofs were torn from buildings, trees were toppled, and flying debris destroyed building accessories and security features: yard gates, air ventilation units, high mast lights, antenna, and sun shelters on the yard. Additional damage at Metropolitan Correctional Center-Miami included:

> Two inmate transport buses and a tractor trailer were rolled over. Some cars literally were picked up and thrown through the air or bounced about like tennis balls; most others sustained damage from flying debris. A trailer housing the associate wardens' offices was flattened and destroyed (Samples 1992:110).

Photo courtesy Federal Bureau of Prisons

Metropolitan Correctional Center, Miami. Inmate dining room following Hurricane Andrew, 1992.

Homestead Air Force Base, including the prison camp, was totally destroyed by Hurricane Andrew.

Level 1 Mitigation. This is achieved through site-location mitigation: building the facility in an area with no history of hurricane activity.

Level 2 Mitigation. If it is not possible to practice site-location mitigation, then a historical analysis, using National Weather Service records, of the hurricane activity in the state may provide a site where the probability of future hurricane activity is the lowest.

Level 3 Mitigation. It is possible to track the path of a hurricane well before it comes ashore. If a facility is built in an area vulnerable to hurricanes, the first priority in level 3 mitigation is to develop an alert system that can provide the maximum amount of advance warning concerning hurricane location and time of arrival on shore:

On September 5, MDC Guaynabo and the Southeast Regional Office opened their command centers in anticipation of Hurricane Luis, a very dangerous storm that was headed directly for the island of Puerto Rico. Contingency plans for emergency logistical support and temporary inmate housing were established with several BOP institutions and other federal agencies. The Southeast Region prepositioned facilities personnel at the MDC to assist in hurricane preparations and to aid in the aftermath (if necessary). MDC and regional staff did an outstanding job of monitoring the storm's progress and preparing for its arrival. Fortunately, Hurricane Luis turned north on September 6, sparing Puerto Rico. High winds and heavy rain associated with the storm caused some damage to the MDC, but disruption of the normal routine at the institution was minimal (Federal Bureau of Prisons 1995:1).

The two elements of a hurricane that represent the greatest threat are the flood surge and high winds:

1. Flood Surge. The wall of water preceding the hurricane can cause massive damage and loss of life. The most effective form of level 2 mitigation for a flood surge is to thoroughly study the flood maps of the proposed site of the new facility, determine the flood zone most open to flood surges, and then build on the site that has the highest elevation above that flood zone. Level 3 mitigation activities in the event of a flood surge are the same as noted for floods.

2. High Winds. Level 3 mitigation of high winds is found in selection of construction techniques and materials. Concrete and steel structures provide the most protection from the winds of the hurricane. All buildings should be constructed to meet the wind-loading requirements for a 200-mile-per-hour hurricane. The most effective building is the all-concrete housing unit.

Renz Prison on August 13, 1993. Structure failure at the Renz Prison. Danger existed from razor wire, chemicals, glass, etc. Power, utilities, etc. were shut before the flood.

Preparedness/Response. If the facility has the ability to maintain physical integrity, then preparedness and response should emphasize maintaining safety by taking cover and protecting staff and inmates from flying debris by covering windows, either with permanent shutters or five-eighths-inch marine plywood. In addition, staff and inmates should systematically tie down every object too big to be moved under shelter. All articles that can be carried inside should be put under cover: buildings and fences that might otherwise withstand the power of the wind can be destroyed when debris piling up against them increase the wind resistance to the point that the structure gives way. Inmates should not be housed in below-ground areas vulnerable to the flood surge.

Recovery. The significant activities for hurricane recovery are contained in the standard recovery protocol and those added under flood recovery.

Tornadoes

A tornado can be spawned from powerful thunderstorms or be the byproduct of a hurricane. Winds can reach 300 miles per hour. Flood surge is generally not an issue in a tornado.

Level 3 Mitigation. Unlike hurricanes, tornadoes often strike with little advance warning. Use of a National Oceanic and Atmospheric Agency weather radio with a warning alarm tone and battery backup can maximize preparedness and response time by alerting staff to two types of warnings: A tornado watch, indicating that conditions are ripe for a tornado at any time, or a tornado warning, indicating that a tornado has been spotted in the immediate area and people should take shelter immediately. Once a tornado watch has been announced, tower and other perimeter staff immediately should be on the lookout for the first signs of a tornado.

Preparedness/Response. A tornado's ability to strike with minimal warning eliminates evacuation as a first option. Given the small amount of time that may elapse between the warning and the strike of the tornado, preparedness and response emphasize taking shelter as soon as a tornado is spotted. Inmates should be relocated to cellblocks or other secure areas if they are housed in wooden-frame modular units. The best protection in a tornado usually is an underground area, such as a basement or storage areas underneath cellblocks. If a basement is not available, possible temporary housing locations include small interior rooms or hallways without windows on the lowest floor; rooms constructed with reinforced concrete, brick, or block with no windows and a heavy concrete floor or roof system; and any areas away from doors and windows (Federal Emergency Management Agency 1993:60). A traditional cellblock may be the safest place to be in a tornado. Staff and inmates should be instructed to crouch down, protect their heads with their arms, and stay beneath any windows to avoid flying glass. Staff in buildings covered with a flat, wide-span roof, lightweight modular offices, or mobile home buildings should be moved to more secure buildings as soon as possible.

Recovery. Critical recovery activities are noted in the standard recovery protocol.

Chapter 16

Earthquakes, Severe Winter Storms, and Forest Fires

*S*eventy million people throughout the United States live with a significant risk to their lives and property from earth-quakes. Another 115 million are exposed to a less significant, but not negligible, seismic risk. Only 8 percent of Americans can safely ignore the earthquake hazard. But most Americans occupy, use, or are served by constructed facilities that were not designed to resist earthquakes and that could collapse in a quake . . . . In the history of the United States there have been approximately 1,300 deaths and 4 billion then-current dollars worth of property damage resulting from earth-quakes (National Research Council 1975:20).

Earthquakes

Earthquakes most frequently occur west of the Rocky Mountains, although the most violent have occurred in the Central United States. Regardless of their location or size, earthquakes occur suddenly and without warning:

> *Earthquakes can seriously dam-age buildings and their contents; disrupt gas, electric and telephone*

services; and trigger landslides, avalanches, flash floods, fires and huge ocean waves called tsunamis. Aftershocks can occur for weeks following an earthquake (Federal Emergency Management Agency 1993:63).

Level 3 Mitigation

Over 95 percent of all deaths in earth-quakes result from building failures (Alexander 1985).

New Facility Design and Construction

The first phase of new prison construction in an earthquake-risk area should be to determine the appropriate safety codes and have a structural engineer assess the status of facility design in terms of those codes. Design and construction of new facilities, and renova-tion of existing facilities, always should be guided by the appropriate safety codes. Profes-sional recommendations for correction of deficiencies should be incorporated into the budget process.

The California Model

The California Department of Corrections provides a model for level 3 mitigation. Its policy requires all new prison construction to include a structural testing and inspection program designed:

> To assure that the structural testing and inspection (T and I) program is developed, monitored and reviewed by the Structural Engineer of Record in accordance with State Seismic Safety Commission recommendations (California Department of Corrections 1991:1).

The responsibilities of the structural engineer of record are to develop and monitor the execution of a testing and inspection program; determine necessary verification tests to be performed by the construction contractor and a construction testing laboratory; verify that any construction, including modifications, was done in accordance with the testing and inspection program; and develop a check sheet to be used by the state construction structural inspector. Department policy sets forth specific responsibilities for contractors, the structural engineer of record, the program manager, the California Department of Corrections construction testing laboratory, the chief state construction inspector, the state construction structural inspector, and the construction manager. The California Department of Corrections' Planning and Construction Division identifies buildings in terms of category of occupancy and use as essential facilities.

Category 1 buildings, such as inmate housing units, food service, and the Armory, have twenty-four-hour occupancy and would be used as essential facilities during an emergency. Category 2 buildings, such as towers and program facility support services, are special occupancy structures not critical to emergency operations. Category 3 buildings are all buildings not designated as Category 1 or 2. Policy requires that buildings be constructed in accordance with comprehensive seismic, wind, and snow design standards (California Department of Corrections 1995).

Existing Facilities

Because of the widespread regional damage an earthquake can produce, evacuation of the facility may not be a possibility. In fact, the facility may be the safest place to be as long as every effort has been made to ensure the housing units will remain standing. Although many correctional facilities have been designed with no consideration given to the possibility of an earthquake, there are measures that can be taken to strengthen such facilities:

> Adding steel bracing to frames. Adding sheer walls to frames. Strengthening columns and building foundations. Replacing unreinforced brick filler walls (Federal Emergency Management Agency 1993:63).

If a building withstands the shock of an earthquake and structural integrity is maintained, there still is a serious potential for injury and loss of life from equipment, furniture, tools, cooking utensils, and nonstructural elements, such as ceilings, partitions, windows, and lighting fixtures:

> In many buildings, the greatest danger to people in an earthquake is when equipment and

non-structural elements such as ceilings, partitions, windows and lighting fixtures shake loose (Federal Emergency Management Agency 1993:63).

To reduce the hazard of flying debris, mitigation should include moving large and heavy objects to low shelves or the floor; hanging heavy items away from where people work; and securing shelves, filing cabinets, tall furniture, desktop equipment, computers, printers, copiers, and light fixtures. Heavy pieces of equipment and machinery should be bolted to the floor or placed on casters and attached to tethers that attach to the wall. Suspended ceilings can be reinforced with bracing, safety glass can be installed, and large utility and process piping can be fastened more securely than is normally done (Federal Emergency Management Agency 1993:63).

Preparedness/Response

Because it is currently impossible to predict earthquakes, response should be immediate. Training drills should emphasize that in the event of an earthquake staff and inmates inside a building should remain there, immediately moving to those areas that are away from exterior walls and windows, taking cover under a sturdy piece of furniture or counter, or bracing themselves against an inside wall. They should protect their head and neck at all times. Individuals who are outside of buildings when the earthquake occurs should move into the open, away from buildings, street lights, and utility wires. After an earthquake, staff and inmates should stay away from windows, skylights, and any items that could fall. If building evacuation is necessary, individuals should use stairways instead of elevators (Federal Emergency Management Agency 1993:64).

Recovery

Earthquake recovery should be in accordance with the activities of the standard recovery protocol. Of particular importance is the determination that the facility is structurally sound and utilities can be used. If the facility is not structurally sound and utilities have been destroyed, evacuation to other facilities will have to be undertaken.

Severe Winter Storms

Severe winter storms create three types of problems for correctional administrators:

1. The heavy snow, ice, freezing rain/sleet, cold temperatures, and heavy winds associated with winter storms can threaten the health and safety of inmates and staff directly exposed to the conditions.

2. Winter storms can prevent employees from leaving the facility at the end of shift or from reaching the facility to start their scheduled shift.

3. Winter storms can cause structural damage and power outages, freeze water pipes, and shorten the life of vehicle batteries.

Level 3 Mitigation

Mitigation includes both physical plant and policy activities.

Physical Plant

The facility should have the following:

• Buildings designed with peaked roofs that will more effectively distribute the weight of heavy snow. Flat-roofed buildings should be avoided because they are vulnerable to collapse once the buildup of snow on them reaches a certain density.

- Insulated inmate housing units and work areas

- Exterior windows large enough to permit visual observation of inmates when necessary, but small enough to limit heat loss

- Exterior doors with seals tight enough to severely restrict or eliminate heat loss

- Exterior entrances consisting of double doors, with an air space in between to restrict heat loss

- Sidewalks between buildings that are enclosed in a glass structure to provide protection from wind and precipitation

- Insulated pipes

- A heating system sufficient to offset the lowest temperatures ever recorded in the region

- Heated garages capable of housing all emergency vehicles

- Mobile patrols provided with roofed stations that have an engine warming capability for those times when the vehicles are turned off

- At least one building with enough space to provide temporary living quarters for staff trapped at work by winter storms. This area should be equipped with a kitchen and bathroom and shower facilities.

- A backup power source sufficient to handle the power requirements for all critical areas of operation

- Adequate storage facilities to maintain an emergency supply of food, water, blankets, clothing, gloves, and all life support supplies, materials and equipment that may not be delivered in accordance with the vendor's routine delivery schedule because of bad weather

- Adequate storage facilities for an emergency supply of gasoline and snow melting/traction enhancing materials

- An adequate inventory of battery-powered radios, extra batteries, and other emergency supplies

Policy Issues

Important policy activities include developing educational programs through which all staff and inmates are informed about the proper measures to reduce the chance of frostbite and hypothermia. As with other types of natural emergencies, there should be a system for alerting staff and inmates to the eminent arrival of a winter storm or a blizzard. A traveler's advisory warning of dangerous driving conditions can accompany the announcement of either type of storm, but a blizzard, generally, is most dangerous because sustained winds of at least thirty-five miles per hour can be expected to be driving the sleet or snow.

Preparedness/Response

Important activities involve (1) releasing nonessential staff early; (2) calling in essential staff early; (3) notifying inmate and staff visitors of the need to leave the facility immediately; (4) activating snow removal crews and snow/ice removal prioritization of all roads, sidewalks, and parking lots; (5) reducing out-of-building activities; and (6) placing Damage Assessment and Damage Repair Teams on alert in case of heating, electrical, plumbing, communication, or security system failures.

Recovery

In addition to the activities of the standard recovery protocol, staff should concentrate on reopening snow-impacted routes to the facility, reestablishing external communications if they have been compromised by the storm, and medical monitoring of staff and inmates for signs of hypothermia or frostbite. It is highly unlikely that evacuation will be necessary, but a blizzard can damage buildings and systems. Inmate count is an essential function, but contraband searches can be conducted in accordance with the routine schedule.

Forest Fires

Many correctional facilities are located in areas where the threat of a forest fire should not be discounted completely.

Level 3 Mitigation

Mitigating the consequences of a forest fire includes clearing as large a fire zone around the facility as possible. If the facility is an institution, this clearing of the fire zone can be an automatic part of site preparation. A large fire zone also serves security goals by increasing visibility for tower officers and perimeter patrols. If the facility is small, such as a boot camp or a forestry camp, there still should be a fire zone cleared around the camp. Every facility should have an easily accessible water supply and proper equipment to spread that water over any buildings in danger of burning. There should be at least two evacuation routes from the facility. Staff and inmates who participate in correctional forestry projects should be trained in proper fire prevention techniques when in the forest. Use of all smoking materials should be monitored carefully by supervisors to ensure this education is put to use.

Preparedness/Response

Each facility should prepare for forest fires by developing, training, and equipping a fire fighting team to establish fire breaks, open evacuation routes, and extinguish burning buildings and burning embers drifting into the facility. All staff should be trained in fire safety, rescue, and evacuation techniques. If evacuation is not undertaken, inmates should be maintained in their housing units until the fire is no longer a threat. A number of states have invested in training and equipping special inmate fire fighting teams for helping fire fighters called to the scene of a forest fire. These inmate teams can be invaluable in the event that a correctional facility is threatened by a forest fire.

Recovery

In addition to the standard recovery protocol activities, staff should monitor carefully the area to ensure no new fires flare up.

Chapter 17

Urban Unrest, Terrorist Activity, Hazardous Material Accidents, and Nuclear Incidents

O ne hot July evening, Ann Miller, our emergency department unit secretary, answered the first of a series of frightening phone calls. The first was short and sweet: "There's a bomb," the caller said, and hung up . . . . A few minutes later, another call came through on the same line. "You better get everyone out; there's a bomb in there," the caller said . . . . "You have 4 hours to get everyone out before the bomb goes off," the man threatened in his third call . . . . Then, a few hours later, another call came in: "You have 29 minutes 'til it blows," the caller said in a calm, deliberate voice (Ferguson 1995:32L).

The external human-created environment contains the potential for four types of threats: urban unrest, terrorism, hazardous material accidents, and nuclear incidents.

Urban Unrest

In May 1992, the acquittal of four white police officers in the beating of black motorist Rodney King "induced a convulsion of

violence in Los Angeles that left 44 dead, 2,000 injured, and $1 billion in charred ruins" (Mathews 1992:5). Entire city blocks were aflame and thousands of people were put at risk during the rioting. Over the past century there have been four cycles of major urban riots (Mathews 1992:38). Correctional facilities located in an urban riot-risk area are vulnerable, although the degree of vulnerability can differ depending on the nature of the facility. Up to this point, the discussion of strategic planning may be applicable to all levels of corrections, although many will consider it most relevant to correctional institutions, many of which are in rural areas. Now the discussion focuses on community corrections (parole and probation offices, correctional residential centers, and contracted residential facilities) and urban jails and prisons.

The Parole and Community Services Division of the California Department of Corrections experienced the full force of the 1992 Los Angeles riots. Its experience can be of value to other community corrections staff:

Traditional disturbance control plans emphasize incident containment and preserving security. Emergency response plans focus on evacuation, medical assistance and survival. Urban riots present several conditions and phenomenon that do not fit readily into either plan. In an urban riot the threat is external and in many cases overwhelming. It usually limits the use of land line communications and geographically separates the responding workforce. Depending on the extent and location of the unrest it can directly impact personnel (DiMaggio 1992:8).

Level 2 Mitigation for Urban Residential Facilities

Locating outside urban areas to eliminate vulnerability to urban unrest (level 1 mitigation) clearly is not a mitigation option for community corrections. When determining a residential facility site, a vulnerability analysis based on the riot history of the city may be useful in placing the facility in an area that has little, or no, history of urban unrest. Unfortunately, this level 2 mitigation activity may be doomed by the Not In My Backyard (NIMBY) phenomenon.

Level 3 Mitigation

If the NIMBY phenomenon prevents location in a low-risk area, the facility administrator should make efforts to harden the facility to make it less vulnerable to urban unrest. The first rule of hardening is no windows at street level. If windows are deemed necessary for staff

morale, they should be small and, if possible, shatter-resistant, bullet-proof, or capable of being shuttered in an emergency. Windows are excellent targets for fire bombs. Other hardening methods include employing exterior steel security doors, limiting exits and entrances, designing secure parking areas that permit safe evacuation, adding fire escapes that can be pulled up above street level to prevent unauthorized access to the building, providing a vault for securing vital records/equipment that might not be possible to remove during an evacuation, and locating in the facility an area that allows two or more avenues of evacuation to minimize the risk of being trapped in a facility that has been breached, and facility construction of brick or stone.

The security of files should be established through a mandatory redundancy system that maintains field and regional parole/probation office files in a secure low-risk location in case both offices have been targeted for destruction by rioters. The files of inmates in residential facilities under the jurisdiction of the parent institution should be duplicated and held within the security of that institution.

Communication can quickly become a problem for community corrections' staff during periods of urban unrest when facility lines become jammed by people trying to determine the safety of friends and family members. An on-hand inventory of hand-held radios and establishment of a corrections base station will mitigate the loss of land-based communications systems. If it is possible to have radios that use police frequencies, then communication with law enforcement authorities can be enhanced.

The establishment of Memorandums of Agreement will allow community corrections' staff to effectively communicate and coordinate operations with law enforcement, emergency medical, and fire personnel, and vendors who can provide multipassenger vehicles immediately. The final element of level 3 mitigation is a system of notification when danger is imminent.

Preparedness/Response for Urban Residential Facilities

Community corrections facilities lack both the physical protection and weaponry available to prison and jail staff. Located in the middle of areas vulnerable to urban riots, these facilities can be ripe targets for rioters, especially rioters who have been inmates and have a particular grudge against corrections. Or, gangs may deliberately target these facilities as symbols of a repressive justice system. Strategic planning should provide for the following:

Reconnaissance Activities. Reconnaissance tours of the area surrounding the community-based facility should be in unmarked vehicles equipped with radios or cellular telephones. Reconnaissance staff should be armed and certified in the use of their weapons. Clothing should be civilian without insignias. The estimated time of the tour and the route always should be known by the supervisor in case communications with the vehicle is lost.

Command Posts. A primary and secondary command site should be established, with at least one of the sites in an area with minimal vulnerability. Crisis staffing should be on a twenty-four-hour basis.

Inmate Management Procedures. Inmate management procedures should address three categories of residents: (1) residents on furlough or work status who are not at the facility for evacuation and need to be retrieved from their home, school, or work site; (2) residents who take advantage of the situation to flee and must be placed on escape status; and (3) inmates in the residential facility who are in danger from community rioters or who appear to be interested in joining in on the riot.

Staff Release Procedures. Staff members whose families have been personally affected by the unrest should be released to go to their assistance as quickly as possible.

Recovery

In addition to standard recovery protocol activities, community corrections staff should rigidly adhere to meeting specific criteria for return to operation of the facility. Returns should not be allowed until a low-profile, on-site inspection has been conducted and there is a certainty that the unrest is not going to flare up in the immediate future. Close coordination with local law enforcement authorities is necessary to make this determination. The interagency agreement with law enforcement agencies should include procedures for identifying parolees and inmates arrested for riot-related activities.

Level 2 and 3 Mitigation for Urban Prisons and Jail

Mitigation activities for these correctional facilities combine the community corrections' mitigation activities with the mitigation activities discussed in chapters 6, 11, and 12.

Preparedness/Response for Urban Prisons and Jails

The primary risk for these facilities is three-fold:

1. The possibility of inmates deciding to respond to the community riot by engaging in an in-house riot

2. Staff being prevented from getting to the facility, or leaving it to return home

3. Assault on the facility itself by community rioters angry at the criminal justice system

The Intelligence Unit can help assess the first risk by increasing contact with staff and inmates (informants and noninformants alike) to determine the mood of inmates. Strategic planning should provide for two options: lockdown or normal operation. Some argue that the best way of maintaining control of the inmate population is a lockdown of the facility at the first sign of inmate agitation. However, if large numbers of inmates are out of their cells, the attempt to lock them down can become the flashpoint for the trouble the staff were trying to avoid in the first place. The Intelligence Unit should determine if lockdown will be a cure worse than the disease.

If the facility is locked down, officer and treatment staff should circulate through the cellblocks talking to inmates, explaining the rationale for the lockdown, providing reassurance, and defusing threats of violence. This can be extremely stressful for staff, but locking down inmates, then ignoring them, promotes the power of rumors and can trigger acting-out. Fears for family safety should be discussed and opportunities for phone calls home should be provided as soon as possible. If the facility is not locked down, staff should increase their time in the cellblocks and work to defuse any talk of rebellion. Inmate access to radio and television means they will see the same riot everyone in the community is seeing. Because it is difficult to know what media coverage will trigger a disturbance, close monitoring of the inmate mood is essential—especially if the decision is not to lock down the facility.

The second risk—staff being prevented from getting to the facility, or leaving it to return home—is quite likely to happen. If it does, an emergency staffing pattern of extended duty should be activated until off-duty staff are able to make it to work.

The third risk—armed assault on a jail or prison—is highly unlikely, but not impossible. Therefore, the Correctional Emergency Response Team staff should be on standby with reinforced perimeter patrols. If such an assault appears to be imminent, the facility should go into a lockdown status and local law enforcement agencies should be notified immediately. Every facility should have a hot-line to both local and state police.

Recovery

If no threat to the facility has materialized, routine activities can resume quickly. If a threat has materialized, the nature and severity of that threat determines which standard recovery protocol activities are necessary.

Terrorist Activity

Terrorism can be either domestic or foreign. Although it is possible that terrorism in the United States could take the form of acts of chemical, biological, or nuclear warfare conducted by organized international terrorist groups, there is nothing in the terrorism literature to suggest that correctional facilities would be the targets of choice. The conventional logic of international terrorist groups that they represent the oppressed peoples of the world makes it unlikely that they would target inmates. It is more likely that a community with some strong symbolism (such as New York City with its World Trade Towers) would be picked and a correctional facility would be caught in the middle of the attack. However, every correctional facility is vulnerable to domestic terrorist activity, and its most likely form is the conventional bomb threat. A bomb threat comes in two forms: the presence of an actual explosive device with no prior warning, or a warning that such a device is in the facility. Both threats are vulnerable to mitigation activities.

Level 2 Mitigation of the Planted Bomb

If an explosive device is physically present, it may be because it has been planted within the facility or on the grounds. The most effective reduction of the probability of a bomb being physically carried into the facility is strict enforcement of all visitor search procedures. All visitor-carried packages, briefcases, and other items large enough to carry an explosive device should be thoroughly inspected before they are allowed into the facility. Tower and perimeter officers should be alert to the presence of civilians on the property. Unknown vehicles parked near the facility should be inspected. Suspicion that a bomb has been planted should activate the emergency plan.

Level 3 Mitigation of the Mail Bomb

If an explosive device has been sent through the mail, level 3 mitigation takes the form of detection. Mailroom staff should be trained by local post office staff to identify suspicious packages and letters. There should be written policy that all suspicious packages and letters are to be held for a law enforcement or military bomb disposal unit with whom there is a prior Memorandum of Agreement.

Preparedness/Response for a Bomb Warning

Although it cannot be guaranteed that a bomb warning is a hoax, it is highly likely that such is the case. If the warning is by telephone, the Intelligence Unit should have an agreement with the local telephone company that will help trace any bomb threat phone calls. If the threat is in writing, the document should be preserved by the Intelligence Unit and given to law enforcement authorities.

The most likely method of delivery of the bomb threat is the telephone. The kind of person capable of making a bomb threat often receives gratification by being in a position to hear the emotional reaction of the recipient of the threat. The most likely member of the staff to receive a bomb threat is the facility switchboard operator or a secretary. The recipient of the phone threat should stay calm. Most bomb threats are false, and remaining calm denies the caller the psychological gratification being sought, but all bomb threats must be taken seriously until investigation has proven they are false. The person answering the call should not hang up on the caller. Threat validity cannot be determined solely from the phone call.

The recipient of the call should listen carefully and record exactly what the caller says. It can be helpful to ask the following (Ferguson 1995:32N):

• When is the bomb set to explode?
• Where is the bomb located?
• What does the bomb look like?
• Why are you doing this?
• What is your name?

Although the caller most likely will make the threat and then hang up without responding to questions, it does no harm to attempt to solicit information. Many institutions use preprinted forms with fill-in-the-blanks that provide a formal historical sequential log of events. This avoids having to rely on memory. After the call has been completed, the recipient should report the call to the facility administrator and no one else unless the administrator is absent. If this is the case, then the deputy for security should be notified. Other staff should not be told about the call. This can promote panic. The administrator should: (1) notify local law enforcement or military units with bomb disposal capabilities, the facility Intelligence Unit, and the agency administrator; (2) arrange with law enforcement to trace any additional phone threats; and (3) evacuate buildings if detonation is supposed to be eminent.

Evacuation creates the potential for panic. If time allows for an Intelligence Unit assessment of the validity of the threat, then a decision should be made whether to delay evacuation. Staff should conduct a thorough search of all buildings even if a specific building has been identified by the caller. If a bomb is located, it should not be touched. Leave disarming to a law enforcement or military bomb disposal unit. Staff should not alert the media,

but their questions should be answered honestly if they call.

Individuals who make bomb threats sometimes like to play a head game with the recipient by making countdown calls in which they warn that time is running out for the facility. If these countdown calls come in over a period of hours, and the recipient can keep the caller talking, a police trace is possible. Apprehension of the caller by the police is the best method of ascertaining threat validity. After the call(s) has concluded, and if apprehension has not occurred, the Intelligence Unit will debrief the recipient of the threat to determine:

• Gender, approximate age, and race of the caller

• Distinctive voice characteristics: tone or accent

• Type of speech: fast, slurred, stuttering, precise, nasal, coarse, slow

• Use of language: educated, profane, degree of familiarity with English, any particularly striking terms, words, slang, slogans, incorrect use of words, repetition of phrases or terms, or use of technical jargon

• Demeanor: calm, agitated, self-righteous, preaching, incoherent, laughing, irrational, angry, hysterical

• Background noises: street traffic, office machines, trains, boats, airplanes, animals, party sounds, bar sounds, voices

If the caller is apprehended, debriefing by the Criminal Prosecution Unit can elicit information useful for prosecution. Strategic plan testing should include a bomb threat even if this situation has never occurred.

Recovery

If the threat is false, the facility can return to normal immediately. The Post-traumatic Assessment Team may have to monitor staff, especially the recipient of the threat. If there has been a bomb, and it was defused without explosion, the Intelligence Unit should conduct a thorough evaluation of all security procedures, especially in the mailroom, visiting room, and any other areas where a bomb can be introduced into the facility. If the bomb was real, and an explosion has occurred, then some or all of the standard recovery protocol activities may be necessary.

Hazardous Materials Accidents

Hazardous materials are substances that are either flammable or combustible, explosive, toxic, noxious, corrosive, oxidizable, an irritant, or radioactive (Federal Emergency Management Agency 1993:53). Title III of the Superfund Amendments and Reauthorization Act of 1986 regulates the packaging, labeling, handling, storage, and transportation of hazardous materials. Detailed definitions and lists of hazardous materials can be obtained from the Environmental Protection Agency and the Occupational Safety and Health Administration. Hazardous material spills can occur within the facility or within the community.

Level 2 Mitigation of In-facility Accidents

All too often inmates and staff alike get sloppy in handling hazardous materials, often because they use them so frequently that they forget how dangerous routinely used chemicals and liquids can be under the wrong circumstances. The Fire Safety Team can initiate mitigation efforts that include:

• Procedures for identifying and labeling all hazardous materials stored, handled, produced, and disposed of by the facility to minimize the possibility of a mistake in identification

• Dissemination and required reading of material safety data sheets for every material used and enforcement of the rule that all government regulations be followed without exception

• Training of all staff and inmates responsible for the use, storage, preparation, or disposal of hazardous materials

Preparedness/Response

In-facility spills can be handled by following the instructions provided on the material safety data sheets, which are provided by the manufacturer. Material safety data sheets provide information on the composition of hazardous substances, safety precautions, and emergency procedures for specific hazardous substances.

Hazardous material accidents that occur within the facility can be serious for the individuals directly involved in the accident, but generally, the threat is confined to a small area of the facility. Most staff and inmates probably will not even know the accident has occurred. The hazardous material accident in the community is another matter. For example, on February 2, 1966, a freight train accident in Cajon Summit, California, resulted in a spectacular fire that spewed noxious fumes into the air and:

> *The derailment forced motorists to take detours of as much as 100 miles around the crash site. The 20-mile section of Interstate 15 was closed in both directions and was not expected to reopen until early morning* (Patriot News 1996:A5).

Community spills represent the greatest threat to the facility because of the quantity of hazardous material that may be involved. A correctional facility near a community accident involving the release of concentrated materials from tank cars may find the entire facility under threat.

Level 3 Mitigation of Community Accidents

Mitigation requires comprehensive identification of all highways, railroads, and waterways near the facility that are used to transport hazardous materials and evaluation of the threat posed to the facility by a hazardous material spill occurring on them. Once these have been identified, procedures to warn inmates and employees of a hazardous material accident should be implemented.

Preparedness/Response

Once the facility has been alerted by media reports or calls from law enforcement of a hazardous material accident in its immediate vicinity, staff and inmates should stay indoors, making certain to close doors and windows. All food containers should be closed and food and beverages put in freezers or other enclosed areas to avoid contamination. If conditions warrant, evacuation may be necessary.

Recovery

If a cloud of hazardous material has engulfed the facility, all food, water, or beverages in open areas should be disposed of as soon as it is safe to do so. Specialized community emergency management teams may have to direct cleanup of the physical plant. Unless evacuation is necessary, the only standard recovery protocol activities necessary will be those involving the Medical Response Team triage of exposure symptoms.

Nuclear Incidents

Incidents involving nuclear technology can be classified as accidents (power plant or military), nuclear attack, or terrorist activities. Any facility near a nuclear power plant should prepare for the possibility of an accident. Facilities near military bases or other targets should prepare for the possibility of nuclear attack. And correctional administrators should not assume that a significant terrorist attack using nuclear materials will not take place in their community. The U.S. Department of Energy budgets $70 million a year for responding to nuclear emergencies and employs over one thousand scientists and technicians on the Nuclear Emergency Search Team. Nuclear Emergency Search Team personnel are trained to respond in the event of terrorist claims of having planted a nuclear device anywhere in the United States. Since 1975, the Nuclear Emergency Search Team has evaluated 110 threats and mobilized to deal with 30 of them: all have turned out to be hoaxes (Waller 1996:39). If the Nuclear Emergency Search

Team were to determine that such a nuclear threat did exist near a correctional facility, the only course of action would be evacuation of the facility.

Level 1 Mitigation

Site-location mitigation of nuclear incidents involves constructing facilities in areas that are not near nuclear power plants, military bases, or other installations (such as airports) that might handle nuclear weapons, be a nuclear attack high-risk area, or offer a tempting target to terrorists. In this age of unfettered prison expansion, site-location mitigation, as well as level 2 mitigation, is difficult, if not impossible.

Level 3 Mitigation

Dangers in a nuclear incident involve the blast, fires, and radioactive fallout, all of which can be lethal over both the short term and the long term. In the event of a nuclear incident, staff and inmates should have immediate access to a protective shelter: "an enclosed area that will protect occupants against specified disaster effects up to a given intensity" (Federal Emergency Management Agency 1990:G-3). Protective shelters may be in-facility or within the community.

In-facility Shelters

The steel and concrete construction of many correctional facilities, especially those with below-ground basements, can provide protection against radioactive fallout. The best in-facility shelters are those that not only provide physical protection, but have ready access to potable water and toilet facilities. Once identified by the Fire Safety Team, in-facility protective shelters should be provided with a radio, fire extinguishers, potable water, canned food, and bedding.

Community Shelters

Every county in America should have a nuclear disaster emergency response plan that includes the location of public fallout shelters. Community shelters can be identified through discussions with local, state, and federal emergency management agencies that include the periodic updating of an inventory of local and/or regional community nuclear attack shelters to which inmates and staff can be evacuated. Some shelters may be off-limits because they are reserved exclusively for military personnel or activities.

Preparedness/Response

In the event of a nuclear incident, the only response options are in-house protective shelter or evacuation (Federal Emergency Management Agency 1990:G-1). Preparedness and response involves:

1. Evacuation to an in-facility protective shelter

2. Assessment of conditions to determine if evacuation to an external protective shelter is necessary

3. Evacuation to an external protective shelter, if necessary

Internal Evacuation

Once an alert has been sounded, staff and inmates should move quickly to in-facility protective shelters. In the shelters, fire prevention actions, such as closing all window shades and blinds, should be mandatory. No one should be permitted to look out of windows, because the blast from a nuclear weapon can cause blindness. Staff and inmates should sit down and protect their heads, but be prepared to extinguish any attack-caused fires immediately. The situation should be monitored by listening to Emergency Broadcast System announcements.

External Evacuation

Very close coordination with local emergency management agency personnel will be necessary to determine whether the degree of in-facility protection is adequate, or if external evacuation is necessary:

> *The time available in which to decide whether to evacuate or shelter in place in a hazardous materials or peacetime nuclear incident is often very limited, and it may be necessary for first responders to make an immediate decision. Factors such as the nature of the material or materials, the atmospheric conditions, the threat of fire or explosion, and estimated duration of toxic effects can influence the final determination* (Federal Emergency Management Agency 1990:G-2).

Problems encountered by correctional administrators in external evacuation will be greatly compounded by the fact that civilians also will be using public shelters and the mixing of inmates and civilians creates a high potential for disruptive activity. If at all possible, specific rooms or areas in public shelters that can be secured should be dedicated to correctional staff and inmates. Rigid security precautions, including the use of handcuffs and leg irons, should be mandatory. Staff should be briefed on the specific conditions under which lethal force is appropriate as a control measure.

Recovery

All the standard recovery protocol activities will be required. Return to the facility will not be possible until a radiation expert has checked the physical plant and surrounding environment for radioactivity and determined that the facility is habitable. Special attention should be paid to sources of potable water and food supplies in inventory. Certification of a facility as habitable is a sophisticated process that will have to be the responsibility of nuclear specialists.

Chapter 18

Evacuation

*A*fter the 1989 Camp Hill riots, over 1,800 inmates had to be kept on the Main Stockade Field from October 27 until October 30 because six cellblocks had been so badly damaged by two days of rioting that they could not be immediately used for inmate housing. Because of extensive damage three of the cellblocks were not habitable for months and approximately 1,000 inmates had to be evacuated and transported during recovery to various state and federal correctional facilities.

An evacuation can be total or partial, occur at any point during the emergency life cycle, and involve any type of correctional facility. A total evacuation involves removal of all inmates and staff. In a large institution, this can involve hundreds of staff and thousands of inmates. A partial evacuation involves the selected removal of part of the inmate population and the only staff leaving the facility will be those necessary to effect evacuation.

The evacuation at Camp Hill occurred during recovery. A response evacuation occurred when Missouri's Central Missouri Correctional Center was no longer able to resist the flooding Missouri River:

> *The prison's 380 inmates were evacuated July 2 to the gym and*

minimum security units of the men's Central Missouri Correctional Center north of Jefferson City. Inmates lost some personal possessions—when they were evacuated they were allowed to bring only what they could stuff into their pillowcases. At the height of flood evacuation activities, staff worked extra shifts ferrying inmates' personal items and whatever facility equipment they could salvage (Spertzel 1993:159).

A level 3 mitigation evacuation occurred in 1992, when Hurricane Andrew bore down on the Federal Prison Camp on Homestead Air Force Base:

> *That evening it became apparent that the hurricane would hit just south of Miami and Homestead would bear the brunt of the storm. FPC-Homestead Superintendent Sam Calbone organized the movement of all 146 FPC-Homestead inmates and 63 institution staff to MCC-Miami. BOP staff, working with Air*

*Force officials, made some efforts
to reinforce the facility. However,
because most of the buildings had
wooden frames, little could be
done to protect them against
winds that were by then expected
to reach 150 miles per hour*
(Samples 1992:109).

Evacuation from an institution and evacuation from a community-based facility have many elements in common, but there are significant differences in procedure that must be recognized if there is to be no unnecessary risk of injury or death.

Evacuation of the Institution

Evacuation is not a decision to be made lightly. The transportation of inmates, even when it is routine activity, such as a hospital trip or transfer to another institution for administrative reasons, always carries a certain degree of risk, but the conditions surrounding an emergency, and the number of inmates to be transported, can raise the degree of risk to high levels. Evacuation planning centers on ten questions:

1. Is the damage that has occurred, or the threat that exists, sufficient to create an inability to:

• Provide safe housing for the inmate population?

• Provide humane conditions of confinement?

• Provide an acceptable level of safety to staff?

• Protect the community by containment of the inmate population?

Physical integrity should be assessed by the Damage Assessment Team and the Architectural Review Team. Working from a complete set of design drawings of the institution that permits a comprehensive structural analysis of the buildings, particularly the housing units, these teams should assess the integrity of a damaged facility or, if the emergency has not yet occurred, predict its structural ability to maintain physical integrity in the face of the impending emergency. If physical integrity has been, or will be, sufficiently compromised, evacuation may be the only reasonable alternative. The decision to evacuate generally is the responsibility of the agency administrator after consultation with the institution administrator. For this reason, the institution should have an emergency means of communication with the central office, such as ham radio, that can be activated if the phone lines are down.

2. What destination sites have the capability to provide:

• Secure inmate housing?

• Adequate levels of support services: food, water, clothing, bedding, personal hygiene items, and medical care for inmates and staff alike?

• Adequate levels of staff assistance?

It is never safe to assume that an institution requires only one destination site, no matter how large that site may be. Particularly in natural emergencies, there is the possibility that a destination site will be destroyed or damaged too severely to provide assistance. Strategic planning always should assume the worst case scenario and develop primary, secondary, and tertiary destination sites. The classification of a destination site as primary, secondary, or tertiary is a function of the site's ability to provide a secure setting with an adequate level of support services. The primary site should provide the most security and services. The tertiary site should provide both security and services, but only at a minimally acceptable level. Preferably, the distance to be traveled will be minimal. The closer the destination site, the less the risk of problems developing during transport, but distance alone should not override the importance of a secure setting.

The most desirable primary sites are local, state, or federal correctional facilities that have sufficient space for housing additional inmates, can create emergency living arrangements quickly, and can be reached with a minimum of travel. Secondary destination sites would include military bases and National Guard armories with the physical structure necessary to keep inmates safely away from any weapons or equipment that cannot be removed from the building. Tertiary sites would include locations such as school gymnasiums or stadiums (weather permitting) that can be secured with a minimum of effort. In a worst case scenario, it can be safely assumed that a large institution will require all levels of destination sites.

3. How many evacuation routes are available? Every evacuation route between the institution and its primary, secondary, and tertiary destination sites should be identified on a strategic planning map. Once evacuation routes have been identified, each should be subjected to a "windshield survey" by the Special Transportation Unit that determines the existence of bridges, tunnels, overpasses, underpasses, high-voltage lines, narrow mountain passes, large bodies of water that can easily overflow their banks, and any other physical feature of the route that has the potential to become an obstacle to evacuation. The mileage from the institution to each potential obstacle should be noted in a written description of each evacuation route that accompanies the map. Determination of the impact of each obstacle on the probability of a successful evacuation should be made. If that impact is sufficient to stop the evacuation, then an alternate route should be identified. If a bridge is on the route, for example, what are the alternate routes if it is destroyed? If there is only one road between the institution and its destination sites, what are the alternatives if that road is destroyed by floods or an earthquake?

4. What are the most effective means of providing convoy security? Staff and inmates are going to be in tight quarters, possibly for an extended period of time, in hazardous conditions that will increase irritability, anxiety, and fear. Always assume that at least some inmates will either give in to their fear and act-out, or consciously view the evacuation as an opportunity to escape or assault staff or other inmates. The possibility of friends or family of an inmate anticipating the evacuation route and making plans to help the inmate escape should be considered. To maximize the safety of all concerned, strategic planning should provide the members of the Special Transportation Unit with:

- All equipment to be carried in evacuation vehicles, including chain saws and pry bars for removing fallen trees or other debris

- Cellular phones as a backup to vehicle radios

- Sufficient handcuffs and leg irons to secure every inmate

- A sufficient quantity of authorized firearms to equip each member of the team

- Policy on the property inmates may take with them. The quantity of items should be severely restricted due to space limitations.

- Convoy escort in the form of correctional officer chase cars and law enforcement vehicles. Escort vehicles should be at the head of the convoy, the rear of the convoy, and interspersed throughout the convoy. At least one "scout" vehicle should travel several miles ahead of the lead vehicle in the convoy to assess road conditions and alert the convoy of any pending obstacles or danger. This scout vehicle should be assisted by a law enforcement helicopter whose pilot has instructions to look for signs of obstacles ahead of the scout car, with special attention paid to any suspicious vehicles of groups of individuals along the convoy route.

- Policy that under no circumstances should any inmate, regardless of classification status, be permitted to contact anybody outside the institution to advise of the impending evacuation. All inmate visitors and nonemergency civilian personnel should be escorted from the institution before any evacuation announcement.

- Sufficient training to obtain any special license necessary to drive the evacuation vehicle

- Procedures for contacting both the institution command post and the destination command post with any deviation from the original plan or route

5. Who will supply evacuation vehicles? It seems obvious that the institution should have immediate access to a sufficient supply of vehicles to safely evacuate all inmates and staff. However, the issue of vehicle supply may be easily overlooked. Evacuation vehicles can come from several sources:

- The institution itself. Emergency fuel supplies should be maintained in a secure, waterproof storage area in sufficient quantity for an evacuation. A program of preventive maintenance of these vehicles should be strictly enforced, with periodic inspections to ensure compliance with the maintenance schedule.

- Other correctional facilities that are not facing evacuation

- Commercial vendors, such as school bus companies. In this case, the institution should have a contract that provides a guaranteed number of buses available to the Special Transportation Unit on very short notice. Drivers of these vehicles may require a special operator's license.

- National Guard or other military units

6. What about equipment, records, and inmate property? If time permits, appropriately assigned staff should remove all records and equipment that can be safely transported from the institution. If removal is not possible, equipment and records should be stored in secure areas, preferably areas that are waterproof. An inventory list of every record and piece of equipment should be maintained. This inventory should note the record or piece of equipment with the name of the person conducting the removal and the destination of the item. All inventory lists should be removed from the institution and given to the institution administrator for safekeeping. However, some think that keeping such an inventory list may be unrealistic because of the large number of tort claims from inmates on the issue of personal property.

If time permits, inmates should be allowed to box up all personal items not being evacuated and advised to develop their own inventory list. These lists should be turned over to the housing unit supervisors for safekeeping. Staff should store the boxes in a secure area within the institution.

7. Is communication possible during evacuation? Strategic planning should require periodic radio checks between each evacuation vehicle and the stricken institution and the destination site to ensure all is going according to plan. In the event of a failure to make the required radio check, there should be procedures for immediate notification of the escort vehicles to promptly assess the situation. Communications should be maintained at all times during the evacuation, ending only when the destination site has been reached and the last inmate has been placed in secure housing.

8. What provisions can be made for inmate management? Inmates can be expected to be frightened during an evacuation. Officers should be alert to any sign of unusual levels of anxiety or fear and be quick to reassure inmates of the measures being taken to ensure their safety. If space permits, members of the Hostage Negotiation Team and Post-traumatic Assessment Team should ride in the vehicles to provide positive reassurance. Once safely housed at the evacuation destination site, a phone call home can do a great deal to settle down a restless inmate.

9. Has the evacuation plan been tested? Evacuation drills should be an automatic part of any test of strategic planning. All staff should fully understand their role during evacuation.

10. Is evacuation feasible? Before making the final decision to evacuate an institution, the agency administrator should establish that:

• The evacuation destination sites are intact. Communications should be established with each destination site to confirm that the physical integrity of the site is intact. In the event of a hurricane or earthquake, it is possible that the destination site also has become a victim and is no longer capable of providing assistance.

• The evacuation routes to each site are open. If evacuation destination sites are intact, then law enforcement agencies should be contacted to determine if evacuation routes remain open. It is possible in certain types of emergencies that evacuation routes will be so severely compromised that it will not be possible to evacuate.

• Law enforcement agencies have the ability to provide convoy escort. In a severe emergency, such as a hurricane, earthquake, or simultaneous riots in major correctional facilities, law enforcement agencies may be stretched too thin to provide adequate convoy security.

• The members of the institution's Special Transportation Unit are available. If these individuals have been trapped in their homes by a natural emergency or injured in a riot, the institution may draft other staff for the evacuation, but the probability of problems being created through lack of training is increased.

• A sufficient number of transportation vehicles are on site and mechanically ready.

• If all of these criteria cannot be met, the decision to evacuate becomes complicated.

Evacuation of a Residential Facility

Evacuation of a residential facility differs from the evacuation of an institution: (1) community corrections staff lack the physical control routinely accepted in an institution because residents are in the community, free of physical restraints to movement, and in a position to exercise considerably more discretion than the institutionalized inmate; and (2) the public can access the facility easily. Evacuation under these conditions can be challenging if the emergency being faced is urban unrest or an emergency that may trigger urban unrest. Community corrections staff may find that they and their residents are in a war zone. Strategic planning for evacuation of residential facilities centers on five specific questions:

1. What is the best way to move through enemy lines? The structure of the evacuation should be different from that of an institutional evacuation. Evacuating staff should maintain a very low profile. They should wear civilian clothing and move inmates in unmarked vehicles, preferably vans with darkened windows. A convoy of correctional officers in marked vehicles can readily draw sniper fire or other forms of assault by rioters. Instead of a convoy shepherded by police escort vehicles, the best approach to residential facility evacuation is to quietly slip out of town by blending into the scenery as much as possible and making every effort to avoid confrontation with community members. Evacuation should be the responsibility of community corrections staff, but if institutional Correctional Emergency Response Team members are available, they should not come into the area wearing riot gear, or any clothing that will identify them as correctional staff.

Administrators should remember that, in an urban riot, there may be several rioters, law enforcement agencies have their hands full, and there is little to be gained by throwing correctional officers to the wolves. Blending into the environment, and quickly exiting the area is the best strategy.

2. Should residents be under physical restraint? The use of restraint equipment on residential facility residents is neither realistic nor appropriate. These individuals are used to being free of physical restraint. To attempt to shackle and handcuff them as a precautionary measure during evacuation may create anger and possibly cause the problems staff are trying to avoid. Use of restraints also may draw the unwelcome attention of rioters who will quickly realize that they have vulnerable correctional staff in their area. This is a situation where inmates should be trusted. Community corrections staff are outnumbered by both the rioters and the inmates. If an inmate decides to walk away, let him or her go. Any attempt to pursue or capture the walkaway may draw the attention of community rioters and endanger staff and inmates alike. There should be no actions taken that will make staff and residents a target.

3. What if residents don't want to evacuate? Inmates may not want to evacuate. They may prefer to remain at their facility to protect it from looters, fearful that once taken to the parent institution for safety, they may not be returned to the community. Assurances that they will be returned to the community quickly can motivate them to leave, but these promises should be honored. Staff may have to manage inmates reluctant to evacuate because they have become intoxicated, or decided to use drugs, because of the stress created by the community riot, and they may fear that return to the institution will result in disciplinary action. Staff should not attempt to force inmates to evacuate if they adamantly refuse to do so. To attempt force can result in an unnerving, dangerous situation for a staff member who, alone, may have to deal with five or ten inmates, some of whom may be inclined to join the community rioters.

4. Will the evacuation route be secure? Evacuation can be especially tricky in the case of urban unrest because the pockets of violence can change constantly, eliminating evacuation routes that may have been safe minutes earlier. As many alternative routes as possible should be identified beforehand. For this

reason, there should be as large a number of destination sites as possible. If the riot spreads, previously safe destination sites may be cut off or put out of action.

5. Are a sufficient number of evacuation vehicles available? Each facility should have enough vehicles to immediately evacuate all staff and inmates assigned to a specific facility. The middle of a community riot is not the time to try to locate evacuation vehicles. Secondary vendors should be identified in case primary vendors are burned out or otherwise unable to get vehicles to the facility.

If urban unrest threatens a residential facility, evacuation may be the only choice.

Chapter 19

Emergency Medical Management

*P*aramedics and emergency medical technicians consider certain vital signs and symptoms basic; they are thought to be most reliable and usually are the first sought: pulse rate, blood pressure, and heart and respiration rates. Other signs thought to be important and looked for are sweating, paleness, labored breathing, skin texture, absence or presence of pain, dilated pupils, and so on. Also considered are any obvious outer signs of injury: stab wounds, lacerations, fractures, bleeding, or other obvious body disturbances (Mannon 1981:35).

The Medical Response Team is organized to intervene in the life cycle of two types of emergency: the nonepidemic emergency and the epidemic.

The Nonepidemic Emergency

Any emergency carries an inherent risk of serious injury or death. The more extensive the emergency, the higher the probability there will be casualties.

Level 3 Mitigation

The Medical Response Team cannot prevent a nonepidemic emergency from occurring, or reduce the probability of occurrence, but it can reduce the consequences of medical injury through Memorandums of Agreement with community hospitals, emergency hospitals, emergency medical services groups, ambulance services, and Lifeflight units, which coordinate medical response and save valuable response time when a medical emergency occurs.

Preparedness/Response

There are three significant elements involved in preparedness and response: specialized training in emergency medicine, a triage system, and medical evacuation and coordination of treatment.

1. Specialized Training in Emergency Medicine. Specialized triage and medical emergency management skills are developed and maintained through an ongoing in-service training program that keeps medical staff up-to-date concerning techniques and approaches to emergency medical management. Community hospital seminars are a valuable educational resource as are weekly discussions of relevant journal articles.

2. A Triage System. There are at least three acceptable definitions of triage. For the purposes of correctional response to emergency situations, triage is most appropriately defined as:

> *A process in which a group of patients is sorted according to their need for care. The kind of illness or injury, the severity of the problem, and the facilities available govern the process* (C.V. Mosby Company 1983:1094).

Triage systems may consist of two, three, four, or five tiers of classification of injury priority (C.V. Mosby Company 1983:1095). Regardless of the number of tiers, an effective triage system will provide initial triage and on-site treatment destination areas where qualified medical personnel can determine the priority of treatment required and priority for evacuation to community or regional hospitals in accordance with established guidelines and a system for triage dispute resolution.

Effective triage depends on establishing an effective color-coded system and initial triage sites with enough space to simultaneously handle large groups of casualties:

> *Each disaster-medical-aid center could be equipped with colored tarpaulins, visible from helicopters flying overhead. A green tarpaulin could indicate that the center was up and running, but had no casualties ready for evacuation. A yellow tarpaulin could indicate that casualties needed evacuation but that the situation was not critical. A red tarpaulin could indicate the presence of seriously injured victims who needed immediate evacuation* (Schultz, Koenig, and Noji 1996: 440).

This system may be used in correctional emergencies if helicopters are available, there is sufficient land available for both triage activities and landing/taking-off activities, and weather and visibility conditions permit immediate evacuation.

However, immediate evacuation may not be possible for a variety of reasons: the area large enough for helicopter access has been filled with debris or is still under inmate control, bad weather is present, or helicopters are not available. Therefore, triage planning should assume there will be a need to use facility physical plant resources with evacuation occurring at a later time. The primary physical plant resource should be the facility hospital or infirmary if there are only a few injuries. If the number of injuries is too large for the infirmary or hospital, a larger area, such as a warehouse or gymnasium, should be designated. As a last resort, cleared exterior areas, such as a parking lot or field, may be used.

Regardless of location, physicians and nurses preassigned to a specific initial triage site will examine casualties as they are received and, borrowing from the tarpaulin color-coding system noted earlier, "tag" each individual with a color-coded tag identifying the priority of treatment, the on-site treatment destination, and priority of evacuation. Red-tag cases will include individuals who have experienced such obvious life-threatening conditions as a state of unconsciousness linked to cardiac arrest, severe blood loss, and/or severe shock; open chest or abdominal wounds; burns involving the respiratory tract; amputated limbs; and general major fractures. Yellow-tag cases will include individuals with severe burns, spinal column injuries, moderate blood loss, and head injuries with no loss of consciousness who may or may not be in an immediately life-threatening condition. Quick visual observation may not be conclusive enough to distinguish between a red-tag and a yellow-tag determination. A more sophisticated method of triage involves the physician talking loudly to the patient while palpitating the carotid and radial pulses:

> *A response indicates airway patency and level of consciousness . . . . If the patient has neither pulse, classify him or her as non-salvageable. If the patient has a carotid pulse, but no radial pulse, then the patient is critical. If a radial pulse is present, then its rate may be the determining factor. A rate greater than 120 indicates serious physiologic derangement, and the patient should be deemed critical. After all patients go through triage, you can allocate remaining resources to non-salvageable patients* (Martinez and Waeckerie 1991:44).

Green-tag cases will consist of the "walking wounded," (Schultz, Koenig, and Noji 1996:440): those individuals who have received minor fractures and sprains, contusions, abrasions, and superficial burns that are not life-threatening or disabling.

The on-site treatment destinations are most appropriately located in the facility hospital or infirmary and designated in terms of the priority of treatment required. Staff at each on-site destination should be responsible for specific activities. Red-tag staff should commence all appropriate life-saving procedures, stabilize vital signs, and prepare the patient for immediate evacuation to a community hospital. Yellow-tag staff should stabilize and monitor vital signs and prepare the patient for evacuation after the red-tag patients have been transported. Green-tag staff should make patients comfortable, monitor vital signs, and schedule evacuation, if necessary, when red- and yellow-tag patients have been transported.

Dental Injuries. Because individuals involved in emergencies may sustain dental injuries, there should be a specific on-site destination for dental injuries. The dentist assigned to this location should assess all injuries to mouth and teeth, treat any injuries in accordance with assessed priority, and schedule the patient for medical evacuation, if necessary.

Psychiatric Casualties. The trauma of an emergency may intensify psychiatric symptoms in those inmates diagnosed as borderline and able to live in general population under normal circumstances, or create acute stress-related symptoms in otherwise stable inmates and staff. Every triage plan should include designation of a psychiatric observation unit, where psychological services staff may identify inmates or staff with emergency-precipitated or exacerbated psychiatric conditions, initiate appropriate treatment, move to appropriate placement in the infirmary, administer indicated medications, and coordinate priority for psychiatric evacuation.

Deceased Casualties. Severely injured casualties brought to the initial triage site may be dead on receipt, die while being evaluated, or die at the on-site destination before evacuation is possible. Every facility should have an on-site temporary morgue where the bodies of the deceased may be stored safely. Medical staff assigned to the morgue should ensure receipt of a death confirmation from a physician and hold the body for the coroner. These staff should work with the coroner's office to determine the cause of death in any fatalities, cooperate in law enforcement investigations into the cause of death, and coordinate removal of the body to a community mortuary. A facility inmate property officer should be assigned to the on-site mortuary for the specific purpose of conducting a thorough inventory and storage of all personal property found on the body of deceased staff and inmates. This person should return all property to the survivor/beneficiary noted in the official personnel or inmate file once authority has been received from the facility administrator to do so, obtain a signed receipt for all property returned, and place the signed receipt in the appropriate personnel or inmate file for subsequent reference if property becomes a subject of post-emergency litigation.

To facilitate triage, every facility infirmary/hospital should maintain prepositioned medical supplies in appropriately designated metal canisters. An inventory list, reviewed every three months, and updated, as needed, should be provided with each canister. The Medical Response Team also should provide any special assistance required by disabled, pregnant, or elderly inmates, even though triage has not indicated they require evacuation and/or hospitalization.

Triage Dispute Resolution. Although medical staff will be operating in accordance with established triage guidelines in an emergency, disputes can arise. Disputes are serious because they consume valuable time and can lead to conflict that will affect the emotions and behavior of staff working under highly stressful conditions. The Society of Critical Care

Medicine Ethics Committee strongly suggests that a single person on the medical staff be in charge of triage decisions and that there be a preestablished method of quickly settling any triage disputes that arise (Society of Critical Care Medicine Ethics Committee 1994:1202).

3. Medical Evacuation and Coordination of Treatment. Strategic planning should provide for an ambulance staging area and an area where medical evacuation helicopters can set down to receive patients. These areas should be outside the perimeter, but as close to the initial triage sites and on-site treatment destination as possible. If a staging area must be inside the perimeter because no other space is available, it should be used only if there is no threat of inmate attack.

Once a patient has arrived at the medical staging area, case management is transferred to the assigned ambulance or helicopter medical crew. These medical personnel should be responsible for providing all necessary patient care and treatment during transport to the hospital. To avoid confusion and costly treatment delays in those areas with more than one local hospital, or a number of local hospitals as well as a regional hospital, there should be a predetermined designation of one of these hospitals as the "medical command" hospital. Emergency medical staff at the medical command hospital should control the assignment of all casualties to local and regional hospitals. This determination should be made on the basis of information provided by the ambulance or helicopter personnel.

Although facility medical staff will no longer have responsibility for inmate patients during transport, the facility does retain responsibility for providing security. A minimum of one officer should accompany any inmate, regardless of the extent of injuries, referred to a community hospital and provide surveillance until relieved. Hospital security always should remain the responsibility of facility staff.

Many correctional facilities have contracted with private medical vendors to provide direct medical services to the inmates. All contracts should include the requirement that the private vendor fully participates in strategic planning.

Recovery

When the facility is declared secure, the Medical Response Team becomes involved in three additional functions: rescue, identification of the dead, and public health monitoring.

1. Rescue. If an emergency has resulted in individuals being trapped in damaged buildings, the Medical Response Team always should be on the scene to provide medical attention as soon as it can gain access to the casualty.

2. Identification of the Dead. If an emergency has resulted in fatalities, the Medical Response Team is responsible for identifying human remains. Although it may be assisted by records staff, physicians and nurses have the training and experience to psychologically handle the often gruesome process of body identification. Although saving lives is the priority, the possibility of death is a reality that should not be avoided in strategic planning. The Federal Emergency Management Agency (1990:H-5) suggests eight recovery functions for civilian emergency personnel that also may be applied to the Medical Response Team:

- Select qualified individuals to establish temporary morgue sites.

- Establish collection points to facilitate body recovery operations.

- Coordinate search and rescue team activities.

- Help coroners determine causes of death.

- Protect the property and personal effects of the deceased.

- Notify relatives. This responsibility may be shared with the counseling staff.

- Establish and maintain a comprehensive recordkeeping system for continuous updating of fatality numbers.

- Coordinate the services of funeral directors and morticians, and assist other agencies and medical personnel in all aspects of body identification.

Special care should be taken to provide counseling and support services to staff involved in recovery and identification of human remains:

> *Mortuary services must be part of all rescue and recovery plans . . . . Having to deal with dead bodies creates many emotional, legal, and psychological problems. These problems have enormous emotional impact not just on relatives and friends of the dead, but on those involved in the rescue and recovery efforts. Too often, the discovery of each lifeless body takes a psychological toll on the rescuers. The important thing for rescuers to keep in mind is that a dead body is not a sign of the rescuers' failure* (Thomas J. Shepardson, as reported by Skolnick 1995:12).

3. Public Health Monitoring. Public health responsibilities include:

- Coordinating with the water, public works, or sanitation departments, as appropriate, to ensure availability of potable water, an effective sewage system, sanitary garbage disposal, and removal of dead animals.

- Establishing preventive health services, including controlling communicable diseases

- Inspecting damaged buildings for health hazards

- Monitoring food handling and mass feeding sanitation services

- Providing general sanitation advice to staff and inmates

Termination of an emergency does not necessarily mean that medical staff can return to the post-emergency routine medical status. During testimony at the Camp Hill riot-related lawsuits, medical staff testified that as late as two-and-a-half years after the riots the facility medical department remained in a recovery status.

Epidemics

There is another type of correctional emergency: the epidemic—acquired immunodeficiency syndrome (AIDS) and tuberculosis. These diseases have three common characteristics: (1) they can be fatal, (2) they are preventable, and (3) they can produce extremely high levels of anxiety and fear among both inmates and staff:

I have to tell you that in my 11 years as a correctional officer, I have never seen my people more scared. They're asking, "Are my kids in danger? Is my family threatened?" This disease is killing people and I'm not confident that the state is going to act quickly and appropriately to protect our people (McFadden 1991:B3).

Acquired Immunodeficiency Syndrome

Acquired Immunodeficiency Syndrome is a serious communicable disease that kills by fatally compromising the human immune system. In terms of epidemics, AIDS is a glacier because transmission of the human immunodeficiency virus (HIV) is relatively difficult in the absence of unprotected sexual intercourse and intravenous drug users sharing dirty needles. However, a study of state, federal, and some county correctional facilities found that the number of known AIDS case in these facilities rose from 766 in 1985 to 6,985 in late 1990, an increase of 800 percent in five years. More than 2,000 inmates died from AIDS during the period of 1985 through late 1990 (Durham 1994:70).

AIDS represents a challenge because infection with HIV usually is fatal and, therefore, staff and inmates alike may be overly fearful of the disease. This fear may create the type of atmosphere conducive to inmate-precipitated emergencies, illegal staff job action, or other unfortunate consequences:

One state reported a recent death by asphyxiation of an HIV-infected inmate who was being transferred—in four-point restraints—from one area of the prison to another. The correctional officers so feared that the inmate might spit on them, exposing them to HIV, that they stuffed a towel in his mouth, and he choked to death (Hammett and Daugherty 1991:32).

Level 3 Mitigation. Mitigation of AIDS transmission and AIDS-related fear can take a variety of forms:

1. Education. The most effective mitigation of the transmission of HIV is mandatory education of all staff and inmates. Knowledge of the transmission vectors of HIV and the simple forms of behavior avoidance that can prevent infection mitigates both transmission and the powerful fear the uninformed experience when they hear the word "AIDS":

> *Because there is no vaccine or cure for the disease, education and training are the cornerstone of efforts to curb the spread of AIDS in prisons and jails, as well as the population at large. Education and training also provide the opportunity to counteract misinformation, rumors, and fear concerning the disease* (Hammett 1986:3).

2. Testing. Testing for the presence of HIV in inmates may be voluntary, as-needed, or mandatory. Voluntary testing is conducted when inmates volunteer to submit to the test. As-needed testing is done on the basis of medical concerns in a specific incident, such as a bite from an inmate. Mandatory testing involves testing all inmates committed to a facility. Testing can be controversial. Legal

review should be conducted before any testing policy is implemented.

Preparedness/Response. Once the presence of HIV has been established, the inmate enters a special status that raises issues in the areas of housing and counseling:

Housing. Where will the inmate live after diagnosis? There are three options: general populations, segregation, and transfer to a dedicated facility.

1. General Population. The HIV-positive inmate remains in the general population and sees the medical staff on a weekly basis for monitoring purposes and aggressive medical intervention as symptoms develop. Population placement terminates only when the inmate's physical functioning is compromised to the point of not being able to live in a regular housing unit.

2. Segregation. The HIV-positive inmate is physically segregated from the general population inmates and the majority of staff to achieve the dual purposes of limiting the opportunity for engaging in risk behavior and improving medical treatment. Segregation can include all HIV-positive inmates, those who are end-stage only, or those whose condition requires specialized medical treatment in a facility infirmary or hospital setting. There is a range of legal issues involved in the issue of segregation, and any such policy should undergo comprehensive legal review and approval. A top corrections medical authority notes:

> *. . . there is no medical . . . rational or scientific basis for the segregation of inmates who are HIV-positive* (Hammett and Daugherty 1991:11).

Alexis Durham (1994:76) argues that segregation may make matters worse by validating inmate and staff fears through reinforcement of the stereotypes about AIDS and HIV-positive people that prevent development of an accurate perception of the disease and the people who carry it, increasing the cost of inmate management, and assigning scarce space to meet the needs of the few instead of the needs of the entire population. Isolation also may have a significant negative psychological effect on HIV-positive inmates by degrading the quality of their lives through denial of the full range of programming and recreational opportunities available to noninfected inmates.

3. Transfer to a Dedicated Facility. If the HIV-positive population is large enough, it may be economically rational to designate an entire facility to HIV-positive inmates. This may be the most practical approach to managing a large number of these inmates, but a host of union and legal issues should be examined before such a step is taken.

Counseling. Counseling should address the need to avoid the high-risk behaviors involved in the transmission of HIV. The more complicated counseling issues will revolve around inmate and family concerns and fears about impending death. Counselors with specialized AIDS-related training are needed to deal with this level of complexity.

Recovery. There is no recovery phase for the vast majority of inmates who are HIV infected in the sense of returning them to their previous disease-free state. At some point, some of them will die in prison from the opportunistic diseases that kill when the immune system has been severely compromised. However, many of them also will be paroled before they develop active symptoms

or die. Comprehensive preparole planning with the HIV-positive inmate, family, and parole staff will be necessary to ensure an adequate continuity of care in the community.

The Connecticut Model. The most humane and effective approach to the question of AIDS may be found in a consent decree in a case that mandates the Connecticut Department of Corrections to provide at all institution: infectious disease service specialists and a coordinator of AIDS-related medical services; systematic intake screening and follow-up monitoring for inmates with, or at risk for, HIV infection; referrals to specialists as part of comprehensive, individualized treatment plans; access to experimental drugs, counseling, and psychosocial services; extensive discharge planning; and quality control assessments throughout the process (Hammett and Daugherty 1991:66).

Tuberculosis

If unprotected sexual intercourse and the sharing of dirty needles is avoided, HIV infection is remarkably difficult. Unfortunately, the same cannot be said for tuberculosis (TB). TB is a communicable disease that attacks the lungs and can result in death. The TB germ is transmitted easily through the air and does not require the close interpersonal contact necessary to transmit HIV: "It is possible for a healthy individual in a closed room with a coughing infected individual to catch the disease" (Durham 1994:86).

A study of inmates in the New York Department of Corrections found that the incidence of TB infection increased from 15.4 per 100,000 in 1976-78 to 105.5 in 1986, an increase of 700 percent (Braun *et al.* 1989:393). A 1991 report asserted that

25 percent of the state's new inmates tested positive for TB and twelve inmates and one correctional officer died of the disease during the first ten months of 1991 (McFadden 1991:B3). Correctional facilities provide the opportunity for the rapid spread of large numbers of TB cases once an infected individual is present, especially if buildings are poorly ventilated.

Level 3 Mitigation. If an inmate arrives at the facility with TB, the emergency has occurred, and the task of mitigation is to reduce the consequences of that arrival, in other words, reduce the opportunity for the disease to spread throughout the population. Reduction of consequences is assisted by (1) a strategic planning requirement that correctional facilities have adequate ventilation systems in every building, (2) mandatory testing of all inmates suspected to be infected, and (3) a policy that infected inmates will not be transferred between facilities unless there are compelling security reasons.

Preparedness/Response. Education about facility policy concerning detection, treatment, and prevention of TB can effectively reduce levels of staff/inmate fear and increase the opportunity for the identification necessary for effective medical intervention. Staff trained to recognize the symptoms of TB should adhere to a policy of immediate referral to the medical department for testing when symptoms are detected.

As soon as a TB-positive inmate has been identified through testing, a previously established medical drug treatment protocol should be initiated and the inmate placed in medical quarantine until treatment has been effective. Quarantine can be in a properly constructed and equipped facility infirmary; a community hospital that has an isolation ward; or, if the system is so equipped, an isolation unit in a designated regional facility.

Recovery. The inmate should be monitored periodically for any signs of reoccurrence of TB after medical release.

Chapter 20

Emergency Management of Public Information

*O*ften on routine matters . . . the temptation is to . . . say that we have to talk to our lawyers first. But you don't have that luxury in a disaster. The press is covering an emergency situation and needs information. Obviously, you can't be irresponsible. You can't go with rumors or hearsay or gossip. But, you have to tell them something; you have to give them what you know, or there will be a vacuum. And, where there's a vacuum, reporters will fill it (Hall 1993:12).

To disseminate information effectively, a public information officer (PIO) should be appointed the official spokesperson for the facility; there should be at least one alternate PIO.

> *Choosing a PIO is relatively simple in theory but difficult in fact. In a nutshell, the PIO must be intelligent, articulate, and attractive and have a sound grasp of both the workings of the media, criminal justice, and the organization . . . . When they fail to do an adequate job, the agency and the public suffer* (Houston 1995:62).

Managing information during response and recovery can become complicated because of the intense demand for information. Much of this demand will be fed by rumors that should be put to rest as quickly as possible to avoid unnecessary confusion. During the second day of the Camp Hill riots, rumors persisted that an officer had been handcuffed to his desk in a modular unit and left to burn to death. There were rumors about inmates dying that created needless suffering for loved ones outside the fence. As soon as it was confirmed that both sets of circumstances represented rumor, not fact, the media and concerned family members were reassured that there had been no fatalities.

Level 2 Mitigation of Rumors

The primary purpose of information management during response and recovery is rumor control. Level 2 mitigation of rumors is accomplished if the PIO is able to provide concise and valid information, control access to the media and the public, and sell a positive message.

Provide Concise and Valid Information

Information about the causes and nature of the emergency and response and recovery activities may be requested by nine groups:

1. Staff—Staff will have concerns about the emergency, especially if it is inmate precipitated. All staff reporting to duty should be briefed at roll call by a senior commissioned officer or department head who has been briefed by the PIO. Staff will arrive with an expectation that the worst has occurred, and accurate information will help reduce anxiety, fear, and anger. Briefers should be alert to any signs that staff may be emotionally incapable of discharging their job responsibilities in a professional manner. Staff who appear to be vulnerable to losing control should be assigned responsibilities that do not bring them into contact with inmates or situations where they may react inappropriately. In addition to checking for signs of emotional vulnerability, briefers should ensure that staff are not bringing unauthorized firearms into the facility. The use of unauthorized firearms can create a legal nightmare.

2. The Media—The PIO should have access to the command post, be present for all discussions of actions to be taken, and function as the leader of the Information Management Team. Only the PIO should be authorized to provide any information to the public and the media, and every statement should be approved in advance by the facility administrator and, if necessary, by the agency administrator. Efficient coordination between the Information Management Team and the PIOs of other response agencies will ensure conflicting information is not released to the media. All

information should be confirmed. Despite the tendency to feel pressured to release information during an emergency, unverified information can do more harm than good. The PIO should set up a media briefing schedule to provide reliable information:

> *Responding to the media during an emergency situation is perhaps the most difficult situation PIOs encounter. The atmosphere of a news briefing or conference or a large-scale interview can be very stressful and intense. The PIO's response can have a major affect not only on the news that results, but also, in some cases, on events inside the institution. Although each emergency seems to move on its own unpredictable course, there are certain general principles that apply to working with reporters during these situations* (Phillips 1993:35).

Information provided to the media should be thoroughly discussed before it is presented. The PIO should read from a written statement and not deviate from that statement with ad-lib answers. The statement should report the known facts and avoid lengthy discussions or explanations that may be construed as defensiveness or an attempt to cover-up staff mistakes. During response no questions should be permitted because questions may fuel speculation that the worst has happened. This is especially true when the PIO must reply with "No comment" or "I don't know." Media questions may be allowed during the recovery phase. If the answer to a question is not known, the PIO should simply state that information is

Lucasville riots, April 1993. During the first days of the riot, the Department of Rehabilitation and Correction received more than 2,000 media information requests.

not yet available, but that every effort will be made to get an answer to the media as soon as possible. The do's and don'ts of responding to the media are succinctly summarized in *Improving Media Relations: A Handbook for Corrections* (Phillips 1993).

Media representatives should be restricted to a predesignated media briefing area equipped with telephones, tables, chairs, a podium, blackboard, bulletin board, and large aerial views of the facility. Strategic planning should include arrangements with a phone company to provide a mobile phone bank for the media.

Restricted access to the facility should be enforced strictly, with personnel staffing roadblocks instructed to identify all media representatives and provide them with an escort to the media briefing area. This area should have

sufficient parking for media representatives. Allowing reporters to circulate freely around the facility may put them at risk physically. It also allows access to individuals who may become the source for the rumors the PIO is trying hard to squash. Be alert to media creativity. During the Camp Hill riots there were reports of police detaining several media representatives who had crawled up to the rear fence of the facility, apparently hoping for an interview with rioting inmates. The risk to reporters in such a situation is high, especially if it is night and armed perimeter officers are in a state of heightened arousal.

At some point during recovery, the media will ask for a tour of the facility. This request should be granted, if safety and security conditions permit, but the tour should be led by the facility administrator and/or PIO, with limited, or no, access to inmates. The positive response actions of staff should be stressed on the tour. All members of the media should be invited to tour, even if some have not made a request for a tour. It is important that there be no perception of favoritism being shown by the facility. This perception, even if untrue, may have consequences in the form of negative future coverage of events.

The Information Management Team always should remember that inmates have access to television and radio and will carefully monitor news coverage of the emergency unless the facility has the ability to cut off all electricity and general policy has prevented inmates from receiving battery-operated radios. As long as inmates can access the media coverage of the emergency, they will be able to hear any rumors or speculation or discussion of possible response activities. The information provided through the media may trigger further negative behavior. During Camp Hill's recovery, a number of inmates advised the author that the second riot had been triggered by the author's statement, after the first riot, that he was going to conduct an investigation into riot causes. This is a statement about an activity that he had assumed to be both reasonable and expected. Apparently, it provided the excuse for the second night of riots.

The PIO should carefully examine every statement before it is given. One cardinal rule: never, under any circumstances, say to the media that inmate threats concerning staff hostages are nothing more than an inmate negotiation tool and, therefore, are meaningless. Inmates caught up in the stress of a riot or hostage-taking situation who hear such a statement on the radio or television may feel they

have to prove that they are serious by taking the life of a hostage.

3. Central Office Staff—The facility administrator periodically should brief both the agency administrator and agency press secretary concerning the emergency. These briefings should, as much as possible, be on a scheduled basis. It is frustrating to be in the middle of an intense discussion about what to do to effect the release of hostages only to be interrupted by a call from Central Office asking, "Is there anything new to report?"

Briefings should provide concise information about the status of response, any resources needed, and any recommended course of action. There should be a candid exchange of information. The facility administrator should focus on responding to the emergency, but the agency administrator should be aware of the larger political picture and advise of decisions or recommendations that may be controversial. For example, an agency administrator advocating the calling in of the National Guard should be made aware that the Governor opposes this action based on a perception that political rivals will term it a sign that the Governor has lost control of the state prison system. If the facility administrator is not aware of this, actions taken during response or answers given to questions at subsequent news conferences may prove embarrassing.

4. Loved Ones of Staff and Inmates—As soon as the media announced the first of the Camp Hill riots, the switchboard was jammed with calls from anxious friends and family of inmates and staff. Many of the callers were frantic because they had heard rumors of sodomy, torture, and death being spread throughout the community by people who had no idea what was really happening. Politicians were trying to reach this author, and well-meaning civilians and staff from other correctional facilities were calling to ask if they could help. Staff evacuated from inside the facility came into the outside administration building to use the limited number of phones to call their families to assure them of their safety, often receiving busy signals because their loved ones were trying to call the facility. Administrative staff who needed to use the phones for directing the response often were greeted by busy signals and could not get their calls through. Calls from loved ones that did get through were answered by a single switchboard operator who had no idea what was happening within the facility. It was chaos. The problem? No thought had ever been given to installing extra phone jacks and having a supply of emergency phones available in the administration building. There simply were not enough telephones available to handle the demand. The result was a total sense of frustration for all concerned.

To prevent this type of frustration, strategic planning should include:

- Installation of extra phone jacks and phone lines and emergency phones in any building outside the facility that may be used during an emergency. If no such building is available, the phone company can provide a mobile phone bank.

- Assignment of Information Management Team members to phone duty, with instructions to provide only authorized information. These individuals can respond calmly and professionally to hostile or frightened callers.

- Key decision makers should have private telephone lines in their offices that the public cannot access. This provides a critical freedom of communication.

- Procedures for issuing a public statement requesting that individuals not call for information about loved ones, that communication will be reestablished as quickly as circumstances permit.

This last approach may be limited in its effect on citizen callers, but more effective with families of staff members who have been advised by means of a paycheck stuffer that, in the event of injury or death on the job, the family will be advised immediately. Families of staff taken hostage should be notified and given the opportunity to come to the facility where they can be informed quickly of breaking developments.

As soon as the facility has entered recovery, inmates should be given paper, pencil, and envelopes so they can write their loved ones. If the phones are still in a usable condition, brief telephone calls should be permitted. Once people are reassured that their loved ones are safe, the volume of incoming telephone calls will drop dramatically.

Other Correctional Facilities. In any emergency, staff of other correctional facilities are eager to help. If the emergency is inmate precipitated, they also will be concerned about the ripple effect that can be caused if their inmates hear rumors about staff brutality at the emergency-stricken facility or are inspired to riot by media coverage of the event. It is important to provide the administrators of other correctional facilities with the information they will need to refute the rumors their staff are receiving. The best method to use is the fax machine. A page or two of faxed information can be extremely helpful. In preparing this information, remember that the document may later show up in court to be used against you. A statement this author made about inmate weapons in a fax after the first riot was used (unsuccessfully) against him in a number of the lawsuits filed by Camp Hill inmates after the riots. The agency administrator always should approve in advance any fax that is sent.

Politicians. Any calls from politicians requesting information should be referred to the agency administrator. The facility administrator should concentrate on the emergency and cannot afford to be distracted. However, the facility administrator should be prepared to personally respond at a later date in public forums, such as the Senate and the House Judiciary Committees, where questions often are raised for the purpose of advancing political agendas.

Union Leadership. At some point, it is likely that the union leadership will want to meet with the facility administrator to discuss concerns that have arisen during response and recovery. This meeting should be held as quickly as possible to ensure that both union and management have all relevant facts, have discussed possible courses of action, and are in agreement concerning staff behavior and future activities. Requests by state union leaders to tour the facility should be honored with no attempt to limit the areas they visit.

Inmate Advocacy Groups. If inmates have been injured or killed, or there is a perception that they were subjected to unnecessary risk, various inmate advocacy groups will request

information. Meeting face-to-face with representatives of these groups can be helpful in correcting misinformation they have received. Any requests for copies of documents should be reviewed first by agency legal staff and receive the approval of the agency administrator before being granted. This is a necessary safeguard given the propensity of inmate advocacy groups that help inmates in litigation filed against correctional administrators.

Inmates. If the emergency is not inmate precipitated, it is important to provide inmates with information that will reassure them that everything is being done to ensure their safety. If inmates can participate in activities (such as sandbagging during a flood), this will give them a sense of control over events, and they should be allowed to do so. Inmates will have concerns and questions during response and recovery that should be responded to truthfully.

Control of Access to the Media. Inmates should be prevented from having unauthorized access to the media during response and recovery. Control of access can take two forms:

1. Every emergency plan should have procedures for cutting off all telephones, especially those cellblock phones used by inmates to make collect calls during their daily routine. The facility should have the ability to ensure there are no "live" telephones inside a facility during an emergency.

2. At no time should correctional staff or visitors be permitted to bring a cellular telephone into the facility. If an emergency occurs, and inmates gain control of the cellular telephone, then they have immediate access to media, friends, and family. Once

the media learn they can talk by telephone to an inmate leader, the facility has lost control of the flow of information. The result can be a stream of incredibly inaccurate information to the public.

Some theorists have suggested that every emergency plan should include an agreement with the Federal Aviation Administration to prohibit all commercial or civilian fixed-wing flights within a ten-mile radius of the facility, especially if the emergency is inmate precipitated. However, others consider this infeasible because of the number of correctional institutions throughout the country. Aerial coverage of rioting inmates can be sensational, but it also can terrify loved ones of both staff and family and provide inmates with intelligence concerning the location of assault and rescue teams. Hovering media helicopters, misidentified by rioting inmates as police helicopters whose presence heralds an assault, can panic inmates into harming hostages.

Staff who are not members of the Information Management Team should not be allowed to talk to the media unless approval has been received from the facility administrator. People uninformed about specific policy decisions or events are not in a position to provide accurate information about those decisions or events.

To Sell a Positive Message. It is possible for the media to be a corrections management tool during response and recovery:

> *The electronic age enables the manager to "sell" his or her organization to the public. This is a point largely ignored by corrections executives. News organizations are hungry for news, and the skillful manager can enhance the image of the organization and educate the public about the needs and special mission of corrections* (Houston 1995:65).

However, there always will be someone who doesn't believe the official press releases or assurances during a news conference. Four years after the Camp Hill riots, this author was visiting a county jail. While talking to a lieutenant about the riots, this author noted that we had been lucky that there had been no fatalities. The lieutenant looked around, saw there was no one within earshot, and said, "Listen, just between you and me and the fence post, how many people really died in your riots?"

Chapter 21

Testing the Emergency Plan

*D*uring the first riot, when I was in the command post in Group I, I received a frantic call. Inmates were pushing a disabled pickup truck toward the Main Gate, apparently in an attempt to try and breach the gate and escape. Should the tower officers fire on them? This was a lethal force issue not covered in emergency planning. Taking a quick consensus of the command staff, it was apparent that there were conflicting opinions on the proper course of action. Finally, I gave the order that if the inmates came within ten feet of the Main Gate they should be fired upon. Fifteen feet from the gate, the inmates stopped pushing the truck, put up their hands and surrendered. In the back of the truck, hidden from view by a tarp, was a badly injured staff member. The inmates had saved him by hiding him in the back of the truck and pushing it to the gate because they couldn't get it started. If the tower officers had fired and killed the inmates, would my order have been legally defensible?

Simply because the process has gone well and a brand new emergency plan has been written, this does not mean the strategic planning process has been completed. Development of the written plan is only the first stage in strategic planning. There also is a second stage. The second stage has four elements:

1. Reviewing the plan from a legal perspective

2. Training staff in specific response and recovery activities

3. Evaluating policy and procedure to identify deficiencies

4. Modifying the plan to correct identified deficiencies

Legal Review of the Plan. Correctional administrators operate in a legal environment. Before authorizing emergency plan activities that may be thoroughly scrutinized by federal courts in the years to come, all relevant state and federal laws governing proposed response and recovery activities should be considered. Before any emergency plan testing, the plan should be formally reviewed by the agency legal team to establish the legality of (1) the authority of the agency administrator to suspend all administrative directives in the event of an emergency; and (2) proposed procedures in sensitive areas, such as using lethal force, confiscating inmate personal property (noncontraband), transferring inmates, interrogating suspected participants in inmate-precipitated emergencies, and any other staff activity that may be subsequently challenged in court.

Standardized guidelines for some issues may not be possible because each facility is different. For example, are the criteria for the use of lethal force by tower officers in an escape attempt influenced by the number of perimeter fences, the distance between them, the amount of razor ribbon used, and the presence (or absence) of mobile perimeter patrols? If so, facility-specific guidelines are necessary before lethal force policy can be formally adopted and disseminated to staff.

Staff Training/Policy Evaluation. A rigorous testing program that teaches staff their role in specific types of emergencies while simultaneously exposing plan deficiencies should include six categories of activity: (1) the tabletop exercise, (2) orientation and education sessions, (3) walk-through drills, (4) functional drills, (5) evacuation drills, and (6) full-scale

exercises (Federal Emergency Management Agency 1993:22-23). As one moves across these categories, the cost in terms of money and time increases, but so does the value in terms of staff ability to perform during response and recovery.

To find deficiencies in the plan, members from another facility's Emergency Planning Team who can look at the plan with a fresh eye should be included in all phases of plan testing. Emergency Planning Team members brought in to review all phases of strategic planning for a facility they are not familiar with are likely to raise issues and concerns overlooked by staff whose familiarity with the facility blinds them to deficiencies.

Operational Review of the Plan: The Tabletop Exercise. Key decision makers, department heads, and union representatives meet in a conference room and evaluate every aspect of the emergency plan, noting any concerns raised by the legal review, or by line staff

Special Response Team exercise, Ohio Department of Rehabilitation and Correction.

with whom the plan has been discussed. Representatives from agencies expected to assist during an emergency also are present. Emergency scenarios are developed and the emergency plan applied.

Although tabletop exercises can be considered a form of training, it is more beneficial to view them as paper reviews designed to catch glaring inconsistencies, errors, or improbabilities through a process of thoroughly examining and challenging all proposed response and recovery activities. An operational review is most effective if it is assumed that the plan has deficiencies that should be identified and corrected. A review that fails to find plan flaws is of questionable value.

Orientation and Education Sessions. All correctional staff should be required to attend the training academy for formal instruction before beginning the job. Academy curriculum should include a full overview of the elements of strategic planning. Once the employee begins work, on-the-job training in the plan should include (1) reading the facility emergency plan; (2) supervisor reviewing employees' understanding of their role in any emergency that occurs; (3) periodic reviewing and updating of knowledge of the plan through written revisions of post orders, reviewing changes at roll call, department meetings, and reorientation sessions (on-post or off-post, depending on union and budgetary restrictions); and (4) actively participating in all tests of the plan.

The Walk-Through Drill. Staff perform the mechanics of their emergency responsibilities: block officers lockdown their units in accordance with an emergency checklist, hostage negotiators assemble in a situation room, Correctional Emergency Response

Team personnel put on their equipment, and so forth. This is a test of the mechanics of response, not decision making, and inmates may or may not be involved. The goal is to uncover unanticipated mechanical or procedural problems. In one instance, a maintenance trades supervisor was surprised to find during a fire drill that the extra fire extinguishers in his department were in a closet that could not be opened because an inmate paint crew had painted the door shut.

Functional Drills. These drills test specific functions, such as medical response, warning and communications procedures and equipment, ability of the local fire department to enter the facility, ease of establishing roadblocks, and the ability to contact vendors and agency representatives. These drills can be conducted independently of the rest of the facility. The goal is to identify problems specific to a department or element of the emergency plan. A basic rule of thumb should be that if at least one significant problem is not detected, staff are not taking the drill seriously enough.

Evacuation Drills. Staff walk the evacuation route, while being timed, and are asked to note any potential hazards along the evacuation route or at the destination site. The process of physically walking the route can detect problems undiscovered during other phases of testing. Evacuation drills are unannounced and evacuation routes are walked by staff who usually are not assigned to that area. A fresh eye can see problems that the habit of routine hides from permanently assigned staff.

The Full-Scale Exercise. This form of testing represents the most effective and valuable test of all elements of strategic planning. Because it also involves an expensive and time-consuming process that disrupts facility routine and inconveniences staff and inmates alike, many administrators give in to the temptation to engage in walk-through and functional drills scheduled at the beginning or end of the shift and avoid the full-scale exercise. The result is a false sense of security and a strong message to staff that administrators are not serious when they talk about the importance of strategic planning for emergencies. An emergency plan that is not fully tested under conditions as realistic as possible is a plan that cannot be relied on in an emergency. It is better to budget money for strategic planning and risk the question, "Is this an appropriate use of the tax dollar?" than it is to lose lives and property when an emergency occurs and the plan fails. Every formal budget request should include a strategic planning line.

A full-scale exercise should be realistic. This means the following:

No Advance Warning. Staff are not warned in advance of the test. Advance knowledge eliminates the element of surprise and the ability to assess how staff react when their daily routine is unexpectedly disrupted. Specific staff activities should be videotaped and reviewed with staff.

Central Office Planning of the Scenario. The emergency scenario should be developed by central office staff, not facility staff. The first notification facility staff have of a full-scale exercise should be when a central office representative walks into the facility administrator's office and says, "Superintendent, inmates have taken over C and D Blocks. They have hostages. You now have a situation." If senior facility staff plan the scenario, it becomes impossible to test their response under pressure or their knowledge of the emergency plan.

External Evaluation. Evaluation of facility staff response to the "emergency" should be conducted by central office staff or representatives of an agency not involved in the drill. Valid critical comment is essential. Facility staff, even strong supervisors, often cannot overcome their reluctance to be critical of the staff they have to work with every day.

Off-Duty Scheduling. Testing is scheduled at times other than those most convenient to staff. This means weekends, nights, and holidays. Being awakened at midnight by a call from the supervisor advising that you should report immediately to your deployment area is a far superior test of personal readiness and plan soundness than a call while you're engaged in the routine of the day and actually may welcome the diversion the drill represents. For safety reasons, the staff member should be told at this point that it is a drill, not an actual emergency. Notification at this point also avoids unnecessary worry on the part of loved ones. Notification and response times should be carefully documented.

The "Wild Card." A wild card always should be introduced by the evaluation team. A hostage negotiation situation that is proceeding in too pat a manner should be shaken up with the sudden announcement that a hostage has just been killed and another death is promised in five minutes. Staff confident that evacuation has proceeded exactly as planned are notified that an officer has been accidentally left behind and is trapped under a burning beam. A superintendent confident that all is going well is told that the state police cannot respond in the expected numbers because another correctional facility has just erupted in riot. A medical director, confident that triage is as efficient as possible, is told that

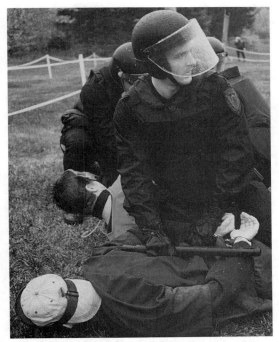

Photo courtesy Anthony Carnevale, Director of Public Affairs, Mass. Department of Correction
Simulation exercises, Massachusetts Department of Correction.

there are no ambulances to transport injured staff and inmates because they have all been diverted to a major pileup on the interstate. Staff constantly must be reminded that in an actual emergency the unexpected always must be expected and adjustments made accordingly. The most effective exercise is one that constantly challenges staff to readjust their thinking.

Counseling Poor Performers. Staff, including those at the highest levels, who perform poorly should be counseled. Team members who do not perform to expectations should be monitored closely in future exercises and removed from the team if performance does not improve. If teams are to perform at peak efficiency in an emergency, the members must believe that they are the best. This occurs only

if high standards are maintained and poor performers are removed.

Maximum Use of External resources. Representatives from the local police, hospital, fire departments, emergency rescue squads, medical lifeflight units, commercial vendors, utilities, state Emergency Management Agency, regional hospitals, National Guard, State Police, and Department of Transportation should be involved in the test and function under the same conditions as facility staff.

Public Recognition. Facilities that respond well to "wild card" situations should receive public recognition in the same way that staff response to an actual emergency would be honored.

When the exercise has been concluded, one critical step in this second stage of strategic planning remains.

The Postmortem and Plan Modification. Strategic planning deficiencies should be corrected as quickly as possible in accordance with a firm deadline established in a postmortem meeting held immediately after the exercise. The seriousness of the postmortem cannot be overemphasized. All too often staff perceive the postmortem as just another meeting to generate more paperwork for the files. A postmortem can save lives in the future if the following questions are asked:

• Are the problem areas and resource needs identified in the preemergency vulnerability and post-emergency vulnerability analysis being adequately addressed?

• Have deficiencies identified in previous drills or responses been corrected in a modified plan?

- Does the plan reflect changes in the physical plant, staff complement, risk assessment, nature of the inmate population, policy, or external environment?

- Have all new staff been adequately trained?

- Are photographs of the facility, archive materials, resource inventories, personnel rosters, and the communications tree directory up-to-date?

- Have new vulnerabilities been identified that are not addressed in the emergency plan?

- Was the community resource response adequate?

- Does the plan reflect changes in key employees' responsibilities within the facility?

- Are all levels of management involved in planning?

- Did team performances live up to expectations?

- What are the overall strengths and deficiencies of the plan and the recommendation for each specific deficiency?

- Are steps being taken to incorporate strategic planning into other facility processes?

There will be those who express concern about the cost, inconvenience, and potential staff resentment of the type of full-scale exercise outlined here. Unfortunately, emergencies are a fact of correctional life: a "pay me now or pay me later" reality. For this reason, every correctional administrator should fight for the budget to conduct at least two full-scale exercises a year in addition to other training activities.

In addition to training staff, and testing the plan, the full-scale exercise has the added benefit of educating inmates to the reality of the response they can expect if they initiate an emergency.

Chapter 22

Communication Failures: The Ultimate Threat to Strategic Planning

A vertical command structure in which some levels are barely on speaking terms with other levels impedes communications, and will inevitably lead to erroneous decisions (Pennsylvania House Judiciary Committee 1990:14-15).

Every facility has at least two levels of communication. The first level is the formal communications structure consisting of the flow of written policy and procedures up and down the chain of command. The second level is the informal communications consisting of the verbal flow of information between staff and inmates and staff and staff. No matter how comprehensive the development and testing of the emergency plan, strategic planning can be short-circuited if there is a failure in communications at either level. A failure in communications can limit the effectiveness of response and recovery or actually be the cause of the inmate-precipitated emergency.

Limiting the Effectiveness of Response and Recovery

The management of any emergency can be hindered because of unexpected basic failures in maintaining preparedness: key response people cannot be reached because the communications tree directory is out-of-date; the need for emergency communications equipment has been underestimated and specialized team members cannot talk to each other; policy and physical plant modifications that change the nature of staff response to a specific type of emergency have not been incorporated into the original emergency plan; staffing patterns and personnel in critical external emergency response agencies have changed with no notification to corrections; or vendors of critical recovery resources have gone out of business and no one at the facility has noticed. These failures can create costly confusion and chaos during response and recovery, but a more serious communication failure can occur that extends the life of the emergency.

Failure to Identify Critical Information

This can occur at any time during the routine operation of a facility, but a particularly critical time occurs after response. Once staff believe an emergency is over, there can be an enormous sense of relief based on the perception that the worst is over: response has ended and recovery has begun. If there is a breakdown in the process of determining the security status of the physical plant, the discovery that recovery activities are premature can be jarring. The first Camp Hill riot was completed at 3 A.M. on October 26. At 10 P.M. that evening the institution was pronounced to be secure. On October 26, 1989, the second riot erupted at 6 P.M. The cause of the second riot is found in the failure to establish that the cellblock cell locking mechanisms had been sabotaged:

> *However, the cell blocks were not secure. Apparently, the reason for this confusion was the failure of the prison staff to realize that the inmates could easily leave their cells by reaching through and above the bars on their cell doors and pulling a lever which opened the cell doors. Many of the panels above the cell doors which hid the mechanism for opening the cells had been removed during the first riot . . . . No one seemed to recognize at the time just how insecure many of the cell blocks were immediately following the first riot because everyone was primarily concerned with getting the inmates back into the cells* (Pennsylvania Senate Judiciary Committee 1990:22).

Disruption in the Flow of Information

The belief that Camp Hill was secure led to the decision to reduce the State Police contingent to twenty-five and delay a shakedown until sufficient staff were available and tensions had cooled:

> *There appeared to be a general feeling among the commissioned officers and among the superintendent and the deputies that the riot was over, and they were simply in a state of gradually resuming normal operations . . . . The commissioned officers have been intent upon blaming the former superintendent and the deputies for the second day's riot, claiming that they notified the deputies of the security problems in the cell blocks, but that nothing was done. The former superintendent and the deputies have been equally intent in blaming the commissioned officers, claiming they were never apprised of the security problems in the cell blocks* (Pennsylvania House Judiciary Committee 1990:14).

Causing the Inmate-Precipitated Emergency

Communication failures can go far beyond interfering with the response and recovery capability of staff. Certain types of communication failure can undermine mitigation so thoroughly that they actually trigger the original emergency. Staff-precipitated emergencies can be caused by a variety of specific communications failures.

Individual Failure to Follow Policy

Administrative staff spend an inordinate amount of time establishing policy and procedures designed to enhance the safe and orderly operation of a facility through mitigation. Policies and procedures are communicated to staff through the methods discussed in chapter 21, but mitigation is doomed to failure if staff do not accept or understand this communication. Failure to follow policy can involve a staff member acting alone, as seen at the State Prison of Southern Michigan in 1952:

> *The only thing that seems clear is that the riot began with a simple security slip committed by an inexperienced correctional officer. Disregarding the rules, the officer opened a cell door for an inmate after the evening lockup. The inmate exited his cell wielding a knife and the disturbance was underway. Such security failures were commonplace at Jackson prison at this time* (DiIulio 1987:26-27).

Collective Failure to Follow Policy

However, all too often the failure to follow established policies represents a collective action. In 1981, at Pennsylvania's State Correctional Institution at Graterford, policy failures involved both treatment and custody staff:

> *It is hard to find anything other than simple security-minded management failures behind the 1981 disturbance at Pennsylvania's Graterford prison . . . . The trouble started when prison authorities mistakenly placed an inmate known to be a security risk in a low-supervision work*

assignment. This inmate led the disturbance. Six prison employees were gone for nearly an hour before anyone recognized or reported that they were missing. Two junior correctional officers and a lieutenant were among the hostages (DiIulio 1987:29).

In 1991, at the New York Department of Corrections' Southport Correctional Facility:

> *53 inmates from . . . A Block break out of their outdoor exercise pens. The inmates immediately take control of the outdoor exercise yard as well as the enclosed fire staircase at the end of A Block, their housing unit. Two Corrections Officers are injured in the takeover, but manage to extricate themselves from the immediate area. Five other Officers are assaulted and taken hostage by the inmates. Two of the Officers sustain puncture wound injuries . . . .* (Coughlin 1991:1).

> *There were no fatalities and the inmates surrendered without further incident at 2:26 p.m. on May 29, 1991. Staff failure to follow established procedures permitted the breach of security: There was a serious breach of security protocol at Southport on the day of the incident. Seven Officers abandoned their assigned posts supervising the inmates in the recreation pens in the yard— so they could eat their lunch*

inside of A Block or in the storage room directly off the yard. At one point, there were no officers in the yard at all . . . .

In addition, officers failed to notice penned inmates unraveling the fencing of the exercise pens while officers were placing other inmates into their pens. Some inmates had been in the pens for 90 minutes instead of the scheduled sixty minutes because officers broke for lunch without returning them to the cellblock. This thirty minute delay in movement prevented detection of the unraveled wiring (Coughlin 1991:3).

Inadequate Rumor Control

Communications involves more than the dissemination, review, and acceptance of written policy. It also involves the ability to communicate on a verbal level. Useem and Kimball (1989) note the role of uncontrolled rumors as a causative factor in the 1981 disturbances in Michigan. At the State Prison in Southern Michigan (SPSM) Central Complex on May 22, rumors spread among the inmates that they were to be locked down for the entire Memorial Day weekend because of inmate disturbances at other institutions. Angered at the thought of losing their holiday privileges, inmates who had not yet been locked down entered block 3 and swarmed over the defenseless officers. Shortly therefore the institution was in a state of riot. By 8 P.M. inmates were quietly returning to their cells.

Photo courtesy Capitol Communications

A key element of successful correctional emergency mitigation is clear and direct communications among mitigation teams and others involved. Communications to inmates, the media, and the public should be carefully planned and delivered.

Then, on May 26, 1981, at approximately 12:10 P.M., after a series of miscommunications and unchallenged rumors, inmates in the Central Complex at SPSM staged a second riot. By 1:30 P.M. most of the Northside Complex was ablaze. Inmates returned to their cells at approximately 8 P.M. However, at the Marquette Branch Prison, at about the time the SPSM riot ended, inmates began the fifth riot Michigan was to experience in five days. This riot was apparently triggered by inmate fear that they were going to go into lockdown because of the riots at SPSM and Michigan Reformatory. These fears were fueled by riot-prevention measures of Marquette's administration, including cancellation of a baseball game with an outside team and an increase in the number of officers on yard patrol. An altercation between an inmate and an officer was the fuse that set off this riot. Fires and looting occurred, inmates were raped, and personal property was stolen.

Impersonal Communication Instead of Personal Communication

A verbal communications failure can occur because of a misperception that written communication about changes affecting inmates is as effective as verbal, face-to-face communication with inmates. Before the Camp Hill riots, the institution held 2,600 adult males in a facility designed for 1,200 juveniles. Nevertheless, the fuse for the riots was found in two policy changes. The first change involved the tradition of Family Days, a holdover from the time when Camp Hill was a juvenile facility. During Family Days, general population inmates were allowed to meet with family and friends for a picnic lunch brought in by the families. This was a perfect route of entrance

for contraband, and it was decided to terminate the practice. Each inmate at Camp Hill was provided with a memo announcing the termination, the rationale, and the fact that changes would be made in the visiting room to allow a wider selection of food and beverages from the vending machines.

The second change was a modification of sick line procedure to permit the doctors an extra day for consultation and evaluation of inmates with particularly difficult cases. Both changes were received with resentment:

> *While several inmates testified about the underlying tensions and frustrations at Camp Hill, there seemed to be a general consensus among the inmates that these changes were . . . "the straw that broke the camel's back . . . freedom was continually restricted and things that we had enjoyed for many years were being taken away"* (Pennsylvania Senate Judiciary Committee 1990:19).

With the luxury of hindsight, it is apparent that inmates were influenced more by rumors than they were by the written revision of policy statements. If the power of these rumors had been recognized, the effect of the changes might have been mitigated by: (1) face-to-face meetings with all inmates filing grievances, (2) formal group meetings with inmates, (3) a staggering of the changes so inmates would have more time to adjust, and (4) systematic circulation of treatment and supervisory staff through the cell blocks to talk to inmates.

Limited Scope of Emergency Planning

Strategic planning is an evolutionary process. It is impossible to anticipate every potential emergency and its response and recovery needs when developing the original emergency plan. This inability to anticipate means staff may not be adequately trained to manage unanticipated emergencies when they occur. However, professional administrators should learn from experience and should expand the scope of the original emergency plan during recovery from each unanticipated emergency.

The Federal Bureau of Prisons Model

Examples of strategic planning as an evolutionary process can be found in the experiences of the Federal Bureau of Prisons. A series of assaults culminating in the murder of two corrections officers at the U.S. Penitentiary in Marion, Illinois, in 1983 demonstrated the need for each federal facility to develop Special Operation Response Teams. In 1987, incidents at Oakdale and Atlanta revealed the weakness of emergency plans that did not provide for institutionwide takeovers in which large numbers of hostages were held and the Bureau of Prisons faced a "monumental task in responding simultaneously to two major riot and hostage situations at different geographical locations; at that time it did not have the benefit of national emergency response guidelines, planning, or equipment" (Federal Bureau of Prisons 1994:14).

A review of the incidents at Oakdale and Atlanta resulted in 107 recommendations dealing with a variety of strategic planning

issues and the creation of the Office of Emergency Preparedness. Particularly significant recommendations concerned the need for Disturbance Control Teams and Hostage Negotiation Teams to work together to create a system of coordinated emergency response. There also were changes in the way Special Operations Response Teams (SORT) trained:

> *Until that time, SORT competitions had been comparatively unstructured, athletically-based tournaments between SORTs from BOP institutions and Special Weapons and tactics (SWAT) teams from State and local law enforcement agencies. After 1988, SORT exercises became organized, week-long regional training events that focused on collaboration between SORTs and featured tests of mental, as well as physical acuity* (Federal Bureau of Prisons 1994:15).

In 1990, the Bureau of Prisons recognized the value in developing guidelines for certifying Special Operations Response Teams' abilities with a focus on problem solving and the use of tactical and firearms skills for emergency response. By the late 1980s the Bureau of Prisons realized the need for development of regional emergency logistics centers that can store the materials and equipment necessary for rapid response to an emergency. Subsequent events have demonstrated the value of having a computer software program to track the availability of stockpiled equipment and supplies and the qualifications and training of all members of specialized teams.

Strategic planning is a process of communications that is evolutionary in nature. Each year should see significant improvements in the capability to address the critical issues of any emergency life cycle.

The Emergency Postmortem

Mistakes rooted in communications failure may be unavoidable given the range of personalities and stresses found in the correctional environment. However, the biggest mistake of all is to fail to understand that mistakes, no matter how personally embarrassing or costly, can provide valuable information for future strategic planning and emergency plan modification. This occurs through a post-emergency communications process called the postmortem. During recovery, in a postmortem conducted by facility and central office staff working together less time should be spent on what worked and instead, participants should concentrate on what did not work. If some element of the emergency plan did not work, chances are good that a communications failure was involved. Strategic planning is an evolutionary process. Each failure, if professionally analyzed, will contribute to the effectiveness of the next generation of emergency plans.

Chapter 23

Raising the Phoenix from the Ashes: Meeting the Physical and Psychological Challenges of Recovery

After Hensley's own capture, he was taken to Cell 62, where he lay on the floor by the bunk, blindfolded with a T-shirt secured by surgical tape, feet tied, listening to all the pandemonium, the screams of inmates being beaten and murdered by other inmates, his clothes all bloodied and the place smelling of excrement (Porter 1995:56).

Conventional emergency planning traditionally emphasizes preparedness and response activities and ignores recovery activities, as though the facility will somehow just spring back into shape like a rubber band that has been stretched out of shape once the emergency is over. Strategic planning understands that the assumption of automatic recovery is invalid. Response may be over in hours or days, but recovery can last for years, especially if there has been major trauma inflicted on property and people. It is during recovery that some of the greatest personal and professional

challenges may arise. Therefore, recovery activities should be a part of every emergency plan.

After the second riot at Camp Hill, we suddenly realized that our problems were just beginning. We had over 1,800 inmates, many of whom had certainly participated in one, if not both, of the riots, and no secure area in which to house them. Six modular units had been burned to the ground and six cellblocks were so badly damaged that it was a year before the last one was available for habitation. We spent long days trying to locate enough single-key padlocks and chain to manually secure the few hundred Group I and II cells that could be used after a frenzied cleanout of destroyed property and equipment. The only area large enough for temporary housing while cleanout was underway was the main stockade field. We had no feeding capability because both kitchens had been destroyed. It was late October, and we knew that the weather could turn bad at any time. There was a shortage of blankets because of the loss of inventory stores to fire. There was one water fountain on the main stockade field. None of these issues had been addressed in emergency planning.

Over one hundred staff had suffered physical or psychological trauma. Some were hospitalized with an uncertain prognosis for complete recovery. The media were swarming over the property, and politicians were racing to see which one could be the first to schedule riot hearings. Inmate families were demanding to see their loved ones. Inmates were demanding that the traditional institutional routine be reestablished immediately even though the institution had ceased to exist as a functional operation. Union officials were vocal in their demand for leadership changes at Camp Hill. Inmate families began to contact outside resources for assistance in filing litigation. Burned-out buildings smoldered while staff tried to determine the priorities and scrambled for equipment and supplies. Evacuation plans had to be hurriedly cobbled together. Recovery became a nightmare.

The primary goal of recovery is to return the facility to normal operations as quickly as possible, a process that involves (1) initiating physical plant restoration, (2) meeting inmate physical needs, and (3) identifying and treating the complex psychological issues involved in staff and inmate post-traumatic stress disorder. The recovery activities to be discussed may be applied to any category of emergency, regardless of origin or size, with appropriate modification.

Meeting the Physical Needs
The Stepdown Committee

Inmates should be placed in secure housing and provided with food, clothing, bedding, hygiene products, and medical care as quickly as possible. The most efficient method of addressing inmate physical needs is to return the facility to normal operations as rapidly as security considerations allow. The most effective tool for returning a facility from emergency to normalcy is the Stepdown Committee. This committee is chaired by the facility administrator, and members include department heads, commissioned officers, and union representatives. Meeting attendance should be mandatory, and formal minutes should be taken. All committee decisions should be made in accordance with seven goals: identifying physical needs, prioritizing needs, developing a formal recovery plan, communicating the plan, assigning responsibility, ensuring accountability, and identifying deficiencies.

Identifying Physical Needs. The information on which to base physical needs identification will come primarily from the Damage Assessment Team, the Damage Repair Team, and the Architectural Assessment Team.

Physical needs generally are the easiest to identify. A visual survey of the facility is the first step. Use a checklist. Check each building in the facility for (1) structural damage; (2) status of utilities, security systems, and communications systems; (3) ability to provide support services (food service, infirmary, laundry); and (4) inventory levels for all essential materials and supplies. The ready availability of archival materials and preemergency inventory information is invaluable during this process.

The physical needs of inmates should be met in a manner that does not represent a security risk. For example, at Camp Hill, a basic inmate need almost immediately identified was the need of inmates to maintain personal hygiene by being allowed to brush their teeth. However, security staff worried about the potential of the traditional toothbrush being converted into a lethal weapon. Because this was a genuine concern, the toothbrushes that had been purchased had to be modified. The hard plastic handles were cut off and replaced by a flexible piece of rubber tubing. For the same reason, hard bars of soap were replaced by liquid soap dispensed in medicine cups. Inmate needs and security concerns should be addressed simultaneously.

Prioritizing Needs. First address those needs that directly affect the health and safety of inmates, the staff, and the public. Once you determine the priority of needs, develop a written priorities list to monitor progress. The priorities list can be modified as events demand, but it always should be in the form of a written document available to all staff.

Developing a Formal Recovery Plan. Once needs have been identified and prioritized, identify the most effective means of addressing them. Marshal resources, outline projects, and propose a written time frame for each project.

Communicating Formal Recovery Plan. During recovery there can be a strong sense of frustration for all concerned, particularly the inmates and their loved ones, especially if it appears that the return to normalcy is taking longer than it should. The formal recovery plan should be communicated verbally and in writing to staff, inmates, and the media. The more information communicated in an accurate and timely fashion, the less the likelihood of additional problems being created by a perception that the administration is deliberately dragging its heels for purposes of retaliation or is too incompetent to do the job properly. Periodic Stepdown Committee briefings of the Information Management Team will ensure the flow of information to the media is consistent and accurate. Periodic briefings provided by the Intelligence Unit will ensure inmate attitudes and behavior are being monitored carefully.

Assigning Responsibility. Every project in the formal recovery plan should be assigned to a specific individual who will be held accountable for completion of the project within the specified time frame. Strict accountability will help prevent unnecessary delay and provide a high level of ongoing assessment of resource needs and problem identification.

Ensuring Accountability. Ongoing written progress reports filed in accordance with a written filing schedule help to monitor progress efficiently and reduce the possibility of miscommunication. Some staff may resent this paperwork requirement on top of all the other recovery demands, but written documentation is the only way to ensure the recovery plan is carried out in the manner intended and important issues are not falling through the cracks. The trail of written documentation also provides a legal defense if inmates file litigation alleging that conditions are not returning to normalcy as quickly as possible. This type of litigation can result in a federal judge intervening during recovery and mandating a court-developed time frame for specific events.

Identifying Emergency-Revealed Deficiencies. As information flows into the Stepdown Committee, deficiencies in mitigation, preparedness, response, and recovery activities should be revealed. The correction of physical plant deficiencies should be incorporated into both short-term and long-term projects. Deficiencies in policy, training, and testing of the plan may be corrected through post-emergency policy modification.

The facility administrator should enter the facility each day and personally determine the rate of progress. The Stepdown Committee will exist and meet regularly until a state of normalcy has been achieved. Depending on the emergency, the Stepdown Committee may exist for no more than a few weeks, or it may become a part of the routine operation of the facility for years to come.

Meeting the Psychological Challenges

Physical needs may be met in a matter of days or months, but the psychological needs of staff and inmates present a more complicated problem, one that is rarely addressed in conventional emergency planning. The Stepdown Committee should address the issue of psychological needs by working closely with the Post-traumatic Assessment Team and the Information Management Team. There are two psychological challenges to be met. The first challenge is to reduce family fear and anxiety.

Reducing Family Fear and Anxiety

The most critical need of staff families and friends is the communication of accurate, timely information about any loved ones caught in the emergency or participating in the response. Depending on the size of the facility, and the nature of the emergency, there are three methods of communication with the

family of staff: the family center, the communications tree, and the media.

The Family Center (if hostages are involved). Post-traumatic Assessment Team members should recognize the uncertainty and fear experienced by the relatives of hostages and the need for emotional support and accurate information. Fagan (1994) suggests the value of establishing a family center at the facility that provides a safe location for the family members of hostages to gather and receive accurate information. Anxiety may be reduced if family members are in a position to immediately question the type of rumors that always swirl around a hostage situation.

The family center allows easy access to Post-traumatic Assessment Team members who are trained to provide counseling and provides a shelter from the media, gawkers, and other individuals prone to intrude on the privacy of people in a state of fear. The center should be located as close to the prison as possible, and its access restricted to authorized personnel, through the establishment of a gatekeeper system. Arrangements should be made for family members sleeping, eating, using the telephone, and recording the television coverage of the event. The families of hostages are starved for information and should have as much access to information sources as possible. Post-traumatic Assessment Team members should recognize the tendency of the media to report rumors as fact and be prepared to respond to family attacks of anxiety. Periodic briefings of the family by the Information Management Team can include information about the agency's policy on hostage negotiation and previous experience with such situations.

During their stay in the center, families will experience varying degrees of stress-related anxiety. Psychological and spiritual counseling may be provided by Post-traumatic Assessment Team members or professionals from community mental health agencies and churches, depending on family preference.

Children represent a special issue because they often react to the stress of the emergency in the same way as the adults they are observing. The approach to children is twofold. First, educators should be informed of the situation and asked to watch for symptoms that can be addressed through referral. Second:

> CIRT members can also establish a child care program at the family center. This allows adults time away from children to work out their own fears and concerns. It also allows children to deal with their feelings away from their parents and other adult relatives. The center should offer activities such as play therapy, story-telling and art therapy to help children cope. Some family members may want to volunteer to work a shift at the child care center (Fagan 1994:81).

The Communications Tree (death or injury situations). In the event of injury or death, the Information Management Team should have as a priority the immediate notification of family members. Once the injury/death status of a staff member has been verified, the person designated in personnel records as the individual to be notified in case of emergency should be called immediately. The information given should be limited to the status of the staff member and the location of the hospital or mortuary to which he or she has been taken. Discussions of the circumstance of death or injury are to be avoided, both for reasons of sensitivity and potential litigation from the family.

The Media (general information). Families who have staff members who were on duty at the time of the emergency, or are part of response activity, also will experience anxiety and fear. The most effective means of allaying staff-specific family anxiety is, if at all possible, to allow each staff member to call home during the tour of duty. Families can be kept up-to-date on general issues through scheduled press conferences.

Post-traumatic Stress Disorder

The second psychological challenge, post-traumatic stress disorder, is more complicated.

At the beginning of the second Camp Hill riot, a staff member this author knew to be level-headed, compassionate, and treatment-oriented rushed past him to the main gate. He was screaming: "I'm going to get a gun from the Armory and kill those bastards. I swear to God I'm going to kill those inmate bastards!" Unable to calm down, this individual had to be removed from the property and driven home.

One of the finest correctional officers the author ever worked with in a twenty-year career was trapped in the Group I Command Post during the second riot at Camp Hill. The terror of that experience apparently reopened old wounds from his service in Vietnam, where he had been severely wounded. This decorated war veteran is now on disability, no longer able to handle the stress and responsibility of correctional life. Some staff and inmates who survive a riot remain among the walking wounded. Physical wounds may heal quickly, but psychological wounds may be permanent.

Post-traumatic stress disorder is a delayed reaction to an abnormal, traumatic life experience (Niles 1991:1663). It is diagnosed in accordance with guidelines set forth in the *Diagnostic and Statistical Manual of Mental Disorders (DSM-III)*. The traditional post-traumatic stress disorder diagnosis requires a personal traumatic event that involves actual or threatened death or serious injury that produced intense fear, helplessness, or horror. However, the elements of diagnosis recently have been expanded:

> *DSM-IV broadens the definition of the event and shifts the emphasis from its severity to the patient's reaction to it . . . . So persons who have had extreme reactions to common events and those who have merely witnessed excruciating trauma are now included* (Bursztajn *et al.* 1995:41).

Post-traumatic stress disorder involves a reexperiencing of the trauma. Recurrent and distressing memories or dreams about the event may occur. A correctional officer beaten during a riot may have difficulty sleeping because every time he closes his eyes he sees the metal bar swinging at him and feels the impact on his jaw, which had been shattered. Staff may unexpectedly feel as if the traumatic event is actually recurring in the form of an hallucination or flashback or experience intense psychological distress when exposed to a cue that symbolizes the event, such as

hearing the word "riot" in an advertisement or seeing a burning building in a movie or newscast. Other symptoms may include amnesia about an important aspect of the event, lack of interest in significant activities (numbing), feelings of detachment, a sense of foreboding about the future, sleep disturbances, concentration problems, hypervigilance, irritability, exaggerated startle response, and survivor guilt (Bursztajn *et al.* 1995:42). Specific symptoms:

> *. . . cannot have been present before exposure to the trauma, must endure for more than a month, and must cause clinically significant distress or functional impairment* (Bursztajn *et al.* 1995:42).

Strategic planning for the diagnosis and management of post-traumatic stress disorder may be hindered by two myths.

Myth Number One. Strong men never cry. The proponents of this myth operate in accordance with the philosophy that a real man can handle anything, and the best way to react to trauma is to get back up on the horse that threw you. These individuals believe that post-traumatic stress disorder is just another term for goldbricking and an easy ticket to a disability pension. What these individuals do not understand is that:

> *In the moment of trauma, fundamental trust in self and others is disrupted, along with basic assumptions about existence. The person is rendered vulnerable and defenseless, and he or she experiences a loss of control in the face of external forces, a fear of*

imminent death, a sense of the inconsistency and purposelessness of existence, feelings of pain and isolation and, ultimately, disintegration of his or her sense of self. . . . It is at this moment that the foundation for post-traumatic stress disorder is established (Niles 1991:1665).

Myth Number Two. You have to be taken hostage, or attacked, or otherwise physically injured to be vulnerable to post-traumatic stress disorder. This is not true. Individuals viewing traumatic events may experience secondary victimization (Figley 1983) that is just as troubling as the trauma experienced by the direct victim. Administrators and supervisors directing the emergency response are not immune to post-traumatic stress disorder:

> *. . . Jim Guilliatt, safety supervisor, was similarly shaken after a recent work place tragedy. Last year, a company driver was killed on the job in a motor-vehicle collision. Afterward, Guilliatt was so upset he sought brief counseling from his company's employee assistance program . . . . Guilliatt was not responsible for the accident . . . . However . . . "If you take this job seriously, you tie yourself into every accident . . . It's tough. You get really emotional"* (Wallace 1993:42).

Witnesses to the emergency, participants who are not physically injured, and individuals who have to make critical decisions are all vulnerable to post-traumatic stress disorder. Strategic planning should account for the possibility of post-traumatic stress disorder as it plans for other emergencies.

Level 3 Mitigation. It is probably impossible to prevent post-traumatic stress disorder in those individuals vulnerable to the disorder, but the consequences may be reduced through education. Academy curriculums should devote at least two hours to the issue of post-traumatic stress disorder. Staff need to be aware that post-traumatic stress disorder is a very real possibility in corrections. They need instruction in causation, symptoms, and treatment options. A specific discussion of strategies for coping emotionally with being taken hostage is very helpful. Members of the Post-traumatic Assessment Team should receive as much training in post-traumatic stress disorder diagnosis and intervention as possible.

Preparedness/Response. Response focuses on short-term counseling services and defusing and debriefing.

Short-term Counseling Services. Staff may experience intense periods of anxiety and/or depression during response. Post-traumatic Assessment Team members can effectively intervene with the use of supportive counseling methods or through immediate referral to community mental health professionals. Staff who have an immediate psychological reaction to the emergency should be monitored carefully for signs of post-traumatic stress disorder.

Defusing and Debriefing. Because this process may be initiated while response is still in effect, it is included as a preparedness/response activity, although, if the emergency is short-lived, it may become a recovery activity. The initial focus of defusing and debriefing is on hostages or injured staff members, although it later may be expanded to all staff and certainly is not limited to inmate-precipitated emergencies. Appropriate modification allows defusing to be a useful process during recovery from any emergency. Defusing has four goals:

1. To engage in psychological and medical screening to determine if treatment or medication is needed

2. To gather relevant information if response has not concluded, especially if that information can aid in continued negotiations, hostage rescue, or general response activities

3. To begin the process of identifying any inmate rule violators for subsequent legal prosecution

4. To allow the opportunity to shower, change clothing, and emotionally prepare for the family reunion

Debriefing sessions occur approximately thirty-six to forty-eight hours after hostage release, involve eight to twelve individuals, and are conducted by at least two facilitators (Fagan 1994:83). The goals of debriefing are as follows:

1. To discuss the traumatic experience and the individual's reaction to it

2. To learn coping mechanisms

3. To provide a list of referral agencies and professionals who can provide long-term therapy

4. To provide an awareness that emotional problems may develop at a later date and staff should not be ashamed to seek help if this occurs

The family should not be ignored by the agency during the debriefing process. Every attempt should be made by the Post-traumatic Assessment Team to educate families about post-traumatic stress disorder. Not only is a strong support system needed for staff recovery from the experience, but:

> *Significant others who live with the person can also develop symptoms of post-traumatic stress disorder. The fundamental concept is that the symptoms of the disorder are often delayed. Changes in family dynamics begin occurring without family members understanding the underlying disorder. In attempting to reestablish balance, the person often feels revictimized, symptoms are exacerbated and family members may be verbally or physically abused, and often develop symptoms themselves* (Niles 991:1668).

Staff family members should be provided with a referral list that contains the names, addresses, and description of community providers of mental health services before they begin to experience stress-related problems.

Recovery. Recovery can last for years because the nature of post-traumatic stress disorder is such that it may be years before symptoms appear. Specific recovery issues include staff return to work, long-term counseling services, and training as therapy.

Staff Return to Work. Staff who have been physically injured or who suffer from post-traumatic stress disorder should not be allowed to return to work until a physician has provided written certification that the employee is physically fit to return to work. Any physical limitations applicable to the work site should be noted and discussed with the employee before an actual return is authorized. Acute flexibility may be necessary in meeting the needs of staff who have been physically and/or psychologically damaged by the emergency. This flexibility should be governed by standardized criteria and include such options as assigning light duty while therapy is ongoing, relocating the employee to other facilities, delaying the return to work, assisting with workers' compensation, or allowing unpaid time off if all earned leave has been used. Every effort should be made to salvage staff. An officer taken hostage in a maximum security facility may not be able to function appropriately in that setting, but may adjust well to working in a community corrections setting. An officer injured in an earthquake in an urban area may be able to function more effectively in a forestry camp.

Long-term Counseling Services. The long-term needs of staff and their families will vary considerably and should be evaluated on a case-by-case basis. A staff assistance center should be established to provide specific contact persons trained to provide on-site or referral assistance to staff who subsequently have difficulty coping with their experiences. For most effective response, the staff assistance center should be the responsibility of a combination of personnel and psychological services staff. The staff assistance center staff should monitor staff behavior and concerns, especially around the anniversary date of the event. A close working relationship between correctional staff and community mental health professionals is essential if staff and their families are to avoid unnecessary pain in the future.

Training as Therapy. Staff who have been taken hostage or injured may become a valuable resource for training purposes, an activity that also may have a therapeutic effect:

> *I tell my students what happened during the Lucasville disturbance. I go into explicit detail because it would be unfair to them to not hear the full story. I also let them know they are the final piece in my healing puzzle.*

> *. . . I sometimes ask myself, "Are you doing this as a benefit and service for the students or as a benefit to Larry Dotson's ego?" But it is something I need to do. Once I work it all out, it will be full speed ahead. Right now, I'm exactly where I need to be* (Unwin 1994:72).

Inmate Post-traumatic Stress Disorder Needs

Inmates also may develop post-traumatic stress disorder. Inmate acting-out, fears, anxiety, and depression that are PTSD-based should be appropriately identified and treated. If facility counseling resources are inadequate, the availability of community mental health resources should be explored. An in-facility inmate-led post-traumatic stress disorder program can help inmates experiencing symptoms. Inmate involvement and leadership in such a program can be therapeutic. Community volunteers, particularly veterans, often are eager to assist in this type of program. Treatment staff receiving inmates from an emergency-stricken facility should develop a comprehensive post-traumatic stress disorder monitoring system.

Inmates who did not participate in an inmate-precipitated emergency, but have lost all their personal property, or were subjected to extraordinary security measures during recovery, may resent those inmates who did participate. They also may resent the staff they came into contact with during response and recovery. Staff should be alert to any signs of resentment aimed at specific inmates, inmate groups, or staff and respond with appropriate counseling and administrative interventions.

Chapter 24

Managing the Tidal Wave of Post-emergency Inmate Litigation

*T**his is a civil action for damages brought by an inmate of a state correctional institution against five (5) supervisory corrections officials under 42 U.S.C. 1983. Plaintiff alleges these officials "witnessed" physical assaults of plaintiff by staff at the State Correctional Institution at Camp Hill, Pennsylvania (SCI-Camp Hill) in 1989 but failed to do anything about it.* (Amended Complaint filed May 14, 1993: Order dated May 14, 1993).

Before the Court are cross-motions for summary judgment. Plaintiff filed his motion and brief on or about October 14, 1993. Following the grant of an enlargement of time, defendants filed their cross-motion on November 15, 1993. This brief is submitted by defendants in support of their motion and in opposition to plaintiff's motion (Camp Hill riot-related litigation 1993).

The normal flow of inmate litigation can be distressing. The flow that occurs after an emergency can be devastating. In the two years following the riots, hundreds of Camp Hill staff were named as defendants in riot-related inmate lawsuits filed in Federal District Court. This author was named in 289 of these lawsuits.

Response to inmate litigation is an administrative responsibility, part of the accepted daily activity of a correctional administrator. During the routine operation of a correctional institution, staff periodically are named as defendants in inmate litigation, often because of behavior or events unknown to the administrator. This litigation requires a legal response from the defendant(s). The administrative response to routine litigation is best described by the routine legal response model:

1. A lawsuit is received and reviewed.

2. Allegations are investigated.

3. An institutional response is submitted.

4. Plaintiff interrogatories are received and responded to through preparation and review of defendant declarations after additional investigation and discussion.

5. The judge conducts a pretrial conference and sets a trial date.

6. Staff are scheduled to testify and review the facts of the case with counsel.

7. Staff testify in court.

The most critical element in any legal response to inmate litigation is event reconstruction. Event reconstruction is an analytical process that is conducted to establish the behavior and decision-making process staff have engaged in during the event or activity. This forms the basis for the litigation.

The routine legal response model requires receipt and review of a lawsuit before a response is possible because most routine lawsuits represent an isolated, unpredictable event. The lawsuit received on Monday may have nothing in common with the lawsuit received on Tuesday. Because administrators cannot predict the filing of most routine lawsuits, and because the content of any given lawsuit may have no relationship to the content of any other lawsuit, the routine legal response model is logical and necessary. This model adequately meets routine administrative needs, especially when there is a low volume of litigation, even though months or years may pass between step one and step seven. This model worked well at Camp Hill in the days before the riots, when routine litigation was processed efficiently as part of the daily routine.

Unfortunately, conventional emergency plans, such as the one in place for Camp Hill in October 1989, typically, do not address a critical issue: preparing cost-effective, efficient legal response to post-emergency inmate litigation. Conventional emergency planning does not address the need for efficient management of a large volume of post-emergency litigation because the focus in planning is the emergency, not anticipation of the legal consequences of the emergency. There often is an assumption that litigation as a result of an emergency can be processed as litigation

always is processed, by using the routine legal response model.

The practical effects of no prior planning for post-emergency litigation are as follows:

• Development of an effective legal response to litigation is not an initial staff priority during recovery.

• Attorneys are not in a position to develop a comprehensive overview of the legal issues before receipt of litigation.

• No procedures are in place for event reconstruction with potential defendants before the receipt of litigation.

• Lawsuits, once received, have to be squeezed into the already heavy workload of busy attorneys.

In December 1989, we received the first Camp Hill riot-related lawsuits. We treated each lawsuit as an individual event. The attorney assigned to the case would discuss specifics with each defendant and prepare the appropriate declarations; the case would move slowly toward a trial date. As the volume of cases increased, and more and more attorneys and staff were drawn into the response process, it became clear that a more efficient method of managing post-emergency litigation was necessary.

Camp Hill riot-related litigation involved alleged violations of the right to Eighth Amendment protection against the infliction of cruel and unusual punishment. Specifically, there were six primary allegation categories:

1. Failure to protect the inmates from harm before the first riot on October 25, 1989, and the second riot on October 26, 1989. Inmates alleged that Camp Hill administrators were

responsible for both riots. This allegation was based on a double premise: administrators should have known that the riots were going to occur, and having knowledge of what was about to happen, administrators failed to take actions that would have prevented the riots.

2. Cruel and unusual punishment after the riots, when approximately 1,800 inmates spent three days on the main stockade field (an outdoor athletic area) while three of the least damaged cell blocks were renovated for habitation. All other areas suitable for indoor housing of inmates had been burned to the ground or otherwise destroyed by rioting inmates. Inmates litigated four primary complaints about their time on the field: *(a)* lack of adequate amounts of food, eating utensils, water, blankets, warm clothing, toilet facilities, and medical care; *(b)* time spent in the "worm farm" (an alleged punishment area); *(c)* being handcuffed and shackled at all times; *(d)* sleeping on the ground at night.

3. Cruel and unusual punishment after the riots. Inmates charged physical and psychological abuses (ranging from physical beatings to derogatory and verbal racial abuse to being made to kiss the rear end of a state trooper's horse) while on the main stockade field, during the return to the blocks, and before transfer to state or federal institutions.

4. Cruel and unusual punishment in the blocks after removal from the main stockade field. Inmates had three main issues: *(a)* too many inmates per cell (each cell held four to five inmates because of the lack of available housing); *(b)* lack of clothing, mattresses, pillows, blankets, soap, toilet paper, toothbrushes, toothpaste, shaving equipment, and showers; and *(c)* being handcuffed and shackled.

5. The wanton and unnecessary destruction by staff of all property belonging to inmates housed in the six cell blocks of Group II and III, where the riots were centered. Inmates alleged that correctional staff destroyed all inmate property in a deliberate act of reprisal rooted in anger about the riots before returning the inmates from the main stockade field. The plaintiffs demanded extensive compensatory and punitive damages amounting to millions of dollars.

6. The malicious removal and disposition of personal wear items (such as watches, neck chains, cigarette lighters, and religious medallions) from Group II and Group III inmates on the main stockade field and all personal property from inmates in the Group I Restricted Housing Unit.

With the clarity of hindsight, all of these themes could have been anticipated quite easily. Staff working the cell blocks after a major disturbance frequently are alerted by inmates of their intention to file litigation. The specific content of that litigation may be spelled out during heated exchanges between staff and inmates. If Camp Hill emergency plans had addressed the issue of post-emergency litigation, appropriate responses to the forthcoming litigation could have been developed immediately. However, advance warning of litigation does not translate into effective legal response unless there is prior development of an appropriate response plan.

Four valuable lessons have emerged from the experience of attempting to manage Camp Hill riot-related litigation through the use of the routine legal response model:

1. After an emergency has occurred, an increased volume of inmate litigation can be

predicted. Common themes of litigation also can be predicted. Inmates charging violation of their civil rights have two years to file a federal lawsuit. Therefore, administrators can predict the filing of post-emergency litigation, the most likely themes of this litigation, and the period during which a higher-than-normal volume of litigation may be expected.

2. Post-emergency litigation event reconstruction using the routine legal response model is not the most efficient model for effective management of a high volume of post-emergency litigation.

3. There are three major routine legal response event reconstruction problems encountered in responding to riot-related litigation: faulty memories, lack of staff supportive physical evidence, and inaccurate documentation. Because of these specific problems, routine legal response to post-emergency litigation may provide an opportunity for undeserved legal victories for plaintiffs. Even when staff actions are legally vindicated in court, the victory comes at considerable financial cost, pressure, and emotional stress for defendants and their attorneys.

4. The routine legal response model should be replaced by a model that can be set into motion before the first lawsuit is received. This model should be more sensitive to the demands of event reconstruction. The post-emergency litigation response model fits these criteria.

The post-emergency litigation response model makes three basic assumptions:

1. Each post-emergency lawsuit will have themes in common with the vast majority, if not all, of the other post-emergency lawsuits.

2. Most, if not all, of these themes can be anticipated immediately through careful post-riot analysis.

3. Event reconstruction of the critical decisions and staff/inmate actions defining each theme can be well under way before the first lawsuit is received and completed long before the first case goes to trial.

Post-emergency litigation response is designed to minimize, or eliminate, the three routine legal response event reconstruction problems identified earlier. Because these problems weaken staff credibility critical to vindication in court, they will be discussed in some detail.

- **Faulty memory.** Riot management is an extremely stressful activity. Psychological trauma and fatigue can blot out critical pieces of information that later will become a significant, and perhaps controversial, issue in court. Good managers attempt to keep a written log of important events during a riot, but decisions have to be made so quickly under such extremely difficult circumstances that accurate record keeping suffers. Line staff caught up in the violence and chaos of the riot cannot be expected to maintain any type of useful log. Information that is not documented may be forgotten or distorted before the first lawsuit is received. The inability to recall critical information years later, or a recall that differs significantly from that of other staff, can produce a "weak link" witness or defendant whose testimony may create holes in the defense presentation that may sway a jury to believe the plaintiff.

• **Lack of staff supportive physical evidence.** Staff must prove that proper procedures were followed; beatings, or other forms of abuse, did not occur; and all decisions being litigated were made on the basis of sound correctional management requirements, not on the basis of retaliation or pettiness. Credibility may be weakened by (1) the lack of a comprehensive staff supportive videotape record, backed up by photographs, of riot damage and key post-emergency inmate management activities, such as moving inmates from one location to another; feeding inmates; taking water to inmates; distributing clothing, bedding, and personal hygiene items; providing toilet facilities; providing medical care; and removing handcuffs that are too tight; (2) the lack of paper documentation, such as medical records, duty rosters, transfer logs, time-on-duty records, identification of videotape and photographic evidence, critical meeting minutes, and incident reports. Defendant credibility problems created by faulty memories may be increased by the lack of staff supportive physical evidence.

• **Inaccurate documentation.** Poorly written reports that contradict other reports, incomplete duty rosters, poorly maintained block logs, poorly organized personnel records, incomplete minutes of step-down meetings, incident reports that leave out critical information, and medical records with conspicuous time gaps will be exploited by opposing counsel at the trial, often with embarrassing results for the defendant. Inaccurate information may, in some cases, create a greater defendant credibility problem than missing information.

Once event reconstruction is complete, there remain two additional areas of potential concern:

• **Staff unfamiliarity with the judicial process, especially regarding the jury.** Many correctional staff are uncomfortable with the formal legal structure of the courtroom. This discomfort may create credibility problems. For example, officers grinning and laughing in the back of the courtroom in an attempt to discharge tension may not realize that the jury seeing this behavior may interpret it as contempt for the judicial process. Staff may not appreciate the role of the judge as he or she attempts to guide an inmate representing himself through the complicated court process, an activity frequently interpreted and resented by staff as constituting judicial favoritism towards the inmate.

• **The psychological stress of appearing in court.** Testifying in court can be an anxiety-arousing experience under the best of circumstances. A response to allegations of inappropriate conduct or faulty decision making that involves cross-examination by an inmate convicted of participating in the riot can be extremely stressful. Staff may be overly aggressive on the stand because of their negative feelings about the inmate, the riot, and the lawsuit. Overly aggressive responses may be misinterpreted by the jury as proof that the defendant is indeed capable of committing the alleged abuses.

Routine legal response event reconstruction and court appearance issues may be addressed successfully by incorporating into institutional emergency plans a post-emergency litigation response model that provides for offering staff preemergency legal training, documenting decisions made during an emergency, developing and activating a multiagency Litigation Response Team, preparing staff before testimony, offering counseling support for staff called to testify, and conducting mandatory post-trial debriefing. This model will be described by taking certain elements and relating them to the Camp Hill riots.

Preemergency Legal Training of Correctional Staff. Training staff about legal issues at the academy level should include an initial exposure to the courtroom experience that goes beyond dry lectures. This initial exposure may include:

• Staging mock trial situations in the academy setting

• Conducting role playing in front of the training class and in small group situations

• Conducting plaintiff role playing by inmates, especially those with actual court experience, or by lawyers with experience

• Observing an actual trial involving correctional staff

• Viewing videotaped testimony (both staff and inmate) in an actual case

• Using case studies, preferably presented by an experienced attorney, that graphically show negative consequences resulting from inadequate testimony

Decision Documentation During the Emergency. Decisions made before, during, and after the riot, especially those decisions made quickly because of time constraints, will be subjected to intensive scrutiny by attorneys and judges for years after the event. Accurate recall of the decision-making process is critical to a successful legal response. Any attempt to

maintain a personal written log, as this author soon discovered during the first riot, is doomed to failure because of time constraints and the sheer number of critical decisions to be made in an atmosphere of chaos, confusion, noise, and fear.

However, two methods of effective decision documentation that will produce a permanent and accurate reference for event reconstruction are available to the decision maker. The first method involves using a portable tape recorder to maintain a running log while moving from decision to decision. A great deal of information may be verbally recorded in a minute or two. Or, if personnel resources permit, a previously identified and trained stenographer can maintain a running written log. Use of both methods ensures maximum accuracy of recall.

The Litigation Response Team. The Litigation Response Team will have several specific post-emergency functions to be performed by correctional officers, attorneys, counselors, psychologists, and clerical staff. The activities of the Litigation Response Team should be coordinated by one person, the litigation response coordinator. This person should be able to organize and manage large amounts of information under trying conditions and be able to communicate with all levels of staff, including those from other agencies.

Representatives of law enforcement and other emergency response agencies called into service during response and recovery should be included in the Litigation Response Team and should help develop an emergency plan that will establish their role in these activities clearly. Each agency should be involved in all emergency plan training, exercises, and debriefing.

The Litigation Response Team is responsible for performing six critical legal response functions:

1. Talk to inmates and line staff as soon as possible after the emergency to determine the common litigation themes being discussed. These themes should be reported to legal debriefing teams immediately.

2. Debrief, *as soon after the emergency as possible*, all administrators and command staff who have played a role in emergency management. The most effective debriefing is accomplished by the team of attorneys who will represent correctional staff. Debriefing by attorneys serves three critical functions: *(a)* review of all decisions from a legal perspective immediately after they have been made; *(b)* establishment of a "decision tree" that defines every major decision made during and after the riots, the participants in the decision-making process, the rationale, and the individuals who implemented the decision; *(c)* preservation of the client-attorney relationship necessary to maintain the confidentiality of debriefing records and correspondence. Debriefing immediately should establish a decision tree for:

• Preemergency administrative decisions that may have helped trigger the event. Camp Hill debriefing would have focused on (1) the preriot decisions to eliminate Family Day visits and restructure medical policy, (2) the decision to not conduct an immediate institutional shakedown and to let most of the state police return to regular duty after the first riot had ended, (3) the perception that the institution was secure after the first riot.

• Emergency management decisions. In the case of Camp Hill, these were not an issue in inmate litigation. However, the shooting, and wounding, of several inmates during the retaking of the institution after the second riot easily could have become a serious issue if fatalities had occurred.

• Post-emergency management decisions. Camp Hill debriefing would have focused on *(a)* moving all Group II and III inmates to the main stockade field after the riots, *(b)* meeting inmate basic needs, including medical needs, while on the field, *(c)* transferring inmates to state and federal institutions, *(d)* removing and disposing destroyed inmate property from the Group II and III cell blocks before renovation, *(e)* meeting needs and maintenance of inmates in lockdown status after return to three of the renovated blocks, *(f)* managing the 800 Group I inmates not involved in the riots, *(g)* removing personal wear items from Group II and III inmates, *(h)* removing restricted housing unit inmate personal property, *(i)* detailing the step-down process that returned the institution to normal operations.

When constructing the decision tree for each decision, all the factors taken into consideration, especially the pros and cons, should be documented. Attorneys should be made aware of any significant differences of opinion among staff before implementation of a particular course of action as quickly as possible. Debriefing results should be maintained by the debriefing team in a central data bank that is systematically updated and cross-referenced. This central data bank will provide the foundation for all future legal response.

As litigation pours into the system, the initial debriefing results can be reviewed. Additional debriefing sessions may be scheduled as subsequent litigation sets forth new allegations and raises additional questions. Staff who did not participate in the initial debriefing may be identified and debriefed. The original data bank may be expanded, as necessary.

This process should be coordinated by the litigation response coordinator. If done properly, event reconstruction for the vast majority of lawsuits will begin while memories are fresh and vital documents are readily available and will be completed long before the first trial date arrives.

3. As soon as the emergency begins prepare a visual record of all major events by using camcorder and photography equipment. In the case of a riot, visual record teams should be filming all inmate riot activities. This film will be invaluable when the rioters are prosecuted in criminal court. Attempts to retake the institution always should be filmed, as should all inmate surrenders. Once the institution is secure, visual record teams should enter the institution and systematically film all physical damage, carefully recording time, date, place, and the name of the camcorder operator or photographer. In several Camp Hill cases, key photographs were not allowed into evidence by the judge because the defense could not establish the factual basis of time, date, specific cell block, and photographer.

All physical injuries to staff, especially those taken hostage or otherwise trapped by rioting inmates, should be filmed and photographed. All activities involving inmates (such as feeding, availability of toilet facilities, distribution of clothing and personal necessity items, medical care, and any other situation with the potential for litigation) should be filmed and all identifying information recorded. The movement of inmates always should be filmed

because it is during movement from location to location that a large number of inmate allegations of brutality will originate. This type of visual record would have greatly improved defendant response to many Camp Hill beating lawsuits.

All filming should be backed up by photographs for easy presentation to a jury. Photographs of the main stockade field conditions were invaluable in winning a number of cases. Many jurors regard visual evidence as concrete proof that staff are telling the truth and the plaintiff is lying. Presenting photographs and videotape evidence can shorten the length of the trial significantly. However, only litigation response team members should have permission to film. Amateur filming should be prohibited. Amateur films tend to be flawed, nonsystematic, and of such poor quality that they can weaken a case by confusing the jury.

The number of visual record teams necessary depends on the size of the institution and the worst case scenario presented in the emergency plan. All equipment and training needs should be established during routine emergency plan training.

4. Ensure that the assignment of all personnel, regardless of agency, is recorded accurately. Event reconstruction that involves tracking down who was where, when, and why they were there, and what they were doing, years after the riot, will waste countless hours. In the case of Camp Hill, numerous correctional staff and state troopers were named, or at least referenced, in inmate litigation, yet their assignment at the time of alleged violations of inmate rights often was unclear.

The frustration and time lost trying to establish assignments and locations after years had passed would have been avoided if specific officers, or clerks, accurately recorded the shift assignments of all personnel who were in contact with inmates.

5. Ensure that officers are properly maintaining all block logs and other documents that will later be shown in court. A Litigation Response Team commissioned officer should visit each housing area (permanent or temporary), including the infirmary, at least twice a day to check the block logs and any other documents used to record staff and inmate activity. All documents should be checked for proper recording of routine officer activities, such as handing out basic necessities; response to inmate medical complaints (there will be an extraordinary number of these after a riot); transfer of inmates within the block, and out of the block; the names of escort officers; reports of inmate aggression or destructive behavior with staff response to those behaviors; and recording of all staff assignments, with the supervisor clearly identified.

Lack of documentation should be pointed out to staff and corrected by submission of a follow-up report. Cross-outs, writing between the lines of a logbook, writing in the margins, and entries placed in the log at a later date than the activity occurred should be minimized, because these practices may be interpreted by jurors as clumsy after-the-fact attempts by staff to falsify the record.

Staff may balk at these requirements because these duties are time consuming and tedious, but if staff don't follow proper procedures immediately after the riot, they may suffer the negative effects of having to defend sloppy log entries in front of a critical jury, or the case may be weakened because of the inadequate entries.

The Litigation Response Team should be especially sensitive to the presence of any derogatory comments, racial slurs, vulgarity, or scatological references to inmates recorded by frustrated staff. This type of material can be extremely damaging to the defense position that staff who write childish log entries are actually professional, competent, and nonvindictive individuals incapable of doing what has been alleged.

6. Ensure that all documentation (log books, personnel time sheets, duty rosters, incident reports, transfer logs, medical records, and so forth) are removed from the origination site immediately and safely preserved in a specified records area under the control of the litigation response coordinator so they are available to the defense team in the years that follow the riot. If this is not done, valuable documentation may be misplaced or destroyed, especially if staff retire or transfer to other institutions. Original documents, not photocopies, should be stored. Photocopies of all documentation should be given to the attorneys as quickly as possible for addition to their central data bank.

Preparation of Staff for Trial Appearance. Staff scheduled to testify always should be provided a pretrial briefing on court protocol by an attorney. The eight basic elements of presenting well before a jury include the following:

1. Dress appropriately. Dark blue or gray suit or sports jacket with white shirt and conservative tie for men. Conservative attire for women. Do not testify in uniform. Many civilians do not respond well to correctional uniforms.

2. Be respectful to both judge and jury. Always stand when the judge or jury enters and leave the room. Do not sit until both the judge and jury are seated.

3. Be professional at all times, not just while in the courtroom. Members of the jury may see staff on the street outside the courthouse, in the hallway before the trial, or during lunch if a common dining area is shared. Horseplay, vulgar language, or wisecracking will offend jurors.

4. Clearly understand the question before responding. If the question is not understood, ask that it be repeated. Do not rush into any answer. If the answer is unknown, or can't be recalled, acknowledge that fact and wait for the next question. Staff are not expected to know everything. Do not try to fake an answer, speculate, or try to recreate from memory a situation or behavior that has faded with the passage of time.

5. Speak slowly and clearly during testimony. Direct all responses to the person who is asking the question, especially if it is the judge. Always address the judge as "Your Honor." Do not address a female judge as "Ma'am." Use correctional jargon only when necessary and immediately explain it in laypersons terms.

6. Do not allow anger or irritation to show during cross-examination. If a defendant can be provoked in a courtroom, this lack of control may convince a jury that the defendant also can be provoked into inappropriate behavior while on the job and, thus, may be guilty of the behavior alleged.

7. When excused from the witness stand, either take a seat or leave the courtroom as

quickly and quietly as possible. If staying in the courtroom, do not joke, talk, or otherwise show disrespect for the proceedings.

8. Be respectful to the plaintiff, no matter how absurd or provocative the allegations made by that individual and his or her inmate witnesses. No matter what the inmate may have done during the riot, no matter how emotional staff may be about the riot and any personal consequences they or their colleagues suffered, disrespect to the plaintiff will only hurt staff credibility.

9. Do not display hostility toward private counsel representing the plaintiff. Even if provoked by the inmate's attorney, do not become hostile. A jury will note the hostility and remember it during its deliberations.

Counseling Support for Staff Called to Testify. Testifying before judge and jury can cause anxiety under normal circumstances. The experience of being cross-examined by a plaintiff who was involved in a major disturbance can be extremely troubling. If the Camp Hill lawsuits are representative of post-riot litigation, there is a high probability that at least some of the plaintiffs will have been rioters convicted of taking staff hostage, brutalizing them, and helping destroy the institution. Having done all that, these same inmates later demand compensation for alleged staff misbehavior. Intense negative emotions can be aroused by just the thought of being in this type of situation. It was this author's experience that being cross-examined by a riot-convicted plaintiff was much more stressful than being questioned by private counsel. The Post-traumatic Assessment Team should be prepared to provide certification of staff inability to testify if that is needed. Sensitivity to the pretrial concerns and issues of staff taken hostage or otherwise injured during the riot is essential.

Post-trial Debriefing. After the last trial is completed, the major participants in the litigation will assess the strengths and weaknesses of the post-emergency litigation response management and make any modifications necessary for future emergencies. This debriefing should be comprehensive, with no artificial time constraints that would serve to limit the process.

Although the focus in this chapter was the Litigation Response Team response to a riot, the post-emergency litigation response model may be applied to any emergency where larger than normal volumes of inmate litigation are expected. The positive results of including a post-emergency litigation response model in the emergency plan are well worth the initial time and energy spent on developing the plan.

Chapter 25

Healing the Silent Wounds

A *personal note which I will share with you, is I found that even the inmates, for the most part, felt a profound sense of loss. They reacted in a true spirit. They were on their best behavior during the evacuation of Renz, as well as when other inmates were used throughout our state to assist with numerous relief operations. Inmates even gave money to relief organizations. At $7.50 per month average wage, a donation of a few dollars represented a sacrifice on the inmates' part. Staff and inmates worked side-by-side . . . .*

At the onset of the great flood, several of our staff even brought their own boats to help remove property from Renz Correctional Facility . . . even though Renz was an old facility, the staff had a sense of ownership in it. They had gone through many less severe floods before. They fought to save Renz Correctional Center. They lost in the end, but their spirit was wonderful. After the water receded, staff returned to view Renz Correctional Center for the final time. Some cried. Many wanted to return and rebuild. This was not possible. They all did their best, above and beyond (Schreiber 1995:2).

A major emergency forever changes a correctional facility. Damaged buildings are demolished and replaced, or renovated; fences are added or removed; the physical reality of the facility is permanently altered. Staff and inmates adjust to the new physical environment and may be openly pleased by the new and improved buildings, although often there is nostalgia for those parts of the physical plant that were unique and now are gone forever. Physical reconstruction issues are easily resolved, especially with the higher-than-normal level of funding that commonly follows an emergency.

However, those connected with facilities affected by emergencies need to heal emotionally, and this is not an easy process. The emotional wounds of fear, anger, and loss of a basic sense of personal security too often are hidden and silent until it is too late to do anything about them. Every employee and inmate who was present at Camp Hill during the 1989 riots now knows with absolute certainty that his or her world can collapse around them at any time, without warning, without mercy. Even staff who were off duty when the riots occurred experience a sinking feeling in the pit of their stomach when they think about what might have happened to them if they had been on duty. And the inevitable question for everyone has become: What if I *am* at work the next time it happens?

There is no easy answer to this question. Many staff accept the uncertainty of their job and give no outward sign of the anxiety that wakes them up in the middle of the night. Other staff accept the uncertainty and function normally because of their religion, or background, or ability to emotionally tolerate uncertainty. Some staff, unable to face the possibility of being caught in the next riot, or the next fire, or the next flood, find they can no longer live with the question and leave corrections. Others try to ignore the possibility of an emergency situation—they may drink a little too much or snap at the family more than they like, but they stick with the job. Some think about suicide; a few attempt it. The healing process faces some potent obstacles: the political aftermath, staff doubt, line staff fear of scapegoating, administrative staff fear of scapegoating, administrative "circling of wagons," public confrontations, inadequate preparation for post-traumatic stress disorder, and community fears.

The Political Aftermath

During recovery from an emergency, especially an inmate-precipitated emergency, there can be a very divisive period of political intrusion (referred to as "dog-and-pony shows" by a perceptive co-worker) into the life of the institution as staff struggle to put the pieces back together. After the Camp Hill riots, key administrative staff had to be on call constantly to repeatedly answer the same questions in investigations being conducted by the Department of Corrections, the Pennsylvania Senate Judiciary Committee, the Pennsylvania House of Representatives Judiciary Committee, the Inspector General's Office, the Adams Commission (representing the Governor), the

union representing correctional officers, politicians interested in running for governor, and the media.

Following the escape of ten inmates from the Ryan Correctional Facility in Detroit, Michigan, the *Detroit Free Press*, in a series of articles under the banner headline of "Police Suspect An Inside Job," ran an article titled "From Governor Down, Accusations Are Flying":

> *Just about anyone involved in the operation, management or oversight of the state prison system had a theory on the breakout Monday. Among the most prominent were spokesmen for Gov. John Engler, who finds himself holding a stick of political dynamite only 10 weeks before he faces re-election . . . . His office went on the offensive Monday, citing negligence by corrections officers at the scene. "It's clear that what happened was staff breakdown," said Engler spokesman John Truscott* (Front page and 3A).

The Governor's position was that the Ryan Correctional Facility was adequately staffed and policies were in place to stop an escape. The failure rested on the staff who had not followed those policies.

In the same article, spokespersons for the Michigan Corrections Organization (the union) claimed that efforts were being made to scapegoat correctional officers for an escape "that was largely attributable to understaffing and poor management" (page 3A). The Department of Corrections did not cite staff failure specifically, but when the director suspended several officers:

> *Indirectly, though, he was critical of the response of three guards who were supposed to be watching the yard. McGinnis said the guards did not attempt to interrupt the escape by force* (page 2a).

Union officials challenged the adequacy of the classification process at the Ryan Correctional Facility at the time of the escape, suggesting that mistakes had been made and the facility was housing dangerous felons it was not equipped to manage. There was a general criticism of inadequate security being provided by administrators. Reporters noted that the Michigan Department of Corrections' efforts to make critical security changes had been tied up in federal court since 1988, as the result of inmate litigation before a judge who was out of town and unavailable for comment.

Investigations are sometimes necessary, but all too often the agenda of the investigators is political, not fact finding. Time that administrators and supervisors should be spending with staff and inmates is consumed by responding to personal attacks and repeatedly defending administrative decisions and actions. Post-emergency political investigations can shatter staff solidarity by encouraging internal finger pointing that can become extremely disruptive if it sets in motion the following process of staff destabilization:

Staff Doubt. Political and public speculation dutifully reported through the media can persuade line staff to believe administrators caused the emergency, made the wrong decisions during response, or were indifferent to the safety of staff.

Line Staff Fear of Administrative Scapegoating. Line staff involved in critical response and recovery activities quickly can develop the perception that legitimate internal investigations being conducted by facility and/or central office Intelligence Units represent the administration's efforts to scapegoat them.

Facility Administrative Staff Fear of Scapegoating. Top administrators at the facility may quickly develop a sense that they are being targeted for scapegoating for political reasons, either by the agency administrator or the governor, or both. Administrative paranoia may develop quickly during recovery as rumors circulate.

Administrative Circling of the Wagons. Facility administrators perceiving that they are under attack from politicians eager to make headlines, a media anxious to sell newspapers and advertising space, a public frightened by the level of uncertainty created by the emergency, line staff with personal survival agendas, and superiors with political agendas tend to focus on career survival, often becoming too suspicious to talk to staff and inmates or anyone outside of their inner circle.

Public Confrontations. Because administrators and line staff come to believe they are under attack from the very people they should be able to depend on for support and assistance, they quickly can be drawn into ugly public confrontations pitting administrators against individual line staff, facility staff against central office staff, and union against management. These public attacks and counterattacks can seriously weaken the public's confidence in correctional staff, increase staff destabilization, and create a massive breakdown in communication that will prevent, or delay, healing.

Inadequate Preparation for Post-traumatic Stress Disorder Management. If post-traumatic stress disorder is not a specific target of strategic planning, staff and inmate personal problems can continue to plague a facility for years:

> *If feelings of guilt and stress are left unresolved, they can lead to even more serious troubles, such as drug and alcohol abuse, marital problems, work absenteeism and severe mood swings . . . . "It's very important not to let yourself get stuck in guilt and blame . . . . It can actually make you sick"* (Wallace 1993:45).

Staff may respond to their symptoms by lashing out at correctional administrators because of a perception that the system does not care. Ugly stories in the local newspaper about system indifference to the battered survivor of a riot, for example, can damage the reputation of corrections, in general, and the emergency-stricken facility in particular. Individuals and organizations with an ax to grind always find post-traumatic stress disorder situations that suggest the system does not care about its employees. Staff returning to work may be fearful of the reaction they will receive from staff not injured in the emergency:

> *My biggest concern was how the other officers would accept me. Would they feel guilty around him? he wondered. Uneasy about not storming the prison to rescue him and the other hostages? "I mean, did the other officers feel that they'd let us down?" he asks. "That they didn't do anything to*

> *save us, didn't come in and get us out of there, and now I'm back to rub it in their face? Anytime you feel embarrassed around a person what you do is you avoid them. Would they do that to me? I didn't know."* (Porter 1995:76).

Inmates and staff who experience post-traumatic stress disorder but don't recognize the symptoms for what they are can become a significant problem long after the emergency, a problem that could be avoided through proper attention during recovery. In the case of post-traumatic stress disorder, recovery may last for years.

A particularly potent issue in post-traumatic stress disorders is anger management. Staff may experience feelings of anger, especially if they were taken hostage or injured, for a long time to come. However, anger does not have to come from personal injury. A maintenance trades supervisor finding his shop in ruins may experience the anger of being violated. That anger may flare up in times of stress and frustration that occur years after the emergency that generated them. Supervisors should be constantly alert for signs of anger surfacing and be ready to talk to the individual affected and make any counseling referral necessary.

Community Fears. When an inmate-precipitated emergency has occurred, the community may experience a sense of fear out of proportion to the actual danger presented by the existence of the facility in the community. Despite the fact that no inmates escaped during the 1989 Camp Hill riots, there was public discussion for more than a year after the riots of the need to level the facility and allow contractors to use the land for private residential development. Inevitably, correctional staff experience a sense of estrangement and isolation from the community. Community concerns often are fanned by politicians and the media as they respond to community concerns. The issue of dangerous inmates at the Ryan Correctional Facility brought a response from the former mayor of Detroit:

> *Young said Monday that then-Gov. James Blanchard personally assured him that no dangerous felons would be kept at Ryan . . . . "That was a specific part of the agreement in 1985," Young said. "It was on the basis of that assurance that I went to that community, argued in favor of the prison"* (page 3a).

Local residents expressed concern about the long-term effects of having a prison located in their community:

> *But community leaders say the prison has undermined the neighborhoods. Willie Segars, who lives in Conant Gardens said many of her friends have moved out because of the prison. Segars fears the escape may hasten the flight and that property values will drop* (page 3a).

Another politician suggested:

> *. . . that all inmates should be required to wear brightly colored uniforms emblazoned with "STATE PRISONER"* (page 3a).

A Plan of Action for Healing the Silent Wounds

The process of emotional healing is time consuming and demanding, but can be encouraged through activities designed to achieve high-visibility communication, foster a positive work environment, help staff regain a sense of control, and regain community trust.

Achieve High-visibility Communication. Administrators should maximize their visibility within the facility during recovery. Staff and inmates alike need the reassurance offered by the high visibility of administrative staff, even if they can't verbalize that need easily. The presence of administrative staff on the grounds provides an antidote to lingering feelings of helplessness and powerlessness. An administrator openly talking to staff and inmates about the emergency, sharing experiences, fears, concerns, and hopes and plans for the future, creates a sense of concern and sharing that can aid in healing:

> *. . . the lessons learned were important. As in other disasters around our country, people from the heartland stood together— worked together, cried together and laughed together* (Schreiber 1995:2).

Foster a Positive Work Environment. In a positive work environment, staff can seek support from their colleagues. The ability to talk to others who have shared a traumatic experience can be invaluable. Sharing should be encouraged by giving staff the opportunity to tell their individual stories to staff at other facilities as well as to each other. The process of telling the story helps develop perspective and relieves bottled-up emotions. In a positive work environment, learning from the experience is encouraged. Mistakes can be the best teacher. They should be admitted, and their lessons applied to strategic planning. Staff should be encouraged to seek therapy if they are experiencing symptoms of post-traumatic stress disorder. There should be no sense of shame, official or otherwise, attached to the need for therapy. Part of emotional recovery is learning to accept what can't be changed (Wallace 1993:45-46).

Help Staff Regain a Basic Sense of Control. An emergency can leave staff fearful that the worst is yet to come. They need to regain their preemergency sense of control:

> *Preparation is one of the best antidotes . . . . If you know what to expect in a crisis—and you've done all that you can to prepare for it—you'll have a greater sense of control if an accident does occur and far less guilt and anxiety* (Wallace 1993:45).

In part, this antidote can be achieved by maximizing staff participation in the application of postmortem information to: (1) modify the original emergency plan; (2) disseminate new knowledge through modifying Academy and in-service training curriculum, publishing articles, presenting papers at national conferences, and making public speaking engagements; (3) renovate the facility; and (4) design and construct new facilities.

Regain the Trust of the Community. Community fears usually are most extreme when the emergency has been inmate precipitated. Administrators should make a conscious effort to reassure the community that lessons

have been learned during response and recovery and are being used for level 2 mitigation. The public information officer can play a significant role in this effort by issuing periodic press releases, appearing on talk shows and at public meetings, and rapidly responding to requests for information. Administrators should be willing to meet with concerned citizens, politicians, and the media.

If the emergency is not inmate precipitated, inmates and staff can increase community acceptance by working with the community as recently happened in Illinois:

> *At Meredosia, 560 convicts have been working 12-hour shifts since last week, shoring up levees, and were on tornado cleanup duty for two weeks before that. "There's nothing wrong with helping people save a town," said Jim Compton . . . . Townspeople have made it clear they appreciate the help of inmates* (Patriot News 1995b).

An emergency does not have to be the end of the world. Adversity can make individuals and staff stronger. The reality is that correctional emergencies are part of the professional learning process. Wise individuals accept that process and use the emergency to become stronger and wiser.

References

Abbott, John. 1991. *In the belly of the beast: Letters from prison.* New York: Vintage Books/Random House.

Adams, Arlin M., George M. Leader, and Leroy K. Irvis. 1989. *The final report of the Governor's Commission to investigate disturbances at Camp Hill Correctional Institution* (21 December).

Alexander, D. 1985. "Death and injury in earthquakes." *Disasters* 9 (1): 57-60.

Allen, Harry E., and Clifford E. Simonsen. 1995. *Corrections in America: An introduction,* 7th Edition. Englewood Cliffs, N.J.: Prentice Hall.

American Correctional Association. 1990. *Riots and disturbances in correctional institutions,* 3d Edition. Laurel, Md.: ACA.

———. 1991. *Vital statistics in corrections.* Laurel, Md.: ACA.

———. 1993. *Gangs in correctional facilities: A national assessment (preliminary results).* Laurel, Md.: ACA. Unpublished.

Arizona Department of Corrections. 1993. *Incident management system manual.* Phoenix, Ariz.: Arizona Department of Corrections.

Associated Press. 1996. "Oops." *The Patriot News,* Harrisburg, Pa. (11 January).

Avoyelles Correctional Center. 1995. *Policy and procedure,* No. 02-05-013. Avoyelles, La.: Avoyelles Correctional Center.

Bartolas, Clemens, and John P. Conrad. 1992. *Introduction to corrections,* 2nd Edition. New York: HarperCollins Publishers, Inc.

Baugh, Dennis G. 1992. "ACA gang survey examines national control strategies." *Corrections Today* 54 (July).

Blaikie, Piers, et al. 1994. *At risk: Natural hazards, people's vulnerability & disasters.* New York: Routledge.

Bone, Roger C., ed. 1994. "Consensus statement on the triage of critically ill patients." *Journal of American Medicine* 271 (15): 1200-1203

Bowker, L. 1980. *Prison victimization.* New York: Elsevier Books.

———. 1985. "An essay on prison violence." In *Prison violence in America,* ed. M. Braswell, S. Dillingham, and R. Montgomery, Jr. Cincinnati: Anderson Publishing Co.

———. 1982. "Victimizers and victims in American correctional institutions." In *The pains of imprisonment,* ed. Robert Johnson and Hans Toch. Beverly Hills, Calif.: Sage Publications.

Boyle, Philip J., and James G. Ricketts. 1992. "Using technology to achieve higher efficiency in correctional facilities." *Corrections Today* 54 (5).

Braun, Mile M., et al. 1989. "Increasing incidence of tuberculosis in a prison inmate population." *Journal of the American Medical Association* 261 (3).

Buentello, Salvador. 1992. "Combating gangs in Texas." *Corrections Today* 54 (July).

Bursztajn, Harold J., et al. 1995. "Recognizing post-traumatic stress." *Patient Care.*

California Department of Corrections. 1991. *Design and Construction Bulletin.* Sacramento: California Department of Corrections.

————. 1995. *Design criteria guidelines.* Sacramento: California Department of Corrections.

Clayton, Susan. 1996. "27 inmates escape Honduran jail." *Corrections Today* 58(1).

Cochrane, H. C. 1975. *Natural hazards and their distributive effects.* Boulder, Colo.: University of Colorado, Institute of Behavioral Science. National Science Foundation Program on Technology, Environment-Man Monograph NSF-RA-E-75-003.

Coughlin, Thomas A., III. 1991. *The Commissioner's investigation: Incident at South Port May 28-29, 1991.* N.Y. State Department of Correctional Services.

Cullen, Murray. 1992. *Cage your rage.* Laurel, Md.: American Correctional Association.

C.V. Mosby Company. 1983. "Triage." In *Mosby's medical and nursing dictionary.* St. Louis, Mo.: The C.V. Mosby Company.

Danto, Bruce L. 1973. "The suicidal inmate." In *Jail house blues.* Orchard Lake, Mich.: Epic Publications.

Detroit Free Press. 1994. "Police suspect an inside job: Chief hints at arrests; one fugitive found dead." *Detroit Free Press* (23 August).

DiIulio, John, Jr. 1987. *Governing prisons: A comparative study of correctional management.* New York: The Free Press.

DiMaggio, Jerome. 1992. *Riot briefing memo.* Sacramento: California Department of Corrections.

Dinitz, Simon. 1981. "Are safe and humane prisons possible?" *Australia-New Zealand Journal of Criminology* (14 March).

Durham, Alexis M. 1994. *Crisis and reform: Current issues in American punishment.* Boston: Little, Brown.

The Evening News. 1995. "Inmates face charges stemming from riot." Harrisburg, Pa., *The Evening News* (9 September): B2.

Fagan, Thomas J. 1994. "Helping hostages and their families through critical response." *Corrections Today* 56(4):78-84.

Farrington, D., and C. Nuttall. 1985. "Prison size, overcrowding, prison violence, and recidivism." In *Prison violence in America,* ed. M. Braswell, S. Dillingham, and R. Montgomery, Jr. Cincinnati: Anderson Publishing Co.

Federal Bureau of Prisons. 1994. *State of the Bureau: Emergency preparedness and response.* Washington, D.C.: U.S. Department of Justice.

———. 1995. "Close call for MDC Guayn-abo." *Monday Morning Highlights*, U.S. Department of Justice (11 September).

Federal Emergency Management Agency. 1990. *Guide for the development of state and local emergency operation plans.* Washington, D.C.: Federal Emergency Management Agency.

———. 1993. *Emergency management guide for business and industry.* Washington, D.C.: Federal Emergency Management Agency.

Ferguson, Diane. 1995. "How to handle a bomb threat." *Nursing* 95 (October).

Figley, C. R. 1983. "Catastrophes: An overview of family reactions." In *Stress and the Family: Coping with Catastrophe* 2, ed. C. R. Figley and H. I. McCubbin. New York: Brunner/Mazel, pp. 3-20.

Fox, Vernon B., and Jeanne B. Stinchcomb. 1994. *Introduction to corrections*, 4th edition. Englewood Cliffs, N.J.: Prentice Hall Career-Technology.

Gaes, G., and W. McGuire. 1985. "Prison violence: The contribution of crowding and other determinants of prison assault rates." *Journal of Research in Crime and Delinquency* 22 (1).

Gershuny, J. 1982. "The choice of scenarios." In *Reaching decisions in public policy and administration*, ed. Richard D. Bingham and Marcuse E. Ethridge. New York: Longman.

Goffman, Erving. 1961. *Asylums: Essays on the social situation of mental patients and other inmates.* Garden City, N.Y.: Anchor Books.

Gondles, James A., Jr. 1992. "Learning to plan for the unplannable." *Corrections Today* (December).

Hall, Betty. 1993. "Terror in the towers: A media relations pro tells his story." *Public Relations Journal.*

Hammett, Theodore M. 1986. "AIDS in prison and jails: Issues and options." *Research in Brief.* Washington, D.C.: National Institute of Justice.

Hammett, Theodore M., and Andrea L. Daugherty, 1991. *1990 update: AIDS in correctional facilities.* Washington, D.C.: National Institute of Justice.

Hawkins, Richard, and Geoffrey P. Alpert. 1989. *American prison systems: Punishment & justice.* Englewood Cliffs, N.J.: Prentice Hall.

Hayes, Lindsay M., and Joseph R. Rowan. 1988. *National study of suicides: Seven years later.* Alexandria, Va.: National Center on Institutions and Alternatives.

Henderson, James D. 1990. *Riots and disturbances in correctional institutions.* Laurel, Md.: American Correctional Association.

Houston, James. 1995. *Correctional management: Functions, skills, and systems.* Chicago: Nelson-Hall, Inc.

Irwin, John. 1970. *The felon.* Englewood Cliffs, N.J.: Prentice Hall.

Jenkins, B., et al. 1977. *Numbered lives: Some statistical observations from 77 international hostage episodes.* Santa Monica, Calif.: Rand Corporation.

Johnson, R. 1987. *Hard time: Understanding and reforming the prison.* Monterey, Calif.: Brooks/Cole Publishing Company.

Kunzman, Eugene E. 1995. "Preventing suicide in jails." *Corrections Today* 57 (6).

Labecki, Lee Ann S. 1994. "Avoiding prison disturbances through environmental scanning." *Corrections Today* 56 (5).

Lockwood, D. 1980. *Prison sexual violence.* New York: Elsevier Books.

Lockwood, Daniel. 1982. "Reducing prison sexual violence." In *The pains of imprisonment,* ed. Robert Johnson and Hans Toch. Beverly Hills, Calif.: Sage.

Mannon, James M. 1981. *Emergency encounters: A study of an urban ambulance service.* Port Washington, N.Y: Kennikat Press Corp.

Martinez, Ricardo, and Joseph P. Waeckerie. 1991. "Catastrophes at sporting events: A team physician's pivotal role." *The Physician and Sportsmedicine* 19 (11):40-44.

Mascari, Ruth B. 1993. "Taking a statewide approach to emergency management planning." *Corrections Today* (April).

Mathews, Tom. 1992. "Fire & fury: America on trial." *Newsweek* (11 May).

Mays, Larry G., and William Taggart. 1985. "The impact of litigation on changing New Mexico prison conditions." *Prison Journal* (Spring/Summer).

McFadden, Robert C. 1991. "Mandatory testing for TB in prisons starts with guards." *New York Times* (19 May).

Mendez, Salvador A. 1992. "Community struggles to prevent youths from joining growing numbers of gangs." *Corrections Today* 54 (5).

Milne, A. 1986. *Floodshock: The drowning of planet Earth.* Gloucester: Alan Sutton.

Nacci, P. L. and T. R. Kane. 1982. *Sexual aggression in federal prisons.* Washington, D.C.: U.S. Department of Justice.

———. 1984. "Sex and sexual aggression in federal prisons: Inmate involvement and employee impact." *Federal Probation* 8:45-63.

Nagel, William G. 1973. *The new red barn: A critical look at the modern American prison.* New York: Walker.

Nanus, Burt. 1974. "A general model for a criminal justice planning process." *Journal of Criminal Justice* 2 (Winter).

National Fire Protection Association. 1995. *Fire extinguishers in the workplace.* Quincy, Mass.: National Fire Protection Association.

National Research Council. 1975. *Earthquake prediction and public policy.* Washington, D.C.: National Academy of Sciences.

———. 1991. *A safer future: Reducing the impacts of natural disasters.* Washington, D.C.: National Research Council.

Niles, David P. 1991. "War trauma and post-traumatic stress disorder." *American Family Physician.*

Patriot News. 1995a. "Allenwood medium-security facility still in lockdown after riot." *Patriot News* (24 October).

———. 1995b. "Inmates help out with Illinois flood." *Patriot News* (31 May).

———. 1995c. "Inmates made clean break of it." *Patriot News* (8 November).

———. 1995d. "Minimum security, maximum risk." *Patriot News* (22 October).

———. 1995e. "Stormwatch: The Hurricane Luis damage report." *Patriot News* (7 September).

———. 1996. "Fiery California derailment kills 2." *Patriot News* (2 February).

Pennsylvania Emergency Management Agency. 1996. "An ounce of prevention." *Recovery Times* 2 (8 February).

Pennsylvania House Judiciary Committee. 1990. *A report on the 1989 prison disturbance and riots at state correctional institutions at Graterford, Huntington, Rockview, and Camp Hill.* Harrisburg, Pa.: Pennsylvania House Judiciary Committee

Pennsylvania Senate Judiciary Committee. 1990. *After Camp Hill: The keys to ending crisis.* Harrisburg, Pa.: Pennsylvania Senate Judiciary Committee.

Phillips, Richard. 1993. *Improving media relations: A handbook for corrections.* Laurel, Md.: American Correctional Association.

Porter, Bruce. 1995. "Terror on an eight-hour shift." *The New York Times Magazine* (26 November).

Quarentelli, E. L. 1990. *Disaster prevention and mitigation in Lada: Problems and options in planning and implementing in a composite country.* Washington, D.C.: The World Bank. Unpublished paper presented at Colloquium on the Environment and Natural Disaster Management.

Report of the Attorney General. 1980. *Riot at Penitentiary of New Mexico.*

Riley, William. 1992. "A dual approach: Washington penitentiary stresses prevention and reaction." *Corrections Today* 54(5):68-71.

Russell, Heidi. 1995. "Ridge gives awards to 4 prison guards: Heroes relied on new training." *Patriot News.*

Samples, F. P. 1992. "Weathering the storm." *Corrections Today* (December).

Schreiber, Mark S. 1995. Personal letter from assistant to the director, Missouri Division of Adult Institutions, 8 Nov. 1995.

Schultz, Carl H., Kristi L. Koenig, and Erik K. Noji. 1996. "A medical disaster response to reduce immediate mortality after an earthquake." *The New England Journal of Medicine.* 334(7):438-44.

Silverman, Ira J., and Manuel Vega. 1996. *Corrections: A comprehensive view.* St. Paul, Minn.: West Publishing Co.

Skolnick, Andrew A. 1995. "First complex disasters symposium features dramatically timely topics." *Journal of the American Medical Association* 274 (1).

Society of Critical Care Medicine Ethics Committee. 1994. "Consensus statement on the triage of critically ill patients." *Journal of the American Medical Association* 271:1200-3.

Spertzel, Jody K. 1993. "Coping with disaster." *Corrections Today* (December).

Stojkovic, Stan, and Rick Lovell. 1992. *Corrections: An introduction.* Cincinnati: Anderson Publishing Co.

Toch, Hans. 1965. *Institutional violence code, tentative code of the classification of inmate assaults on other inmates.* Report prepared for the California Department of Corrections Research Division.

———. 1977. *Living in prison: The ecology of survival.* New York: The Free Press.

————. 1985. "Social climate and prison violence." In *Prison violence in America*, ed. M. Braswell, S. Dillingham, and R. Montgomery, Jr. Cincinnati: Anderson Publishing Co.

Trout, Craig H. 1992. "BOP Overview: Taking a new look at an old problem." *Corrections Today* 54 (5).

United Nations Disaster Relief Organization. 1989. "Editorial." *UNDRO News* (May-June): 2.

Unwin, Tessa 1994. "Hostage recounts 11 days of terror." *Corrections Today* 56 (August): 66, 68, 70, 72.

USA Today. 1995. "Danish Jail-break." *USA Today.*

Useem, Bert, and Peter Kimball. 1989. *States of siege: U.S. prison riots, 1971-1986.* New York: Oxford University Press.

Wallace, Jean. 1993. "When bad things happen to good safety directors." *Safety and Health.*

Waller, Douglas. 1996. "Nuclear ninjas." *Time* (8 January).

Weiner, Ronald I. 1982. "Management strategies to reduce stress in prison: Humanizing correctional environments." In *The pains of imprisonment,* ed. Robert Johnson and Hans Toch. Beverly Hills, Calif.: Sage.

Wilbanks, William. 1973. "Review of Attica—My story by Russell Oswald." *Criminal Law Bulletin* 9, No. 2: 124-39.

Wiley, William. 1992. "Taking a two-pronged approach to managing Washington's gangs." *Corrections Today* 54 (5).

Wilkinson, Reginald A. 1994. "Lucasville—The aftermath." *Corrections Today* 56 (5):64-65, 74, 76, 101, 143.

Winfree, L. Thomas. 1996. "Attica." In *Encyclopedia of American prisons*, ed. Marilyn D. McShane and Frank P. Williams III. New York: Garland Publishing, Inc, pp. 43-45.

Wright, Erik. 1973. *The politics of punishment.* New York: Harper, Colophon Books.

Wright, Kevin N. 1994. *Effective prison leadership.* Binghamton, N.Y.: William Neil Publishing.

Zausner, S. 1985. *Unusual incident report 1984 calendar year.* Albany, N.Y.: N.Y. State Department of Correctional Services.

Sample Emergency Procedures Checklists

Courtesy the Maryland Department of Corrections

Key to Acronyms:

SERT Special Emergency Responses Team

TAC Tactical Team

VAC Volunteer Activities Coordinator

Revised: 8-1-92

Code 10-33
Mass Disturbance and Hostage Recovery
Emergency Procedure Checklist
Warden/Assistant Warden

Date:

Time:

	Time Task Completed	Initials
1. Report to master control center to be briefed by the shift commander.	_____	_____
2. Assume command of the disturbance situation and direct all activities immediately connected with the situation.	_____	_____
3. Ensure the emergency procedure checklist for the shift commander is being used.	_____	_____
4. Warden or designee will notify and appraise headquarters of division duty officer Phone: (phone number) HDU.	_____	_____
5. Establish situation command team consisting of the following:		
A. Warden/assistant warden	_____	_____
B. One major (from shift on which the incident occurred)	_____	_____
C. Maryland Emergency Management Agency	_____	_____
D. Anne Arundel County Emergency Management	_____	_____
E. Case management supervisor (historian)	_____	_____
6. Establish emergency operations center. Designate security chief as officer in charge.	_____	_____
7. Seek approval from commissioner for the use of force in both mass disturbance and hostage situations unless it is apparent that physical harm has been or is being rendered to hostage and/or third party.	_____	_____
8. Mass Disturbance Plan: Before using force, and when security provisions have been made, announce via the public address system for all those who desire to exit the troubled area to proceed to a designated area.	_____	_____
9. Hostage Recovery Plan: Above information will be relayed by hostage negotiators after consulting with negotiators and the chief psychologist.	_____	_____
10. Mass Disturbance Plan: When prepared to take action, make it known by the public address system or bull horn to the involved inmates: "Authority prevails and order will be maintained. Force will be used if necessary to maintain order."	_____	_____
11. Mass Disturbance Plan: If appropriate, attempt to reason with involved inmates before applying force. **Do not bargain.**	_____	_____
12. Mass Disturbance Plan: If #9 fails, a direct order will be given to terminate the disturbance. This order will not be given until it can be effectively enforced.	_____	_____
13. Hostage Recovery Plan: Establish and maintain an open line of communications with the hostage takers. Negotiators will be the only ones in contact with the hostages.	_____	_____
14. Hostage Recovery Plan: The warden or designee will determine which demands made by the hostage takers, the negotiators should grant. He or she will determine the need and time for introducing those who might be able to grant other demands in negotiations.	_____	_____
15. Hostage Recovery Plan: When notified that the situation has deteriorated or negotiations have reached an impasse, initiate the use of force.	_____	_____

Post Disturbance Activities—Ensure the Following Is Done:

16. Provide medical and psychological treatment to all staff and inmates. All injuries will be photographed.   _____   _____

17. Count Inmates.   _____   _____

18. Account for all staff.   _____   _____

19. Debrief and release assisting agencies   _____   _____

20. Isolate disturbance participants.   _____   _____

21. Debrief and initiate reports from staff.   _____   _____

22. Interview suspects and witnesses.   _____   _____

23. Gather and preserve all evidence, photograph affected areas.   _____   _____

24. Develop an institutional damage report.   _____   _____

25. Deactivate Command Post.   _____   _____

Comments:

_____

Signature   Date

Revised: 8-1-92

Code 10-33
Mass Disturbance and Hostage Recovery
Emergency Procedure Checklist
Chief of Security

Date: _____
Time: _____

	Time Task Completed	*Initials*

1. Report to master control and be briefed by the shift commander/ situation commander: _____ _____

2. When ordered, activate the emergency operations center and establish operations command team consisting of the following.
   - A. Chief of security _____ _____
   - B. Majors (operations communicator & assistant operations commander) _____ _____
   - C. Utility captains (misc. assignments) _____ _____
   - D. Allied agency coordinators _____ _____
   - E. Operations lieutenants _____ _____
   - F. Case management supervisor (historian) _____ _____
   - G. Personnel officer _____ _____
   - H. Psychologist _____ _____
   - I. Public information officer _____ _____
   - J. Medical officer _____ _____
   - K. Maintenance supervisor _____ _____
   - L. Locksmith _____ _____
   - M. Social worker _____ _____
   - N. Food service supervisor _____ _____
   - O. Clerical staff _____ _____
     1. Security chief's secretary _____ _____
     2. Operations clerical staff _____ _____

3. The emergency operations center is established to coordinate operations in the institution and ensure support functions are mobilized around the immediate disturbance situation and provide support and assistance to other staff. _____ _____

Post Disturbance Activities—In Concert with Warden Ensure the Following Are Done:

4. Provide medical and psychological treatment to all staff and inmates. All injuries will be photographed _____ _____

5. Notify all staff that incident is resolved. _____ _____

6. Count Inmates. _____ _____

7. Account for all staff. _____ _____

8. Debrief and release assisting agencies. _____ _____

9. Isolate disturbance participants. _____ _____

10. Debrief and initiate reports from staff. _____ _____

11. Interview suspects and witnesses. _____ _____

12. Gather and preserve all evidence, photograph affected areas. _____ _____

13. Develop an institutional damage report _____ _____

14. Deactivate the emergency operations center. _____ _____

Comments:

_____   _____
Signature of Individual Completing Checklist   Date

Revised: 5-1-92

Code 10-33
Mass Disturbance and Hostage Recovery
Emergency Procedure Checklist
Shift Commander

Date:

Time:

	Time Task Completed	*Initials*

1. Locate and verify incident.

2. Isolate the incident by establishing initial cover group with available staff.

3. Lock down the institution.

4. Establish command center and set up initial emergency operations center.

5. Through Operations, provide extra personnel to secure the perimeter and assist in inmate movement and other needed areas.

6. Order Operations to initiate full custody call-in, if needed.

7. Evacuate all inmates in program and activate areas to secure locations. (Alternate secure location for inmates within the institution in Appendix E. Alternate secure locations outside the institution are located in Appendix F.)
❏ Visiting Room ❏ Kitchen Chapel ❏ Dispensary ❏ Education Bldg. ❏ Gym

8. Identify and evacuate all visitors from the institution.

9. Evacuate civilian personnel from the following areas:
❏ Chapel ❏ Lower K Bldg. ❏ Education Bldg.
❏ Print Shop ❏ Gym
All other areas evacuated without specific shift commander authorization.

10. Advise Operations of what services are needed from outside agencies.

11. In concert with TAC commander, place intelligence officers.

12. In concert with TAC command and Operations use TAC officers to relieve initial cover group. Designate a cover group leader and supply this officer with a walkie-talkie.

13. In concert with TAC commander and Operations use non-TAC officers to establish perimeter group. Designate perimeter group leader and supply this officer with a walkie-talkie.

14. Have all persons with first-hand knowledge of the incident available for interview.

15. Ensure that all emergency procedure checks are proceeding smoothly.

16. Brief arriving command center members.

17. Assign staff person to coordinate assistance with outside agencies.

18. List contact persons of outside agencies as they arrive and duties to which they are assigned.

NOTE: 19 through 27 are identical to the emergency procedures checklist for the warden. If necessary, in the absence of the warden, assistant warden and security chief complete these duties. Also, the warden or senior officer in charge will authorize use of chemical agents and use of force in 20 through 26.

19. Seek approval from commissioner for the use of force in both mass disturbance and hostage situations unless it is apparent that physical harm has been or is being rendered to hostages and/or third parties.

20. Mass Disturbance Plan:
Before using force, and when security provisions have been made, announce via the public address system for all those who desire to exit the troubled area to proceed to a designated area.

21. Hostage Recovery Plan:
Above information will be relayed by the hostage negotiators after consulting with the negotiators and the chief psychologist.

22. Mass Disturbance Plan:
When prepared to take action, make it known by the public address system or bull horn to the involved inmates: "Authority prevails and order will be maintained. Force will be used if necessary to maintain order."   _____   _____

23. Mass Disturbance Plan:
If appropriate, attempt to reason with involved inmates prior to application of force. **Do not bargain.**

24. Mass Disturbance Plan:
If 23 fails, a direct order will be given to terminate the disorder. This order will not be given until it can be effectively enforced.   _____   _____

25. Hostage Recovery Plan:
Establish and maintain an open line of communication with the hostage takers. Negotiators will be the only ones in contact with the hostages.   _____   _____

26. Hostage Recovery Plan:
The warden or designee will determine which demands made by the hostage takers, the negotiators have to grant. He or she will determine the need and time to introduce those who might be able to grant other demands in negotiations.   _____   _____

27. Hostage Recovery Plan:
When notified that the situation has deteriorated or negotiators have reached an impasse, initiate the use of force.

Post Disturbance Activated—In Concert with the Warden, Ensure These Are Done:

28. Provide medical and psychological treatment for all staff and inmates. All injuries will be photographed.   _____   _____

29. Notify all staff that incident is resolved.   _____   _____

30. Count inmates.   _____   _____

31. Account for all staff.   _____   _____

32. Debrief and release assisting agencies.   _____   _____

33. Isolate disturbance participants.   _____   _____

34. Debrief and initiate reports from staff.   _____   _____

35. Interview suspects and witnesses.   _____   _____

36. Gather and preserve all evidence, photograph affected areas.   _____   _____

37. Develop an institutional damage report.   _____   _____

38. Deactivate command center.   _____   _____

Comments

_____

Signature of Individual Completing Checklist   Date

Revised: 5-1-92

Code 10-33
Mass Disturbance and Hostage Recovery
Emergency Procedure Checklist
Master Control Center Initial Information

Date:

Time:

Time Task Completed   *Initials*

On Initial Contact Ascertain and Note:

1. Nature of the disturbance.

2. Location of the disturbance.

3. Number of Inmates involved/extent of disturbance.

4. Number of staff involved.

5. Number of injured or dead.

6. Hostage situation/number and identity of hostages number and identity of hostage takers/harm or threat of harm.

7. No hostage situation but destruction or threat of destruction.

8. Weapon, number and type.

9. Location and name of reporting officer.

Comments

Signature of Individual Completing Checklist   Date

Revised: 5-1-92

Code 10-33
Mass Disturbance and Hostage Recovery
Emergency Procedure Checklist
Master Control Center Initial Information
Master Control Center

Date:

Time:

Time Task Completed   *Initials*

1. Control center will notify the shift commander at ext. 285/287 or by walkie-talkie.

2. Announce code "10-33" twice over the radio and the public address system.

3. Announce over the radio and the public address system that all radio and telephone communications will be kept to only those necessary.

4. Transfer information to situation status board and keep this information up to date.

5. Notify shift commander when all noncustody staff are accounted for.

6. Prepare to log and distribute equipment (walkie-talkies, restraints, weapons, etc.).

7. Use intercom system to try to eavesdrop on the incident.

8. Ensure all equipment returned is logged and checked for damage.

9. Notify all units via radio and the public address system when incident is resolved.

Comments

Signature of Individual Completing Checklist   Date

Revision #2
February 1995

Code 10-33
Mass Disturbance and Hostage Recovery
Emergency Procedure Checklist
Operations Staff

Date:

Time:

	Time Task Completed	*Initials*

1. Begin TAC and SERT recall (see emergency phone lists)

2. Notify Command Personnel
   A. Warden:
      Beeper: (Number)
   B. Assistant:
      Beeper: (Number)
   C. Chief of Security:
      Beeper: (Number)

3. Confirm with shift commander when lockdown and evacuation is complete:
   Chapel ❑ Gym ❑ Rec. & I.D ❑ AHU ❑ BHU ❑ CHU ❑ DHU ❑ EHU ❑
   FHU ❑ GHU ❑ HHU ❑ Kitchen ❑ Dispensary ❑ Ed. Bldg. ❑ Voc. Bldg. ❑
   Visiting Room ❑ L-1 Dorm ❑ L2, 3 Dorm ❑

4. Account for and notify shift commander when all custody staff are accounted for and evacuated.

5. Prepare to receive count and notify master control of count results.

6. In concert with shift commander, provide extra personnel to secure perimeter and other areas.

7. Station a supervisor at time clock to direct incoming staff. Provide this supervisor with a walkie-talkie.

8. Post armed guard at main entrance to admit authorized personnel only.

9. Have on-duty TAC personnel relieved and report to TAC room.

10. Assign armed officers to seal off road entrances to institution at Maryland Correctional Institute-Jessup access road, admitting only authorized personnel. Place one officer at the main entrance and one at the Herman Boot Camp Road.

11. Provide personnel to assist with evacuation where needed as directed by shift commander.

12. Notify additional personnel & agencies:
    A. Hostage negotiators—Beeper:
       (Name, Number)
       (Name2, Number2)
    B. TAC Capt. (Name, Number)
    C. Psychology Staff: Beeper: (Name, Number)
    D. Support Agencies:
       1. Maryland State Police (number)
       2. Anne Arundel County Sheriff's Dept. (number)
       3. Anne Arundel County Police (number)
       4. Univ. Hospital Emergency (number)
       5. Ambulance: (911)
       6. Fire Dept.: (911)
       7. Maryland Emergency Management Agency (number)
       8. Department of Corrections Investigative Unit (number)
       9. Anne Arundel County Emergency Management (number)

E. Other Department of Corrections agencies:
    1. Headquarters (number) _____ _____
    2. Headquarters duty officer (number) _____ _____

F. Department Heads:
    1. Medical _____ _____
    2. Maintenance (number) _____ _____
    3. Food service (number) _____ _____
    4. Investigative captain _____ _____
    5. Warden's secretary _____ _____
    6. Assistant warden's secretary _____ _____
    7. Key control _____ _____
    8. VAC _____ _____
    9. Clerical _____ _____
    10. Social worker _____ _____

13. Notify Patuxent Institution (phone number) of situation and advise it to put information on the Jessup Community Hot Line. _____ _____

14. Initiate full custody call-in, if ordered by senior officer in charge. _____ _____

Signature of Individual Completing Checklist   Date

Revised: 5-1-92

Code 10-33
Mass Disturbance and Hostage Recovery
Emergency Procedure Checklist
Tactical Unit Commander

Date:
Time:

	Time Task Completed	*Initials*
1. Report to the emergency operations center and be briefed by the emergency operations coordinator.	_____	_____
2. In concert with officer in charge, place intelligence officers and maintain communications with them.	_____	_____
3. Assemble and brief TAC Unit personnel in the visiting room.	_____	_____
4. In concert with the emergency operations center, officer in charge uses TAC officers to relieve initial cover group. Designate a cover group leader and supply this officer with a walkie-talkie.	_____	_____
5. In concert with shift commander and Operations use non-TAC officers to establish perimeter group.	_____	_____

Comments

Signature of Individual Completing Checklist   Date

Revised: 8-1-92

Code 10-33
Mass Disturbance and Hostage Recovery
Emergency Procedure Checklist
SERT Unit Commander

Date:

Time:

	Time Task Completed	Initials

1. Report to the emergency operations center and be briefed by the shift commander/situation commander.
2. Brief SERT personnel.
3. Check personnel and equipment for readiness.
4. Position snipers with established intelligence officers if appropriate.
5. Coordinate with TAC commander.
7. Continue to receive updates and pass information on to SERT personnel.

Comments

Signature of Individual Completing Checklist   Date

Revised: 5-1-92

Code 10-33
Mass Disturbance and Hostage Recovery
Emergency Procedure Checklist
Sallyport

Date:

Time:

	Time Task Completed	Initials

1. Stop all entry into the institution.
2. Assist in the evacuation of noncustody staff.
3. Collect and inventory all keys from evacuating staff, and when evacuation is complete, send all keys to master control.
4. Admit vehicles and persons only when ordered by the emergency operations center.
5. Log-in and inspect all returned weapons, prepare report on any and all weapons having been fired and missing or damaged equipment.

Comments

Signature of Individual Completing Checklist   Date

Revised: 8-1-92

Code 10-33
Mass Disturbance and Hostage Recovery
Emergency Procedure Checklist
Lobby Officer

Date:

Time:

	Time Task Completed	*Initials*
1. Instruct all visitors in the lobby to leave the institution.		
2. Coordinate the evacuation of all visitors from the institution.		
3. Identify all those leaving the visiting room as visitors.		
4. Observe departing visitors on sidewalk. Notify Tower #1 when last visitors are clear.		
5. Notify the emergency operations center when evacuation is complete. Dial ###, ###, ###, or ###.		
6. Notify the emergency operations center that you are available for further assignment. Dial ###, ###, ###, or ###.		

Comments

_____

Signature of Individual Completing Checklist   Date

Revised: 8-1-92

Code 10-33
Mass Disturbance and Hostage Recovery
Emergency Procedure Checklist
Visiting Room Officers

Date:

Time:

	Time Task Completed	*Initials*
1. Terminate all visits, coordinate with lobby officer in the evacuation of all visitors from the visiting room. Notify front lobby when visitors are clear.		
2. Place inmates in the strip search room and identify them, if necessary.		
3. Keep inmates under observation until directed to assist in evacuation of these inmates by the emergency operations center.		
4. Notify the emergency operations center when evacuation is completed and that you are available for further assignment. Dial ###, ###, ###, or ###.		

Comments

_____

Signature of Individual Completing Checklist   Date

Revised: 8-1-92

Code 10-33
Mass Disturbance and Hostage Recovery
Emergency Procedure Checklist
Dispensary Officer

Date:

Time:

	Time Task Completed	Initials

1. Lock outside entrance to dispensary.

2. Alert medical staff and have them secure all dangerous tools and utensils. Also have medical staff lock all access doors to drug storage area.

3. Have medical department initiate their emergency plans.

4. Account for and evacuate nonmedical staff through stairwell to Lower K building north door (secretaries, pharmacy tech., dental staff).

5. When evacuation is complete, notify the emergency operations center and advise that all medical staff in dispensary are accounted for and nonessential staff have been evacuated.

6. Keep inmates under observation until directed to assist in evacuation of inmates to their housing units or other secured area by the emergency operations center.

7. Notify the emergency operations center when evacuation is complete. Dial ###, ###, ###, or ###.

8. Position yourself at officer's station, await further instructions.

Comments

_____
Signature of Individual Completing Checklist   Date

Revised: 8-1-92

Code 10-33
Mass Disturbance and Hostage Recovery
Emergency Procedure Checklist
Kitchen Officer

Date:

Time:

	Time Task Completed	Initials

1. Secure outside doors and door leading to the food preparation area.

2. Account for all tools and utensils and secure area.

3. Account for all inmate workers and secure them in hallway between the kitchen and officers dining room.

4. Observe these inmates until directed to evacuate them to their housing unit or other secure location.

5. Notify the emergency operations center when evacuation is complete. Dial ###, ###, ###, or ###.

Comments

_____
Signature of Individual Completing Checklist   Date

Revised: 8-1-92

Code 10-33
Mass Disturbance and Hostage Recovery
Emergency Procedure Checklist
Food Service Supervisor

Date:

Time:

	Time Task Completed	*Initials*

1. All tools and dangerous utensils will be returned to the kitchen area where they will be counted and secured. Report any discrepancy to the emergency operations center.

2. Secure all doors leading to kitchen area, and secure all supply areas.

3. Account for all inmate workers and secure them in hallway between kitchen and the officers dining room. Post CDOs to observe these inmates.

4. The emergency operations center will direct the evacuation of the inmates to their housing units or other secure area.

5. Notify the emergency operations center when inmates are evacuated. Dial ###, ###, ###, or ###.

6. Account for all staff, and evacuate through sallyport.

7. Coordinate evacuation of inmate workers with kitchen officer.

8. Refer to food service supervisor's checklist for the emergency operations center command.

Comments

_____   _____

Signature of Individual Completing Checklist   Date

Revised: 8-1-92

Code 10-33
Mass Disturbance and Hostage Recovery
Emergency Procedure Checklist
Education Officer

Date:

Time:

	Time Task Completed	*Initials*

1. Secure outside doors.

2. Notify staff of emergency situation.

3. Have all teachers step out of classrooms and secure inmates in their rooms.

4. Observe inmates until directed by the emergency operations center to evacuate them to their housing units or other secure location. Evacuate inmates one room at a time.

5. When education area is evacuated, begin evacuation of vocational area one room at a time.

6. In concert with the department supervisor, evacuate noncustody staff. Primarily evacuation route is through shop area to sallyport.

7. Assist chapel officer in evacuation of noncustody staff from chapel.

8. Notify the emergency operations center when evacuation is complete and request further assignment. Dial ###, ###, ###, or ###.

Comments

_____   _____
Signature of Individual Completing Checklist   Date

Revised: 8-1-92

Code 10-33
Mass Disturbance and Hostage Recovery
Emergency Procedure Checklist
Education Supervisor

Date:

Time:

	Time Task Completed	*Initials*

1. Ensure all dangerous tools and utensils are secure.

2. Have all education staff in the building gather in staff lounge area.

3. When all education staff are accounted for, notify education building officer and receive the evacuation instructions.

4. When evacuation is complete notify the emergency operations center if all education staff are accounted for, or if not, last known location of those not accounted for. Dial ###, ###, ###, or ###.

Comments

_____   _____
Signature of Individual Completing Checklist   Date

Revised: 8-1-92

Code 10-33
Mass Disturbance and Hostage Recovery
Emergency Procedure Checklist
Vocational Shop Officer

Date: _____

Time: _____

Time Task Completed   *Initials*

1. Secure outside doors. _____ _____
2. Notify staff of emergency situation. _____ _____
3. After instructors have accounted for all tools, secure inmates in their respective rooms. _____ _____
4. Begin evacuation of shop areas one room at a time after education areas has been evacuated. _____ _____
5. Advise the emergency operations center when inmate evacuation is complete. Dial ###, ###, ###, or ###. _____ _____
6. Evacuate noncustody staff through north door to sallyport and then request further assignment from the emergency operations center. Dial ###, ###, ###, or ###. _____ _____

Comments

_____

Signature of Individual Completing Checklist   Date

Revised: 8-1-92

Code 10-33
Mass Disturbance and Hostage Recovery
Emergency Procedure Checklist
Library Officer

Date: _____

Time: _____

Time Task Completed   *Initials*

1. Secure outside doors. _____ _____
2. Notify staff of emergency situation. _____ _____
3. Have librarian leave the room and secure inmates in the library. _____ _____
4. Coordinate evacuation of library inmates with education officer. _____ _____
5. Evacuate noncustody staff through shops to sallyport. _____ _____
6. Notify the emergency operations center when evacuation of inmates is complete, and request further assignment. Dial ###, ###, ###, or ###. _____ _____

Comments

_____

Signature of Individual Completing Checklist   Date

Revised: 8-1-92

Code 10-33
Mass Disturbance and Hostage Recovery
Emergency Procedure Checklist
Print Shop Officer

Date: _____

Time: _____

	Time Task Completed	Initials
1. Secure outside doors.	_____	_____
2. Notify staff of emergency situation.	_____	_____
3. After all tools have been accounted for and secured, secure inmates in the old print shop.	_____	_____
4. Begin evacuation of inmates, coordinating with vocation shop officer.	_____	_____
5. Advise the emergency operations center when inmate evacuation is complete. Dial ###, ###, ###, or ###.	_____	_____
6. Evacuate civilian personnel through the vocation shop north door to sallyport.	_____	_____
7. Notify the emergency operations center when evacuation of inmates is complete and request further assignment. Dial ###, ###, ###, or ###.	_____	_____

Comments

_____

Signature of Individual Completing Checklist   Date

Revised: 8-1-92

Code 10-33
Mass Disturbance and Hostage Recovery
Emergency Procedure Checklist
Chapel Officer

Date: _____

Time: _____

	Time Task Completed	Initials
1. Ensure all outside doors are locked.	_____	_____
2. Place all inmates in the main chapel and wait for directions from the emergency operations center for evacuation to housing units or other secured area.	_____	_____
3. Have all noncustody staff together in a secure area prepared to evacuate only at the direction of the the emergency operations center.	_____	_____
4. After all noncustody personnel are safely evacuated and the inmates are secured notify the emergency operations center of such and request further assignment. Dial ###, ###, ###, or ###.	_____	_____

Comments

_____

Signature of Individual Completing Checklist   Date

Revised: 8-1-92

Code 10-33
Mass Disturbance and Hostage Recovery
Emergency Procedure Checklist
Social Work Supervisor

Date:

Time:

	Time Task Completed	Initials

1. Ensure all dangerous tools and utensils are secure.

2. Have all social work staff in the building gather together in a secure area.

3. When all social work staff are accounted for, notify Lower K Building officer and receive evacuation instructions.

4. When noncustody staff evacuation is complete, notify the emergency operations center if all social work staff are accounted for, if not, last known location of those not accounted for.

Comments

_____

Signature of Individual Completing Checklist   Date

Revised: 8-1-92

Code 10-33
Mass Disturbance and Hostage Recovery
Emergency Procedure Checklist
Gym Officer

Date:

Time:

	Time Task Completed	Initials

1. Secure all outside doors.

2. Notify noncustody staff of emergency situation.

3. Order all inmates into the bleacher area of main gym.

4. Have all noncustody staff together in a secure area, and prepared to evacuate when ordered by the emergency operations center.

5. Keep inmates under observation until directed by the emergency operations center to assist in evacuation of inmates to their housing units or other secured area.

6. After all noncustody personnel are safely evacuated and the inmates under control are secured in housing units, notify the emergency operations center that you are available for further assignment. Dial ###, ###, ###, or ###.

Comments

_____

Signature of Individual Completing Checklist   Date

Revised: 8-1-92

Code 10-33
Mass Disturbance and Hostage Recovery
Emergency Procedure Checklist
Barber Shop Officer

Date:

Time:

Time Task
Completed   *Initials*

1. Secure all dangerous tools and utensils in the barber shop.   _____   _____
2. Order all inmates into bleacher area of main gym.   _____   _____
3. Keep inmates under observation until directed by the emergency operations center
to assist in evacuation of inmates to their housing units or other secured area.   _____   _____
4. After all inmates under your control are secured in housing units, notify the
emergency operations center that you are available for further assignment.
Dial ###, ###, ###, or ###.   _____   _____

Comments

_____
Signature of Individual Completing Checklist   Date

Revised: 8-1-92

Code 10-33
Mass Disturbance and Hostage Recovery
Emergency Procedure Checklist
Commissary Officer

Date:

Time:

Time Task
Completed   *Initials*

1. Evacuate inmates to the bleachers in the main gym.   _____   _____
2. Secure the commissary.   _____   _____
3. Assist gym officer as directed.   _____   _____

Comments

_____
Signature of Individual Completing Checklist   Date

Revised: 8-1-92

Code 10-33
Mass Disturbance and Hostage Recovery
Emergency Procedure Checklist
Housing Units A Through H

Date:

Time:

	Time Task Completed	*Initials*

1. Secure all exit and tier doors.

2. Lock down the unit.

3. Account for all staff.

4. Count inmates.

5. Notify Operations that #1 through #4 are complete. Dial ###, ###, ###, or ###.

6. Send staff where ordered.

7. Continue half-hour tier rounds, being especially alert for inmate mood swings and unusual activities.

Comments

_____
Signature of Individual Completing Checklist   Date

Revised: 8-1-92

Code 10-33
Mass Disturbance and Hostage Recovery
Emergency Procedure Checklist
L Dormitories

Date:

Time:

	Time Task Completed	*Initials*

1. Secure all gates and doors and keep inmates in the dormitory.

2. Account for all staff.

3. Count inmates.

4. Notify Operations that #1 through #3 are complete. Dial ###, ###, ###, or ###.

5. Continue frequent security rounds, being especially alert for inmate mood swings and unusual activities.

6. Perform other assignments as ordered by Operations.

Comments

_____
Signature of Individual Completing Checklist   Date

Revised: 8-1-92

Code 10-33
Mass Disturbance and Hostage Recovery
Emergency Procedure Checklist
Tower #1

Date:

Time:

	Time Task Completed	Initials
1. Stop all entry to the institution.	_____	_____
2. Coordinate the evacuation of visitors with lobby officer.	_____	_____
3. Coordinate all other movement with the officer assigned to the main gate.	_____	_____
4. Observe compound and surrounding area, report any unusual activity.	_____	_____

Comments

_____

Signature of Individual Completing Checklist   Date

Revised: 8-1-92

Code 10-33
Mass Disturbance and Hostage Recovery
Emergency Procedure Checklist
Tower #2-6

Date:

Time:

	Time Task Completed	Initials
1. Observe compound and surrounding area. Report any unusual activity.	_____	_____

Comments

_____

Signature of Individual Completing Checklist   Date

Revised: 8-1-92

Code 10-33
Mass Disturbance and Hostage Recovery
Emergency Procedure Checklist
Case Management Manager

Date:

Time:

	Time Task Completed	Initials

1. Ensure all dangerous tools and utensils are secure.

2. Have all inmates present secured in one area and coordinate evacuation with Lower K building officer.

3. Secure all records doors.

4. Have all case management staff gather in the hallway of the classification department.

5. When all case management staff are accounted for, notify the Lower K building officer and receive evacuation instructions.

6. When evacuation is complete notify the emergency operations center if all case management staff are accounted for or if not, last known location of those not accounted for.

7. Report to command center, and assume position of historian.

Comments

_____
Signature of Individual Completing Checklist   Date

Revised: 5-1-92

Code 10-33
Mass Disturbance and Hostage Recovery
Emergency Procedure Checklist for Operations Command
Majors (2)

Date:

Time:

	Time Task Completed	Initials

1. Maintain the flow of information between command center and emergency operations center via priority phone in the conference area.

2. Provide assistance and advice to operations commander.

3. The major who is not acting as communicator will complete any duties assigned by operations commander. Maintain written log of duties assigned and disposition.

Comments

_____
Signature of Individual Completing Checklist   Date

237

Revised: 8-1-92

Code 10-33
Mass Disturbance and Hostage Recovery
Emergency Procedure Checklist for Operations Command
Majors (2)

Date:
Time:

	Time Task Completed	Initials
1. As allied agencies arrive or call, identify yourself by name and rank and establish yourself as the communications link between the Maryland Correction Institute-Jessup and its agency.	_____	_____
2. Log the name and rank of the supervisor of each reporting agency.	_____	_____
3. In concert with emergency operations center direct allied agencies to stand and/or deploy.	_____	_____
4. Have the supervisors of each agency position themselves at the emergency operations center if possible, and have a means of communication with agency.	_____	_____
5. If the supervisor of any agency cannot be positioned at the operations center, establish a means of communication with this supervisor by walkie-talkie or telephone.	_____	_____
6. Pull ten walkie-talkies from either the master control center or equipment room.	_____	_____

Comments

_____
Signature of Individual Completing Checklist   Date

Revised: 5-1-92

Code 10-33
Mass Disturbance and Hostage Recovery
Emergency Procedure Checklist for Operations Command
Utility Captains

Date:
Time:

	Time Task Completed	Initials
1. Assist where needed in the establishment of emergency operations center.	_____	_____
2. Perform duties as assigned by emergency operations center/communicator. One of these duties is supervision of the Operations area.	_____	_____
3. Maintain written log of duties assigned and disposition.	_____	_____

Comments

_____
Signature of Individual Completing Checklist   Date

Revised: 5-1-92

Code 10-33
Mass Disturbance and Hostage Recovery
Emergency Procedure Checklist for Operations Command
Operations Lieutenant

Date:

Time:

	Time Task Completed	Initials

1. The Operations lieutenant on duty at the time of the incident will be assisted by the other reporting Operations lieutenant.
2. Coordinate the staffing of the institution as directed by the emergency operations center.
3. Maintain a record of where officers are assigned, either TAC unit or other duties.
4. Supervise all inmate moves and recording of same.
5. Verify all inmate counts.
6. Carry out duties as assigned. Keep log of these duties and disposition.

Comments

_____
Signature of Individual Completing Checklist   Date

Revised: 5-1-92

Code 10-33
Mass Disturbance and Hostage Recovery
Emergency Procedure Checklist for Operations Command
Case Management Supervisor

Date:

Time:

	Time Task Completed	Initials

1. Set up assistant warden's office.
2. On clearance from command center, access base files and psychological files of involved inmates. Before releasing the files, again obtain clearance from command center. ###, ###, ###, or ###.
3. Interpret information from base file.
4. Gather further information on inmates by contacting agencies and/or persons listed in base files, offender-based computer management system, visiting cards, and adjustment records; housing area staff also may be used for source information.
5. Collaborate with psychologist, medical department, and clerical staff in preparing Personal Fact Sheet.
6. Submit two copies of Personal Fact Sheet to the emergency operations center commander/communicator.

Comments

_____
Signature of Individual Completing Checklist   Date

Revised: 8-1-92

Code 10-33
Mass Disturbance and Hostage Recovery
Emergency Procedure Checklist for Operations Command
Personnel Associate I and II

Date:

Time:

	Time Task Completed	*Initials*

1. Access personnel files of staff held hostage. _____ _____

2. Review information in these files and ascertain:
names of family members and phone numbers _____ _____
names of physicians and phone numbers _____ _____
family members or physician, if involved staff has any medical or psychological
problems _____ _____

3. When directed by the emergency operations center, call family members and
advise them generally of the situation. Ascertain information for the Personal Fact
Sheet and then have family members report to the Jessup Community Hall. _____ _____

4. In concert with clerical staff, prepare Personal Fact Sheet on each involved
staff member. _____ _____

5. Submit two copies of Personal Fact Sheet to the emergency operations center. _____ _____

6. Provide a list of family members reporting to Jessup Community Hall. Submit
two copies to the emergency operations center. _____ _____

Comments

_____

Signature of Individual Completing Checklist   Date

Revised: 8-1-92

Code 10-33
Mass Disturbance and Hostage Recovery
Emergency Procedure Checklist for Operations Command
Psychologist

Date:
Time:

	Time Task Completed	*Initials*
1. Set up in assistant warden's office.	_____	_____
2. If not previously accomplished by classification, obtain clearance from the emergency operations center and access base files and psychological files of involved inmates. Before returning to Operations area with the files, again obtain clearance from operations center, ext. ###, ###, ###, or ###.	_____	_____
3. Interpret information from these psychological files.	_____	_____
4. Gather further information on inmates by contacting agencies and/or persons listed in the psychological files. Other staff also may be used for source information.	_____	_____
5. Collaborate with classification, medical department, and clerical staff in preparing Personal Fact Sheet.	_____	_____
6. Submit two copies of Personal Fact Sheet to operations commander/communicator.	_____	_____
7. Assist social worker with family members, but do not leave the Operations area without clearance from the emergency operations center.	_____	_____

Comments

_____

Signature of Individual Completing Checklist   Date

Revision #1
February 1995

Code 10-33
Mass Disturbance and Hostage Recovery
Emergency Procedure Checklist for Operations Command
Public Information Officer

Date:
Time:

	Time Task Completed	*Initials*

1. Attempt to contact the Department of Corrections public information officer at (Phone Number) and advise him/her that the media will be located at the Brockbridge Training Building at (phone number) ext. ###.   _____   _____

2. Advise all media to go to the Maryland Correctional Institute-Jessup Training Building and inform them that regular press releases will be given from this area. Set up a schedule with the media for press releases and tell them up front that certain information may be withheld to protect hostages and other staff.   _____   _____

3. Collaborate with the Department of Corrections public information officer and clerical staff to draft written press releases.   _____   _____

4. Have all press releases reviewed by the operations commander before release to the media.   _____   _____

5. Take steps to limit other sources of information to the media, i.e., family members, other staff, North Arundel Hospital, University Hospital staff.   _____   _____

Comments

_____

Signature of Individual Completing Checklist   Date

Revised: 8-1-92

Code 10-33
Mass Disturbance and Hostage Recovery
Emergency Procedure Checklist for Operations Command
Social Worker

Date:

Time:

	Time Task Completed	*Initials*
1. Report to the emergency operations center.	_____	_____
2. Proceed to Jessup Community Hall and prepare to accommodate family members of staff held hostage.	_____	_____
3. Keep family members isolated from media and as comfortable as possible. Bring food, drink, and whatever is needed.	_____	_____
4. Communications will be maintained with the emergency operations center and status updates will be given to family members.	_____	_____
5. Provide medical and psychological assistance as needed. Make request through the emergency operations center (phone number, ext. ###, ###, ### or ###).	_____	_____
6. Provide referral to community assistance program to those family members who exhibit or indicate a need for it. (Phone Number) or (Phone Number).	_____	_____
7. Collaborate with the emergency operations center psychologist when necessary (Phone Number).	_____	_____

Comments

_____   _____

Signature of Individual Completing Checklist   Date

Revision #1
February 1995

Code 10-33
Mass Disturbance and Hostage Recovery
Emergency Procedure Checklist for Operations Command
Medical Supervisor

Date:

Time:

	Time Task Completed	Initials

1. Pull medical files of involved inmates. Classification specialist or psychologist will have a listing of inmate names, phone # ###.   _____ _____

2. Collaborate with classification, psychology, and clerical staff in preparing Personal Fact Sheet.   _____ _____

3. Ensure staff do not give out any information in regards to the incident or the medical condition of staff or inmates.   _____ _____

4. Advise the emergency operations center (phone number) of the name of any staff member transported to the hospital.
   Reminder: Do not transport inmates until security escort is provided.   _____ _____

Note: Medical Department functions under the CMS Manual subject heading, Emergency Medical Service Activation Plan. Above items are specific duties.

Medical supervision will not report to Operations as a general procedure.

Comments

_____

Signature of Individual Completing Checklist   Date

Revised: 8-1-95

Code 10-33
Mass Disturbance and Hostage Recovery
Emergency Procedure Checklist for Operations Command
Maintenance Supervisor

Date:

Time:

	Time Task Completed	Initials

1. Check out walkie-talkie and maintenance key sets from master control.   _____ _____

2. Stand by in Maintenance Department (ext. ###).   _____ _____

3. Account for all on-duty maintenance staff and call in those needed that are not on duty.   _____ _____

4. Contact the emergency operations center by walkie-talkie or by phone with questions (ext. ###, ###, ### or ###).   _____ _____

5. Under the direction of the emergency operations center, access electrical and water feeds to the incident.   _____ _____

6. Maintain the rest of the institution.   _____ _____

7. Assist in damage control and damage assessment following incident.   _____ _____

Comments

_____

Signature of Individual Completing Checklist   Date

Revised: 8-1-95

Code 10-33
Mass Disturbance and Hostage Recovery
Emergency Procedure Checklist for Operations Command
Locksmith

Date:

Time:

	Time Task Completed	*Initials*

1. Check out walkie-talkie and needed key sets from master control.

2. Have available schematic diagram showing location of instructional locks and the identification number of keys to those locks.

3. Disable and able various phones from the switchboard room as requested by the emergency operations center.

4. Collaborate with maintenance to ensure the proper function of all doors, locks, and gates in the institution.

Comments

_____

Signature of Individual Completing Checklist   Date

Revised: 5-1-92

Code 10-33
Mass Disturbance and Hostage Recovery
Emergency Procedure Checklist for Operations Command
Food Service Supervisor

Date:

Time:

	Time Task Completed	*Initials*

1. Initiate emergency food service plan.

2. Coordinate feeding schedule with Operations lieutenants (ext. ### or ###).

Note: Food service supervisor will not actually report to the Emergency Operations Center area as a general procedure.

Comments

_____

Signature of Individual Completing Checklist   Date

Revised: 8-1-95

Code 10-33
Mass Disturbance and Hostage Recovery
Emergency Procedure Checklist for Operations Command
Secretaries and Clerks

Date:

Time:

	Time Task Completed	Initials
1. The assistant warden's secretary will maintain log of events of the operation command post (historian).	_____	_____
2. Clerical staff will operate the phone in the master control center in the absence of the operator.	_____	_____
3. Clerical staff will maintain the count boards and verify inmate counts with the Operations lieutenant.	_____	_____
4. Assist in the typing of material requested by the emergency operations center.	_____	_____

Comments

_____

Signature of Individual Completing Checklist   Date

Index

A

Abbott, J.
learned violence, 69
state-raised inmates, 69

AIDS. *(Acquired Immune Deficiency Syndrome)*
definition, 156
fear of, 156-157
management, 157-158
statistics of occurrence, 156

Alpert, G.
inmates most likely to commit suicide, 79

Alternatives to Violence program, 73-74

Architectural Assessment Team
deployment phase, 39, 118, 144
goals of, 40
membership selection criteria, 40

Arizona Department of Corrections. *See Emergency plan activation incident management system*

Aryan Brotherhood, 84-85

Attica riot
friendly fire deaths, 31
response problems, 29
staff retaliation, 96

B

Bayside State Prison
reduction of inmate victimization rates, 74

Blair County Prison
escape from, 4

Bowker, L.
effects of sexual victimization, 78
modification of prison environment for violence reduction, 72-73

Budget planning
and mitigation, 9, 16, 17, 55, 56

Bureau of prison. *See Federal Bureau of Prisons*

C

Cajon Summit, California
train derailment, 139-140

California Department of Corrections
parole and community services division, 133-134

California earthquake mitigation model
categorization of buildings, 128
structural testing and inspection program, 128

Camp Hill riots
causes, 32, 50-51, 52-54, 179
cellblock locking mechanisms, 56, 176
communication problems, 91-92, 161, 163
evacuation of, 143
events, 1-2, 4-5, 43, 169
external resources, use, 26

litigation. *See Camp Hill riot litigation.*
recovery problems, 94-95, 98, 183-184, 185, 197, 205-206
response to riot, 92
staff fatigue, 48-49

Camp Hill riot litigation
lessons learned from, 195-197
nature of inmate allegations, 194-195

Central Missouri Correctional Center
evacuation, 143
flooding, 143

CERT. *See Correctional Emergency Response Team*

Civil Rights Act, Section 1983
basis for inmate litigation, 70, 193

Command posts
location, 42-43
staffing, 43
types of, 42

Communications
communications tree, 41-42, 187
coordination of community resources, 15-17, 26, 28, 38
levels of, 175

Communications, problems with. *See also* **Camp Hill riots, Graterford correctional institution,** *and* **Southport Correctional Facility**
cause of inmate-precipitated emergency, 176-179
collective failure to follow policy, 177
information flow disruption, 176
failure to identify critical information, 175-176
individual failure to follow policy, 176-177
impersonal communication, 179
rumor control, inadequate 178-179

Connecticut model of AIDS management, 155

Contract vendors, 16, 17

Correctional emergency categories, definition of
facility fires, 107
human, 18
inmate precipitated, 18
natural, 18
technological, 19, 112

Correctional Emergency Response Team (CERT)
deployment phase, 30, 39, 61, 84, 91, 92, 112, 117, 118, 136, 148
goals of, 30
selection criteria for membership, 30

Criminal Prosecution Team
debriefing of victims, 37
deployment phase, 36, 39, 78, 84, 94
goals of, 36
selection criteria for membership, 36-37
use of specialized equipment, 37

Crowding. *See also* **Camp Hill riots, causes; Farrington, D.; Nuttall, C.**
relationship to violence, 71, 72,

D

Damage Assessment Team
deployment phase, 33, 39, 84, 112, 113, 118, 130
goals of, 33
selection criteria for membership, 34

Damage Repair Team
deployment phase, 34, 39, 84, 112, 118, 130
goals of, 34
selection criteria for membership, 35

Debriefing victims. *See also* **Criminal Prosecution Team**
goals of, 37, 188-189
support system for family, 189

Defusing goals, 188-189

Denmark, 3

DiIulio, J.
poor management as a cause of inmate violence, 70

E

Earthquakes. *See also* **California earthquake mitigation model**
location, 127
mitigation of, 127-128
preparedness/response to, 129
recovery from, 129
training drills, 129

Emergency. *See also* Correctional emergencies
definition of, 7

Emergency life cycle. *See* Mitigation; Preparedness;
Response; Recovery

Emergency plan
need for, *v-vi*

Emergency plan activation
incident management system, 12-13, 45-46
location of staff during, 43-44
traditional command and control structure, 12, 45
twelve-hour emergency staffing schedule, need for,
46-47

Emergency plan testing. *See also* Full-scale exercise
categories of testing, 170
evacuation drills, 171
full-scale exercises, principles of, 171-173
functional drills, 171
legal review of, 16, 169
orientation/education sessions, 17, 171
postmortem and plan modification, 16, 173-174, 181
table-top exercises, 170-171
walk-through drills, 171

Emergency Planning Committee, role of
central office committee, 15-16
facility committee, 16-18

Emergency prevention. *See* Mitigation

Emergency resources. *See* Internal Resources Inventory
and External Resources Inventory

Emergency teams. *See* Architectural Assessment Team;
Command Post Recording Team; Correctional
Emergency Response Team; Criminal Prosecution
Team; Damage Assessment Team; Damage Repair
Team; Escapee Recovery Team; Fire Safety Team;
Hostage Negotiation Team; Information
Management Team; Intelligence Unit; Litigation
Response Team; Media/community Information
Team; Medical Response Team; Post-traumatic
Assessment Team; Special Transportation Unit;
Stepdown Committee

Employee strike. *See* Strike of employees

Environmental scanning, inmate
as mitigation, 57
inmate informants, 59-60

long-term statistical indicators, 58
role of the administrator, 60-61
short-term behavioral observation indicators, 60-61

Environmental scanning, staff
labor relations climate, 102-103
personnel statistical data, 103-104
quality of work performance, 101-102

Epidemics. *See* AIDS; Tuberculosis

Escapee Recovery Team
ability to think like an escapee, 35
deployment phase, 35, 39
goals of, 35
selection criteria for membership, 35

Escapes
cooperation of friends and family, 69
escapee information packet, 69
mitigation of, 67-68
preparedness/response to, 69-70
recovery from, 70

Evacuation, institutional
communication, 147
convoy security, 145
critical planning questions, 144-147
inmate management during, 147
sources of evacuation vehicles, 146
types of evacuation, 143

Evacuation, residential facility
critical planning questions, 148-149
difference from institutional evacuation, 147-148
inmate refusal to evacuate, 148-149
use of inmate restraints, 148

External Resources Inventory
human resources, 26
material resources, 27-28

F

Farrington, D.
crowding and inmate violence, 70

Fatigue, staff. *See* Camp Hill riots; Emergency plan
activation twelve-hour emergency staffing schedule

Fires. *See* Facility fires *and* Forest fires

Facility fires
  causes, 107
  classes of fires, 110-111
  evacuation routes, 19, 109, 112
  fire extinquishers, types of, 111
  fire inspections, 109
  flammable substances storage, 108-109
  housing unit combustible materials, 108
  mitigation of, 108-109
  preparedness/response to, 110-112
  recovery from, 112

Federal Bureau of Prisons. *See also* Federal Correctional
  Institution, Atlanta; Federal Correctional Institution,
  Oakdale; Federal Correctional Institution, Talladega;
  U.S. Penitentiary in Marion, Illinois
  direct supervision of inmates, 51-52
  emergency planning model, 180-181
  riots at, 3-4, 41
  security threat groups tracking, 87
  unit management of inmates, 51

Federal Correctional Institution, Atlanta
  strategic planning issues, 180

Federal Correctional Institution, Oakdale
  strategic planning issues, 180

Federal Correctional Institution, Talladega
  hostage situation, 180
  regional emergency logistics centers, 180

Federal Prison Camp on Homestead Air Force Base
  effect of Hurricane Andrew, 2, 123, 124

Federal Emergency Management Agency
  definition of emergency life cycle, 8
  earthquake mitigation guidelines, 128-129
  evacuation guidelines for nuclear emergency, 142
  flood mitigation guidelines, 120-122
  hazardous materials definition, 139
  hurricane preparedness/response guidelines, 126
  medical recovery functions, 155

FEMA. *See* Federal Emergency Management Agency

Fire Safety Officer. *See also* Fire Safety Team
  duties of, 107, 108-109

Fire Safety Team
  deployment phase, 29, 39, 107
  goals of, 29
  selection criteria for membership, 30

Flammable substances, 108-109

Flash (rapid-onset) floods. *See* Floods, classification of

Floods
  classification of, 120
  mitigation of, 120-122
  preparedness/response to, 23, 122
  recovery from, 23, 122
  warning system for, 122

Foreign examples of emergencies
  Copenhagan, Denmark, 3
  Honduras, 4
  Puerto Rico, 3

Forest fires
  mitigation of, 131
  preparedness/response to, 131
  recovery from, 131

Full-scale exercise
  advance warning issue, 172
  counseling of poor participant performance, 173
  external evaluation of staff response, 172
  off-duty scheduling, 172
  planning, 172
  postmortem and plan modification, 173-174
  public recognition of participant performance, 173
  wild card, 172-173
  use of external resources, 173

G

Gaes, G.
  prison crowding and violence, 80

Gangs. *See also* Aryan Brotherhood; Gang-related
  disturbances; Texas DCJ gang initiatives
  contribution to prison violence, 84-85
  membership identification, 85, 87
  mitigation of, 85-87
  preparedness/response to, 87
  recovery issues, 87-88

Gang-related disturbances
  nature of, 84-85

Goffman, Erving
  primary adjustment of inmates, 7
  secondary adjustment of inmates, 7-8
  total institution, 7

Graterford (Pennsylvania) Correctional Institution
  escape from, 69-70
  staff retaliation after Camp Hill riots, 99

Grievance flooding. *See* Environmental scanning,
  inmate, short-term behavioral observations

H

Hawkins, R.
  inmates most likely to commit suicide, 79

Hazardous material accidents. *See also* Cajon Summit,
  California
  community accidents, 139-140
  facility accidents, 139
  material safety data sheets, 139
  recovery from, 140
  superfund reauthorization act of 1986, 139

HIV-positive. *See* AIDS

Homestead Air Force Base. *See* Hurricane Andrew

Honduras, 4

Hostage Negotiation Team
  coordination with CERT, 31, 89
  deployment phase, 31, 39, 89
  goals of, 31
  need for bilingual negotiators, 32
  selection criteria for membership, 31

Human emergencies. *See* Hazardous materials
  accidents, Nuclear accidents, Terrorist activities, *and*
  Urban unrest

Hunger strikes
  administrator memo to inmates, 66
  daily medical report, 66
  mitigation of, 65
  preparedness/response to, 65-66
  recovery from, 66-67

Hurricane Andrew
  effect of, 121, 143

Hurricanes
  federal facilities affected, 121, 123
  flood surge, 125
  high winds, 125-126
  mitigation of, 9, 124-126
  preparedness/response to, 23, 126
  recovery from, 23, 126

I

Ice. *See* Winter storm

Information Management Team
  deployment phase, 38, 39, 162, 164, 170
  division into groups, 38
  goals of, 38
  selection criteria for membership, 38

Inmate control equipment
  non-use in residential facility evacuations, 148
  types of, 24-25, 27-28, 142

Inmate control issues
  community access, 55-56
  tools, weapons, flammable substances, vehicles, 54-55
  within facility movement, 52-54

Inmate discontent. *See* Environmental scanning,
  inmates

Inmate informants
  intelligence unit use of, 61-62

Inmate labor teams. *See* Internal Resources Inventory,
  inmate labor teams

Inmate litigation. *See* Camp Hill riots litigation; Civil
  Rights Act, 1983; Routine Legal Response model;
  Post-emergency Litigation Response model

Inmate precipitated emergencies. *See also* Escapes;
  Gangs; Hostage situations; Hunger strikes; Inmate
  control issues; Inmate work stoppages; Minor
  disturbances; Riots; Sexual assault; Suicide
  classification of, 49
  difference from other emergencies, 49-50
  general mitigation principles, 50-56

Intelligence Unit
chain of evidence, 32
deployment phase, 32, 39, 65, 73, 78, 84, 118, 136
goals of, 32
monitoring of inmate activities, 32, 50-51, 65, 73
selection criteria for membership, 32
staff disciplinary action, role in, 32

Internal Resources Inventory. *See also* **Inmate control equipment**
inmate labor teams, 23-24, 45, 117-118
material and supply inventory, 25-26
physical plant, 19, 21, 25-26
security response inventory, 24-25
staff, 23

Irwin, J.
learned violence, 71
state-raised inmates, 71

J

Johnson, L.
modification of prison environment to reduce violence, 72-73

K

Kane, T.
target hardening for inmate violence reduction, 78

Kimball, P.
poor management as a cause of prison violence, 78

King, Rodney. *See* **Los Angeles riots**

L

Labor unrest. *See* **Strike of employees**

Legal issues. *See* **Inmate litigation**

Litigation Response Team
debriefing of staff, 37, 199
deployment phase, 37, 39
functions of, 198-203
goals of, 37-38
selection criteria for membership, 38, 198

Litigation Response Coordinator. *See also* **Post-emergency Litigation Response model**
role of, 198

Lockwood, D. *See also* **Alternatives to Violence program**
sexual assaults in prison, 77
violent inmate model of violence, 71

Los Angeles riots
cause of, 133
impact on residential correctional facilities, 2, 133-134

Lucasville Riot. *See also* **Wilkinson, Reginald; Vallandingham, Bobby**
casualties, 2
significance of riot, 2
use of external resources, *v*

M

Marquette Branch Prison
riot, 179

Maryland Division of Corrections
directive, 12, 112-126
emergency plan check list system, 12, 218-246
standardization of emergency categories, 12

Maryland Emergency Management Agency
assistance to Maryland DOC, 15

McGuire, W.
prison crowding and violence, 72

Media. *See also* **Public Information Officer; Rumor control**
control of inmate access to, 166-167
problems with, 163
selling a positive message to, 167
sources of information requests, 162-166
strategies for media management, 162-164

Media/community Information Group
deployment phase, 38, 39
goals of, 38
selection criteria for membership, 38

Medical Response Team. *See also* **Triage**
deployment phase, 32, 39, 94, 112, 118, 122, 151, 154, 155
evacuation of injured, 154-155
goals of, 32-33

identification of the dead, 155
public health monitoring functions, 156
rescue involvement, 155
selection criteria for membership, 33
treatment functions of, 151-154

Memorandum of Agreement. *See also* External resources
Inventory coordination of resources
establishment of, 134-135, 137

Metropolitan Correctional Center, Miami
effect of Hurricane Andrew, 117, 123

Michigan. *See* Marquette Branch Prison; Michigan
Reformatory; Ryan Correctional Facility; State Prison
in Southern Michigan

Michigan Reformatory
riot, 179

Minor disturbances. *See* gang-related disturbances;
non-gang related disturbances

Mississippi
county jail escape, 4

Missouri. *See* Central Missouri Correctional center;
Renz Correctional Center

Mitigation
definition of, 8
levels of, 8-9
proactive nature of, 8
site-location mitigation, 9
zero probability of occurrence, 9, 49

N

Nacci, P.
target hardening for inmate violence reduction, 78

Nagel, W.G.
physical plant mitigation of violence, 74

Natural emergencies. *See also* AIDS; Earthquakes;
Floods; Forest fires; Hurricanes; Tornadoes;
Tuberculosis; and Winter storms
community consequences of, 118
magnitude of, 115-116, 134
mitigation of fear, 116-117
source of, 115
recovery from, 118-119

NEST. *See* Nuclear Emergency Search Team

Newgate Prison
first U.S. riot, 89

New Jersey. See Bayside State Prison

New Mexico Prison riot
nature of, 89
physical plant failures, 89
snitches, 62, 89

New York. *See* Southport Correctional Facility

NIMBY
source of, 134

Nonepidemic emergency. *See also* Triage
mitigation of, 151
preparedness/response to, 151-155
recovery from, 155-156

Non-gang related disturbances
mitigation of, 83
preparedness/response to, 83-84
recovery from, 84

Nuclear accidents. *See also* Nuclear Emergency Search
Team
community shelters, 141
external evacuation, 141-142
in-facility shelters, 141
internal evacuation, 141
mitigation of, 140-141
preparedness/response to, 141
recovery from, 142

Nuclear Emergency Search Team (NEST)
role of, 140

Nuttall, C.
crowding and inmate violence, 72

O

Ohio. *See* Lucasville riot

Ohio Department of Rehabilitation and Correction.
See Lucasville riot

O. J. Simpson trial
as a potential riot cause, 20

P

Pennsylvania. *See* Camp Hill; Graterford Correctional Institution; Blair County Prison; State Correctional Institution at Coal Township; State Regional Correctional Facility at Mercer

Post-emergency Litigation Response model. *See also* Litigation Response Team
assumptions of the model, 196
counseling support for testifying staff, 202
decision documentation during the emergency, 198
debriefing of decision makers, 37-38, 199
establishing a decision tree, 37, 199-200
event reconstruction problems, 196-197
mandatory post-trial debriefing, 202-203
pre-emergency legal training of staff, 198
preparation of staff before testifying, 37, 198, 201-202

Post-emergency vulnerability analysis
inmate management issues, 22
physical plant issues, 21

Post-traumatic Assessment Team
deployment phase, 36-37, 39, 73, 78-79, 84, 112, 117, 118
goals of, 36
selection criteria for membership, 36

Post-traumatic Stress Disorders (PTSD)
definition of, 187-188
myths about, 188-189

Post-traumatic Stress Disorders, counseling. *See also* Debriefing victims; Defusing
family center, 186-187
family needs, 186-187
inmate self-help groups, 191-192
long-term staff counseling needs, 191
short-term staff counseling needs, 189-190
training role as therapy, 191
staff return to work, 190-191
use of community volunteers, 191

Preemergency vulnerability analysis
archiving, 17
geographic element, 19
historical element, 18
human error element, 19
physical element, 19
prioritization of emergencies, 17, 19-21

resource availability, 17
technological element, 19

Preparedness
definition of, 10
goals of, 10

Prevention of emergencies. *See* Mitigation

Prioritization of emergencies
probability ranking, 19-21

PTSD. *See* Post-traumatic Stress Disorders

Public Information Officer
duties of, 161, 162, 164

Puerto Rico, 3

R

Recovery. *See also* Recovery healing issues; Recovery plan of action for healing; Post-traumatic Stress Disorders
definition of, 10
goals of, 10, 184
physical plant needs identification, 184-186
psychological needs identification, 186-192
role of stepdown committee, 184-186
identification of emergency-related deficiencies, 185-186

Recovery healing issues. *See also* Recovery plan of action for healing
community fears, 208-209
fear of scapegoating, 207
inadequate preparation for PTSD, 208
political aftermath of emergencies, 206-207
public confrontations, 207
union issues, 206-207

Recovery plan of action for healing
fostering a positive work environment, 209-210
high-visibility communication, 209
regaining a sense of control, 210
regaining community trust, 210

Renz Correctional Center
evacuation of, 205
flooding of, 119, 120, 125, 205

Residential facility. *See also* Evacuation, residential facility
coordination with other agencies, 147
difference from prisons and jails, 147-148
inmate control issues, 148-149

Response
definition of, 10
goals of, 10

Riots. *See also* Camp Hill riots; Newgate Prison; New Mexico Prison riot; Attica riot; Urban unrest
classification of, 89
frequency, 89
ripple effect of, 11

Riots, recovery phase. *See also* Violence, staff; Evacuation, institutional
assessment of security status, 95-96
clearing the count, 94
evacuation, 96
inmate planning of future disturbances, 28
inmate property procedures, 97, 195
shakedowns, 94-95, 176
supervision in the disciplinary unit, 97

Riots, response phase. *See also* Violence, staff; Staff retaliation
containment, 90-91
freeing the hostages, 92-94
retaking the facility, 92-94

Routine Legal Response model. *See also* Camp Hill riot litigation
definition of, 193-194
event reconstruction, 194, 196-197
problems with RLR model, 195-197

Rumor control
as primary purpose of information management, 161
techniques of, 161-167

Ryan Correctional Facility
inmates escape from, 2-3, 206

S

Schreiber, M.S.
flooding in Missouri, 119, 205

Sexual assault
characteristics of victims and aggressors, 77
effects of sexual victimization, 78-79
mitigation of, 77
preparedness/response to, 78
recovery from, 78-79
target hardening approach to mitigation, 78

Site-location mitigation. *See also* NIMBY
floods, 120
hurricanes, 124
urban unrest, 134

Slow-Onset floods. *See* floods, classification of

Snowstorms. *See* Winter storm

Social-cultural model
as source of inmate violence, 73

Southern Ohio Correctional Facility at Lucasville. *See* Lucasville riot

Southport Correctional Facility
breakdown in security procedures, 177-178
hostage situation, 177
personnel data warning signs, 103

Special Transportation Unit. *See also* Evacuation, institutional
deployment phase, 33, 145
goals of, 33
selection criteria for membership, 33

Staff discontent. *See* Environmental scanning, staff

Staff retaliation. See also Riots, recovery phase
administrators at receiving institutions, 98-99
brutality ripple effect, 98-99
examples of, 92, 96
mitigation of, 96-99
environmental scanning for inmate psychological abuse, 97-98
high management visibility, 98
monitoring of noncorrectional staff, 98
supervision of outside correctional officers, 98

Staff training. *See* Emergency plan testing

Standard recovery protocol
definition of, 118-119
recovery implementation, 122, 126, 129, 130, 131, 134, 139

State Correctional Institution at Coal Township
inmate disturbance, 3

State Police
at Camp Hill, 92

State Prison in Southern Michigan
riot, 101, 178

State Regional Correctional Facility at Mercer
perimeter security issues, 56

Stepdown Committee
accountability, 185
deployment phase, 39, 40, 112
goals of, 40
physical plant challenges, 184-185
psychological challenges, 186-192
recovery plan, formal, 185
role in standard recovery protocol implementation, 118
selection criteria for membership, 40, 184

Strategic planning. *See also* Federal Bureau of Prisons, emergency planning model
as an evolutionary process, 181
assumptions of, 11
definition of, 5
rules of, 7-13
types of emergency plans, 15

Strike of employees
cross-training, 105
mitigation of, 105
preparedness/response to, 105
recovery from, 106

Suicide. *See also* Alpert, G.; Hawkins, R.
behavioral warning signs, 79-80
ecology of, 79
mitigation of, 79-81
preparedness/response to, 81
screening device for, 81
recovery from, 81

T

TB. *See* Tuberculosis

Technological emergencies
definition of, 19, 112
mitigation of, 112-113
preparedness/response to, 113
recovery from, 113

Terrorist activities
bomb threats, 137-138
mail bombs, 137
planted bombs, 137
recovery from, 138-139
threat recipient role, 137-138

Texas Department of Criminal Justice gang initiatives
membership identification, 86
policy initiatives, 86-88

Toch, H.
contextual payoffs as causation, 71-72
hot spots, 73
reduction of prison violence, 72-73
sexual assaults in prison, 77
social climate model of violence, 71-72

Tornadoes
mitigation of, 126
preparedness/response to, 126
recovery from, 126

Traditional command and control structure. *See* Emergency plan activation

Train derailment, 139

Training of staff. *See* Emergency plan testing; Full-scale exercise

Triage
classification of treatment needs, 32, 152-154
color-coding system, 152-153
coordination with community hospitals, 32, 154-155
deceased casualties, 32, 153-154
definition of, 151-152
dental injuries, 153
evacuation, 154
initial triage sites, 152-153
on-site treatment sites, 153
psychiatric casualties, 153
triage-dispute resolution, 154

Tuberculosis
difficulty of infection, 158-159
management issues, 159
mandatory testing, 159
mitigation of, 159

preparedness/response to, 159

quarantine of infected inmates, 159

recovery from, 159

statistics of occurrence, 158-159

U

Union

nature of grievances, 103-104

relationship with management, 102, 166

Unit management. *See* **Federal Bureau of Prisons**

United States Bureau of Prisons. *See* **Federal Bureau of Prisons**

United States Congress

crack cocaine laws, 20-21

United States Penitentiary in Marion

assaults at, 180

Urban residential facilities

command posts, 135

inmate emergency management procedures, 135

mitigation of emergency, 134-135

preparedness/response to emergency, 134

reconnaissance activities, 135

recovery from, 135

staff release procedures, 135

Urban unrest. *See* **Los Angeles Riots; Urban jails/prisons; Urban residential facilities**

Urban jails and prisons

lockdown versus normal operations, 136

mitigation of emergency, 135

preparedness/response to, 135-136

primary risks, 136

recovery from, 136

Useem, B.

poor management as a cause of inmate violence, 72

V

Vallandingham, Bobby

fatal casualty in Lucasville riot, 2

Violence, inmate. *See also* **Alternatives to violence program; Toch, H.**

causes, 71-73

physical plant mitigation issues, 74

social climate model of causation, 71-73

societal-cultural model of causation, 73

staff training/orientation to, 74

target hardening approach, 78

use of technology to reduce, 74-75

violent inmate model of causation, 71

Violence, staff. *See* **Staff retaliation**

Violence, theories of. *See* **Abbott, J.; Bowker, L.; Irwin, J.; Johnson, R.; Kane, T.; Lockwood, D.; Nacci, P.; Nagel, W.G.; Toch, H.**

W

Walkaways

definition of, 67

mitigation of, 68-69

preparedness/response to, 69-70

recovery from, 70

Washington State Penitentiary in Walla Walla

gangs, 85-86

Wilkinson, Reginald A.

emergency teams, *vi*

Lucasville riot, *v-vi*

need for emergency planning, *v-vi*

Winter storms

mitigation of, 129-130

preparedness/response to, 130

recovery from, 130-131

Work stoppages. *See* **Labor unrest and Work stoppages, inmate**

Work stoppages, inmate

level 2 mitigation of, 65

preparedness/response to, 65-66

recovery from, 66-67

Work stoppages, staff. *See* **Strike of employees**

About the Author

From 1970 to 1990, Robert M. Freeman served as superintendent of two Pennsylvania Department of Corrections adult men's facilities, including the 2,600-bed Camp Hill Prison, where he served during the riots. He has extensive experience in every phase of correctional management, including prison riots. Currently he is an assistant professor in the Department of Criminal Justice at Shippensburg University in Shippensburg, Pennsylvania.

Dr. Freeman earned his bachelor's and master's degrees in psychology from Indiana University of Pennsylvania. His doctorate is in criminal justice and criminology from the University of Maryland.